FROM THE GROUND UP

FROM THE GROUND UP

Six Principles for Building the New Logic Corporation

Edward E. Lawler III

 Jossey-Bass Publishers
San Francisco

Jossey-Bass books and products are available through most bookstores. To contact Jossey-Bass directly, call (888) 378-2537, fax to (800) 605-2665, or visit our website at www.josseybass.com.

Substantial discounts on bulk quantities of Jossey-Bass books are available to corporations, professional associations, and other organizations. For details and discount information, contact the special sales department at Jossey-Bass.

 Manufactured in the United States of America on Lyons Falls Turin Book. This paper is acid-free and 100 percent totally chlorine-free.

Library of Congress Cataloging-in-Publication Data

Lawler, Edward E.
   From the ground up : six principles for building the new logic corporation / Edward E. Lawler III.
      p.   cm. — (The Jossey-Bass business & management series)
   Includes bibliographical references and index.
   ISBN 0-7879-0241-1
   ISBN 0-7879-5197-8 (paper)
      1. Organizational effectiveness. 2. Complex organizations. 3. Communication in organizations. 4. Organizational change—Management. I. Title. II. Series: Jossey-Bass business and management series.
   HD58.9.L387 1996
   658.4′063—dc20   96-19552

FIRST EDITION
HB Printing   10 9 8 7 6 5 4 3 2
PB Printing   10 9 8 7 6 5 4 3 2 1

The Jossey-Bass
Business & Management Series

98949

Contents

Preface

Like a snowball rolling down a steep hill, the mass of new management trends, practices, and buzzwords seems to get bigger every month. Reengineering, delayering, downsizing, empowerment, agility, learning, open-book management, boundaryless and total quality management are just a few prominent examples. There is little question in my mind why this is happening. Technology, political change, and economic change have created more complex work and a more demanding global business environment. In order to be successful, corporations must both respond quickly to change and develop ever-higher levels of productivity, quality, and innovation.

Many corporations are struggling to adapt their organization designs to this global era of hyper business competition. The result is a growing market for new management practices and ideas. In today's competitive environment, corporations can no longer rely on a bureaucratic management approach based on nineteenth-century technology and ideas. They must reinvent themselves and rebuild their organizations from the ground up to form a twenty-first-century organization.

The changes taking place in corporations raise a number of important questions: How effective are they? What will be their impact on jobs and individuals? How can companies implement these new management practices and make them work? Although these questions and their answers are important and will be considered in this book, I believe they do not address the fundamental change issue—the development of a new logic of how complex organizations should be managed and designed.

A new logic is developing—an approach to organizing corporations that will shape them for decades. This new approach draws on employee involvement, total quality management, reengineering, and other approaches, but it goes beyond what any of them consider and propose. The six principles that form the foundation of the new logic are detailed in Chapter One. The principles assert that a corporation's approach to organizing can be the ultimate competitive advantage if it includes all of the following features:

- Involvement is used as the source of control.
- Work is structured so that all employees add significant value.
- Lateral processes are emphasized.
- The organization's structure is designed around products and customers.
- Effective leadership is practiced throughout the organization.

The new logic is not just a passing fancy that will lose its popularity as have management fads of the past—and as will those of the present. Rather, it is a new, long-term approach to creating organizations that can be competitive in the business environment of the twenty-first century. It uses new principles to help organizations change every significant element of how they operate, from how people are paid, how work is designed, and how people are hired and trained, to what kind of information systems are used.

The promise of a quick fix is often very seductive. People understandably hope to find silver-bullet programs that will cure their organizations' ills and make them more effective. Unfortunately, such quick fixes often lead to an organization going through a succession of short-term change efforts that lead to little improvement in the organization's effectiveness, and result in a considerable waste of the organization's resources, energy, and the commitment of its employees. In order to transform an organization, changes must be made in most or all of its important practices, policies, and structures. It is not enough, for example, simply to introduce teams or pay-for-performance plans, or to restructure. Change from the ground up is needed.

When somebody asks me whether employee involvement is good or TQM is good or open-book management is good, and so on, I almost inevitably respond "Yes, but. . . ." The "but" here always emphasizes that by themselves, such techniques are simply foreign elements that enter into an organization and are often rejected because they do not fit with the rest of the structures, practices, and policies of the organization. As a result, at times in this book it may seem that I am overly dismissive of ideas such as empowerment, open-book management, reengineering, and total quality management, but this is not my intention. I do not want to reject them; rather, I want to put them in the context of the larger reality of what it takes to make an organization successful in today's and tomorrow's highly competitive, global business environment. TQM, reengineering, and a number of other programs and practices can be effective, but they are not by themselves an adequate response.

From the Ground Up is especially written for people who are tired of quick-fix programs and are ready for transformational change based on a new logic of organizing. These people realize that changing an organization from the ground up is complex, but is the only kind of change that can produce a long-term competitive advantage based on organizational excellence.

In fact, the principles of the new logic can be a very effective inoculation against quick-fix faddism. If individuals ask themselves whether the new management practices they are considering fit the six principles of the new logic, they can see whether the latest management ideas and practices will move their organization toward the higher levels of performance that the twenty-first century will demand. The principles are also tools that individuals and corporations can use to assess how much progress they have made in transforming themselves into high-performance organizations and to determine what they have to do to finish the task.

It is time for those who face the challenge of developing effective organizations to understand what it will take to make organizations and individuals successful in the future. It is also important that every manager, every employee, every union leader, and every public official understand the implications of the new management logic that I outline in this book. They need to actively use the six principles of the new logic in making decisions about how they manage their organizations and how they think about their careers, work lives, and futures.

I firmly believe that those individuals who grasp where work is going and who develop the right skills and competencies can, in fact, have more rewarding jobs and better lives in the future. They will, for example, have more choices in their lives and have a much greater opportunity to use their decision-making skills and to act as mature, self-managing adults. I also believe that they will have the opportunity to work for—and be served by—much more effective organizations.

From the Ground Up focuses not just on how to improve organizational performance, but on how individuals can develop the skills and competencies they need for twenty-first-century careers. It provides guidelines and approaches for those who create and manage organizations as well as for those who face the challenge of developing meaningful careers and lives in our rapidly changing world. It provides information on how people should be paid, how work should be designed, how individuals should be selected, and what kind of information systems are needed; in short, on how all the major features and systems of an organization should operate.

Acknowledgments

In writing this book, I have drawn heavily on the research work of the Center for Effective Organizations at the University of Southern California. I have had the good fortune to be a member of this center for the last seventeen years and have profited enormously from it. It has given me the opportunity to do organizational research that is relevant to both theory and practice. I am very appreciative of the support the center and I have received from the business school of the university and the many companies that have contributed to the center's research mission.

Being at the center has allowed me to collaborate with a very talented group of researchers whose work has contributed tremendously to this book. I cite and draw upon their work throughout this book, but I would like to individually mention them and thank them for their support: Susan Cohen, Jay Galbraith, Gerry Ledford, Gary McMahan, Allan Mohrman, Susan Mohrman, and Ram Tenkasi. I would also like to thank Liza Starr and Georgia Marinelli for their help in preparing my manuscript. Sheryl Fullerton and Michael Verespej helped me with the development of my manuscript. Special thanks to them for making it much clearer and more interesting.

Last, but certainly not least, I would like to thank my wife, Patty, who has, from the beginning of my work on this book, offered ideas, thoughts, support, and love. The first three of these have helped me greatly, the last is her special gift.

Los Angeles
June 1996   EDWARD E. LAWLER III

The Author

Edward E. Lawler III is professor of management and organization in the business school at the University of Southern California. He joined USC in 1978 and during 1979 founded and became director of the university's Center for Effective Organizations.

After receiving degrees from Brown University (B.A., 1960), and the University of California, Berkeley (Ph.D., 1964), Dr. Lawler joined the faculty of Yale University. He moved to the University of Michigan in 1972 as professor of psychology and program director in the Survey Research Center at the Institute for Social Research.

Dr. Lawler is a member of many professional organizations in his field and is on the editorial board of five major journals. He has consulted with over one hundred organizations on employee involvement, organizational change, and compensation and has been honored as a top contributor to the fields of organizational development, organizational behavior, and compensation.

The author of twenty-five books and over two hundred articles, Dr. Lawler has had his works translated into ten languages, and has given speeches in twenty-eight Asian, South American, European, and African countries. His writings have appeared in the leading academic journals as well as in *Fortune, Industry Week,* and *Harvard Business Review.* His most recent books include *Strategic Pay* (Jossey-Bass, 1990), *The Ultimate Advantage* (Jossey-Bass, 1992), *Organizing for the Future* (Jossey-Bass, 1993, with J. Galbraith and associates), *Creating High Performance Organizations* (Jossey-Bass, 1995, with S. A. Mohrman and G. E. Ledford, Jr.), *Tomorrow's Organization* (Jossey-Bass, 1998), *Strategies for High-Performance Organizations* (Jossey-Bass, 1998, with S. A. Mohrman and G. E. Ledford, Jr.), *The Leader's Change Handbook* (Jossey-Bass, 1999, coedited with J. Conger and G. Spreitzer), and *Rewarding Excellence* (Jossey-Bass, 2000).

FROM THE GROUND UP

The New Realities of Business Competition

When we look around the business landscape, we see many giant corporations that were once very successful—General Motors, Westinghouse, IBM, Kmart, Digital, and Sears—trying to regain their glory days. At the same time, we see much younger corporations such as Compaq, Wal-Mart, Intel, and Microsoft competing with them and thriving. How did these successful giants of the 1960s and 1970s—praised by researchers and consultants, including myself, for their exemplary management practices—end up with major competitiveness problems in the 1980s and 1990s? The answer is both simple and extraordinarily complex.

These once very successful corporations remained good at operating well-managed, bottom-line-oriented hierarchies, and as a result they continued to make small improvements in performance. Their fiercest competitors, on the other hand—often other U.S. companies—were, and still are, redefining the rules for business success and achieving dramatic improvements in their performance. Until recently, many of these formerly very successful companies have stubbornly clung to the old ways of doing things and refused to accept that a new era of management thinking—what I call the *new logic* of organizing—is beginning. As a result, the IBMs, Westinghouses, and Sears Roebucks of the world are behind in the race to reinvent themselves and the way they are managed.

The new logic of organizing is based on a set of principles that redefine how a business needs to be structured and managed from the ground up. It identifies the foundations on which effective twenty-first-century organizations should be built. The new logic is based on the belief that organizational design and management can provide the ultimate competitive advantage. It argues that in order to be successful in tomorrow's highly competitive business environment, organizations need to be built to maximize involvement and lateral processes and should be managed by visionary leaders.

Corporate America need look no further than organizations such as Nucor, Intel, Southwest Airlines, L.L. Bean, Land's End, Home Depot, Wal-Mart, Compaq, and MCI to see how using the new logic to structure an organization can pay off. Lands' End and L.L. Bean virtually destroyed the Sears catalog business by understanding their customers better and offering superior service. Personal computer manufacturer Compaq has succeeded where General Electric, Xerox, Honeywell, and RCA failed: in competing with IBM. It has done so by offering high quality, high-performance products, and good service. MCI has been a thorn in AT&T's side partly because it does not use the traditional management approaches that dominate in AT&T.

Another example is Nucor, an innovative steel company that succeeded while the giants of the steel industry, U.S. Steel, Republic, LTV, and National, crumbled. Under CEO Ken Iverson, it has grown from $20 million in sales in 1965 to over $3.5 billion. Iverson structured Nucor around customers and pioneered the use of highly productive mini-mills (Nucor now has eight). Operations employees make day-to-day decisions, and employee teams can increase their compensation as much as 200 percent based on weekly output. Iverson, who answers his own phone, is a fanatic when it comes to keeping his corporate staff small.

Likewise, Southwest Airlines, from its inception in 1973, defied conventional industry thinking by flying between city pairs instead of using the airline industry's hub-and-spoke system. It also trained its employees to do multiple jobs, and it has emphasized non-bureaucratic approaches to customer service: employees can resolve customer service problems without having to consult a supervisor first, and it is OK for employees to be humorous. Southwest has been profitable since its first full year of operation, and it still enjoys a competitive advantage, because no one has been able to duplicate its customer service and operational capabilities.

It came as no surprise to me that both Nucor CEO Ken Iverson and Southwest CEO Herb Kelleher—who at age sixty-five still works the ticket counter, mans the baggage ramp, and serves drinks and snacks when flying on business—were among 1995's five most admired CEOs worldwide as chosen by *Industry Week.*

Foreign competition is often mentioned as a major cause of the problems of some of today's troubled American and European companies. There is little doubt that it has drastically affected competition in many industries and has contributed to the problems of some companies, including Kodak and General Motors. Foreign competition, however, cannot account for many of the problems of IBM and Sears. Their fiercest and most troublesome competitors were and are onshore: Lands' End, Eddie Bauer, L.L. Bean, and Wal-Mart for Sears; Dell, Compaq, Intel, and Microsoft for IBM.

What Wal-Mart, Nucor, Southwest, and many other successful newcomers realized is that the world of business is in an era of transformation that is as dramatic as when transcontinental travel in the United States changed from trains and cars to airplanes. Information technology, the global economy, and foreign competition have changed forever the way companies need to make, market, and sell products and services as well as structure their organizations. They responded to this transformation by creating organizations and business strategies that take advantage of the new logic of organizing. On the other hand, IBM, Sears, and a host of other companies continued to do business as usual and as a result lost out to better managed corporations, not to foreign competition.

Change: Risks and Rewards

I am convinced from my research and consulting with companies of all sizes and types that this is a period of great risk for both individuals and organizations. Organizations that stick with the old management logic are bound to fail. If companies are organized according to traditional principles, even inherent advantages such as superior technology, a skilled work force, and the ability to raise low-cost capital may not be enough to ensure success—particularly when they face new high-performance organizations that have superior organizational capabilities, better core competencies, and a more customer-focused approach.

Similarly, individuals who fail to adapt to the new order risk career failure, because changes in the way corporations are managed are fundamentally reshaping the way that people work as well as the way they are educated and governed. New types of careers, different approaches to career management, new pay systems, pressures for changes in legislation and public policy, demands on schools for new types of skills and training, and a new role for unions are all developing as a result of the increasing use of the new logic. Those of us who sit on the sidelines and assume that the changes are really not that fundamental, that they will pass like other fads of the past, run an enormous risk of being left behind during a critical transition period in the management of large-scale organizations.

Some time ago, in the heyday of the old hierarchical AT&T, I was interviewing managers there to see why they were not supporting a new program. One manager explained it to me clearly: he said that he was neither supporting nor opposing the new program; to do either would not be smart. According to him, when programs were launched, active opponents were often moved aside and dismissed. When new programs failed, active proponents often failed, too. Thus he felt the correct position on most change was carefully positioned neutrality. As he pointed out, this approach had worked for him for thirty years; he assumed it would work for him during the rest of his time at AT&T. Although the managed-neutrality approach may have worked in the past, it will not work as companies like AT&T shift the way they are managed. The person who does not support the new is likely to be a leading candidate for downsizing and outplacement.

As the new logic takes hold, it will dramatically change the relationships between individuals and their work. The future of work looks more like a typical cross-functional product design team at Hewlett-Packard than an engineering group in a traditional organization that works one step in the product design process and then passes the product on to the next group. In design teams, engineers, marketing experts, and manufacturing experts are all put together to develop new products. They have the power to make decisions about the product. When they finish their design, they disband as a team and look for a new assignment.

More and more, pay will be based on competencies and performance, raising the market value of individuals with critical skills. In the new logic, it is much more important for managers to be able to lead groups and teams. Likewise, individuals who can learn different skills and adapt to new organizational forms should do well. But the future is not bright for individuals who are unable to develop marketable skills or learn how to manage themselves.

Some signs of the new logic are already visible:

- Hierarchy is being dramatically reduced. It is increasingly common for large organizations to have single-digit management levels and double- and triple-digit reporting relationships (often called *spans of control* in the old logic).
- Jobs, as we know them today, are disappearing. As a result, individuals need different skills and different concepts of what constitutes a successful career.
- Education is focusing more on peer learning, lifetime learning, self-management, and problem solving.
- Millions of individuals have lost their jobs as troubled corporate giants have struggled to become more competitive.
- Governments are struggling to serve a work force that is increasingly made up of individuals who are essentially self-employed and who, as a result, need to keep learning and to have a safety net for health care and retirement.

At this point doubters may be wondering, What's so different about the innovations and changes in management that are occurring today? Haven't there been new fads and fashions as long as I have been a manager? Weren't a host of "new" practices—such as zero-based budgeting, management by objectives, job enrichment, empowerment, cross-functional teams, and quality circles—supposed to revolutionize management in the 1970s and 1980s?

While I certainly agree that there is a long history of fads and fashions in management, I don't agree that we are just seeing more of the same. For the first time we are in a change-or-die environment. Further, the changes today are not just micro fine-tunings of traditional systems; they represent a new paradigm for management thinking that is bringing an end to the command-and-control, old logic approach that has dominated organizations since large bureaucracies first emerged. This is a classic example of a sea change, a paradigm shift, a transformational change—in short, a change that is rewriting the rules of how organizations should be organized and managed.[1]

As a result, those who sit on the sidelines are risking not only their careers and economic security but also the competitive capabilities of their companies. Staying the same is now a greater risk than changing. It is the organizational equivalent of driving across the country when your competitors are flying in jets. To me, the obvious conclusion is that the only way troubled giants can attain new competitive performance levels is to switch to a jet. They need to transform their organizational approach completely, fundamentally, and radically; they need to move from the old management emphasis on hierarchical, top-down control to a new logic that is based on involvement, leadership, lateral process, and customer focus.

The movement away from the traditional organizational approach and toward a new paradigm or logic of management thinking is not now—and will not ever be—a simple and painless change. It is more than a change in thinking. It requires a change in the behaviors of all individuals as well as a shift in how organizations are designed, structured, and run. This is the challenge; it is also the necessity for any company that wants to thrive in the future and for individuals who want to thrive in the world of new logic corporations.

So far, few companies appear to have aggressively adopted the new logic. A 1993 survey by my Center for Effective Organizations at the University of Southern California asked each Fortune 1000 company what percentage of its operations have been organized to support business involvement and customer focus, key elements of the new logic.[2] On average, the answer was about 10 percent. What's more, 50 percent of the firms had few, if any, of their employees operating according to the new logic. (The highest use was among large manufacturers, organizations facing foreign competition, and highly capital-intensive manufacturers such as those involved in chemicals and food processing.)

The finding—that only 10 percent of the work force in the Fortune 1000 is managed according to the new logic—is surprising to me. I had expected the percentage to be higher, given the amount of attention that is devoted to organizational change and new approaches to management by the *Wall Street Journal, Business Week, Fortune, Industry Week,* and a host of magazines and newsletters that focus on the corporate world. If one were to read only the popular press, one might believe that all large U.S. corporations were already embracing the principles of the new logic.

But before condemning the Fortune 1000 for their slowness in adopting the new logic, it is important to consider two crucial factors. First, we all know that just because things are reported in the business press does not mean that they are actually being widely practiced. Indeed, it is "newness" and uniqueness that make something newsworthy; something that everyone is already doing is hardly news. Second, the longer-term trend is toward greater adoption; thus by now the percentage is likely to be significantly higher. Further, in 1993, over 75 percent of the Fortune 1000 companies were either adopting the new logic completely in some part of their organization or adopting some programs which fit the new logic—for example, quality management or employee involvement—throughout their entire organization.

What most large corporations do not have is a corporation-wide, systematic effort targeted at changing the total logic of how they are organized. They tend to concentrate their efforts on small parts of the organization or try limited programs that don't change the overall way they operate.

The relatively low adoption of the new logic leads to an obvious question: If it is so powerful and provides such a strong competitive advantage, why isn't everyone doing it? There are many, many reasons for this, but perhaps the major reason lies in the analysis of who is likely to lose in a move to the new logic. Many of the individuals who stand to lose the most if the new logic is adopted—that is, senior and middle management—have the power to slow or prevent change. They can be, and often are, major obstacles to change.

There is an upside to the slowness of organizations to switch to the new logic: significant opportunities still exist for firms that want to be leaders in putting it into practice. This is true for both new organizations and existing ones. What's more, those that do an effective job of creating high-performance organizations based on the principles of this newly emerging logic can gain a competitive advantage that is difficult to duplicate.

The Competitive Demands of Today's World

If organizations need evidence that it is time for them to create a new approach to organizing and managing their businesses, they need only look around them to see how the business environment has changed. Simply stated, the level of competition today requires high levels and continuous improvement of organizational performance in four critical areas:

- The quality of goods and services
- The cost of producing goods and services
- The speed with which products and services are brought to market
- Innovation in the development of new products and services

In the past, companies had some slack in one or more of these four performance areas. If an organization could get a product out quickly, customers would pay more for it and would tolerate defects. Or, if the price was low enough, customers would accept poor quality, some slowness in delivery or service, or both. Today, however, there is little tolerance for substandard performance in any area. Customers want value, and that means speed, cost, quality, and innovation. Even more significantly, they do not have to tolerate shortfalls in performance; they can readily turn to alternative sources that offer faster, cheaper, better, more innovative products and services.

General Motors once stonewalled complaints about their cars and refused to improve quality while AT&T only made black phones in one style. And when AT&T did offer color phones, they charged extra for them. Such unresponsive behavior is disastrous today, because intense competition has produced an excess supply of virtually every product and every service. As a result, consumers can demand and get levels of service and product performance that are unprecedented in the history of business. For example:

- If you want to ship a package overnight, both United Parcel Service and Federal Express provide overnight delivery service that is superior to anything that the traditional supplier, the U.S. Postal Service, has to offer.
- Television sets today are essentially problem-free and have almost eliminated the TV repair business. I remember all too well—and I am sure you do, too—lugging my TV to a service center or waiting for someone to make a house call to fix it.
- World-class automobiles of the 1990s are essentially defect-free. During the first three years of operating my present car, I have

only taken it in for service once every six months for an hour or two of minor maintenance. No parts to replace, no manufacturing defects; in short, no problems in a car that is much more technologically complex than anything that was produced just a few years ago. When U.S. car companies dominated the market, I seemed to be making monthly trips to my local garage for oil changes, tune-ups, repairs, and so on.

• Wal-Mart and Home Depot provide good service and a wide array of merchandise at low prices, so consumers get more choice and cheaper prices with little or no sacrifice in service. Nordstrom's department stores provide a unique combination of price, quality, and personal service that simply was not available anywhere a few decades ago.

• I am spoiled now by being able to look through several catalogs for clothes that fit my rather large frame. Once I find something that I like, I can call a toll-free number and get delivery from one of a number of companies within forty-eight hours. If I do not like the product, I can send it back with no questions asked and get a complete refund. Years ago, the best that I could do was to go to a store miles from home that handled large sizes and choose from their very limited stock.

• Perhaps the most dramatic change has occurred in the computer industry. Personal computers now come to market in less than a year, virtually defect-free and with a price-performance ratio that improves 20 to 30 percent annually.

To avoid losing out in this new competitive business world that asks companies to simultaneously improve quality, lower costs, bring new products to market faster, and be innovative, organizations must respond by dramatically improving performance. And they must achieve that improvement in a business environment that is rapidly changing.

Why It Is So Tough: The New Environment

Why is business competition so different today? Why does it take ever higher performance levels to be successful? The explanation rests in four major changes in the business environment: a boundaryless economy, worldwide labor markets, instantly linked information and communications, and agile new companies.

1.   *A boundaryless economy* and the globalization of business have brought new competitors with both new and different management styles and powerful competitive advantages (for example, strong government support and relatively cheap skilled labor) into many markets. Japanese organizations such as Toyota and Honda have succeeded in large measure because they have a very different way of thinking about management, organizing work, relating to suppliers, and managing employees. Previously the importance of management and organization in building a competitive advantage was not evident to many in the industrialized democracies of the world because U.S. and western European companies all used the same management style and competed only with each other. Now that we see others using management and organization as a source of competitive advantage, it is clear that they can be powerful sources of advantage.

2.   *Worldwide labor markets.* Because work forces in different countries have different skills and wages, organizations can now draw on a wider variety of workers and working conditions. This has led to the creation of organizational structures and business strategies that are global in their reach. Because of the increasing ease of moving information and, in some cases, production around the world, work is moving to wherever needed skills exist at the best price. For example, a significant amount of electrical engineering work has already moved to Israel, and software development is increasingly being done in India and the former Soviet Union. Low-skilled jobs are moving to less developed countries where individuals are willing to work for low wages. Ultimately, this is likely to mean that the only work that will remain in more developed countries will require relatively high levels of skills or involve face-to-face contact for service delivery.

3.   *Instantly linked information and communication.* Information technology is enabling organizations to be designed and managed in dramatically different ways. Personal computers, company networks, the Internet, World Wide Web, expert systems, and a host of voice and video communication devices make it possible for more people in complex organizations to have more information. Individuals and teams can easily and quickly gain access to large data bases concerning particular products, processes, and customers. Networks can help workers and managers form a consensus for action,

produce innovative decision-making models, make it easier for individuals to work together on products and services, and reduce the time to respond to customer requests. This is in sharp contrast to the conditions that shaped traditional organizations: information was expensive to obtain and difficult to move around. Thus organizations sought ways to create efficient chains of command to move information up the line for centralized decision making, and they created specialized functions that could operate independently to perform single steps in production and service processes.

4.   *Agile new companies.* Many newly formed companies find it easy to adopt new organizational approaches and to reach high levels of performance. Simply put, when it comes to adopting new approaches to organizing and managing complex organizations, creation is easier than resurrection. New organizations do not have to unlearn and bury old habits or ways of doing business in order to create new ones. They do not have to dismantle existing systems, deal with individuals who stand to lose out because of change, or even change the psychological contract between employees and the organization. They also do not suffer from an "experience handicap" that is based on what has worked in the past. They just have to learn the new. For example, instead of having to unlearn the behaviors associated with the belief that quality can be inspected in, they can start from the principle that it has to be built in by high-performance teams.

This does not mean that traditionally managed organizations cannot change to the new logic or will always lose out to new competitors who start without any organizational baggage. Harley-Davidson, Xerox, Corning Glass, General Electric, and others who have transformed their existing organizations to world-class levels provide clear evidence that older large corporations can win in today's environment. But it can take years to rebuild organizations from the ground up. It takes time for the foundation of the new logic to be put in place and for it to dominate.

The Way Things Were: The Traditional Logic of Organizing

You might ask, what's wrong with the traditional organizational approach? It seems to make sense to assign carefully specified simple work to employees at the bottom of the pyramid who then report through a supervisor up a hierarchical chain of command to a group of senior executives who provide direction, coordination, and control.[3]

After all, the hierarchical approach enabled many organizations to grow to a size and scope that was unprecedented before it was developed. AT&T, for example, at its high point in the 1970s, had over one million employees functioning in an integrated and effective manner. Over 100,000 telephone operators across the United States, just one part of that system, answered the phone in the same way and dealt with customers in a consistent and professional manner—a powerful example of what is possible with the bureaucratic approach to management.

Unfortunately for many of those who use it, the hierarchical, command-and-control approach works best only as long as work is simple and stable. As work becomes more complicated and more knowledge based, it runs into problems. For example, it is difficult for a supervisor to control individuals doing knowledge work. It is one thing to supervise a group of telephone operators all doing essentially the same task every few seconds. It is quite another for a supervisor to monitor programmers writing software. The software writers often know more about the technology than the supervisor, and much of the work cannot be observed while they are doing it.

Often the response of a hierarchical organization to the challenge of managing individuals doing knowledge-intensive tasks is to increase the number of managers and the levels of management. So supervisors end up micro-managing a relatively small number of employees, and in turn they need to be micro-managed themselves. Instead of improving control, all this overhead adds to the cost of doing business and slows decision making. With the instability, complex work, and demands for speed, cost, quality, and innovation that exist in today's business environment, it is simply impossible for companies to operate effectively with a command-and-control approach to management.

The Way Organizations Need to Be: Focused on New Organizational Capabilities

In order to be successful, organizations must have capabilities that allow them to coordinate and focus behavior in ways that are tuned to the marketplace and produce high levels of performance—ways that differentiate them from their competitors. Every organization must understand what capabilities it needs to compete in its market and then develop them by creating the appropriate organizational designs and management systems.[4]

What are some key organizational capabilities? They include the ability to focus on quality or customers, operate on a global basis, be a low-cost operator, learn, respond quickly to the business environment, speed products to market, and a host of other capabilities that we will discuss throughout this book.

Organizational capabilities don't exist in one place, in the heads of a few technology gurus, or in a set of patents. They rest in the systems, culture, relationships, and overall design of an organization and typically require the coordination of many individuals and systems in an organization.

Much of 3M's success and growth over the years has to do with its organizational capability to innovate and to develop and market new products—not just with its technical competency in the chemical properties of a variety of materials. Scotch tape, Post-its, and thousands of other products are the result of its ability to innovate. This capability does not reside in one department or one set of procedures; it resides in all of its organizational systems, practices, and structures. For example, 3M's budget allows individuals time to experiment, and its reward system recognizes innovative behavior when it occurs.

When I interview people who have visited 3M to study how it maintains such an outstanding record of innovation, their reaction is always the same: they are very impressed by what they have seen but also unsure how they can create 3M's capability in their firms. They correctly recognize that 3M's organizational capability to innovate does not rest in a single or limited set of practices that other organizations can easily copy. In fact, the only way other organizations can duplicate 3M's capability to innovate is to systematically build practices and systems that fit their situation.

Similarly, Motorola's much-discussed superior capability in quality exists because of the design of all of its systems and structures, including its employee selection process, training programs, corporate vision statement, and senior management's behavior. In short, it is not based on any one system or practice; it permeates the organization. That's why an organizational capability that is developed as an integral part of a corporate strategy is virtually impossible to copy. And that is what makes it a distinct and highly valuable competitive advantage that can often provide a long-term strategic advantage.

Today, organizational success frequently requires not just a single world-class organizational capability but the right combination of several. It may take two or three that are exceptional and a number of others that are at least at a world-class level.

Successful corporations such as Motorola, Hewlett-Packard, 3M, Procter & Gamble, and Wal-Mart are able to both innovate and focus on quality at the same time. Motorola, for example, has won the Baldrige National Quality Award and is world-famous for its 6-Sigma quality program. Its capabilities do not stop with quality, however. They are also excellent at getting products quickly to market and at technological innovation. For example, Motorola has consistently been the first to introduce new cellular phone technology and has developed the ability to manufacture custom pagers in a matter of hours. Other companies are able to operate globally while staying tuned in to local customers.

Core Competencies and Organizational Effectiveness

It is important to note that organizational capabilities are not the same thing as core competencies.[5] Core competencies, also a possible source of competitive advantage, are technical areas of expertise such as 3M's knowledge of chemical processes, Xerox's knowledge of copier and imaging technology, Honda's competency in making gasoline engines, and Sony's ability to miniaturize products.

The longevity of the competitive advantage that an organization gains from its core competencies depends on how easy they are to copy. There is always the risk that others can duplicate an organization's core competencies when they rest in the minds and skills of a small number of employees.

For example, other organizations can gain the same competencies by hiring key employees away from the organization that has developed them. Apple did just this when it started. It hired people from Xerox's Palo Alto, California, research facility who had developed the software operating system for Xerox's innovative personal computer, the Star. They went on to develop the Apple operating system, which provided Apple with a significant competitive advantage.

Employees may also leave on their own and take core competencies with them to create new, competing organizations. One of the most dramatic examples: during the 1970s, Fairchild Electronics—which pioneered the development and production of semiconductors—combined a high level of technological competence with a well-deserved bad reputation for the way it managed and treated employees. This combination made it difficult for Fairchild to maintain a technological advantage despite the pioneering development work it did on semiconductors. Employee after employee simply took knowledge of Fairchild's core competency in semiconductors with them and used it to start competing businesses that were better managed. While its spin-offs Intel, AMD, and others are among the most successful semiconductor firms in the world today, Fairchild is now out of business.

While it is important to acquire, develop, and protect core technological competencies, it is clear that they are neither enough by themselves for success nor necessarily the best source of a sustainable competitive advantage. Organizational capabilities oriented toward understanding customers and speeding technology to market with the best possible quality and at a reasonable cost are often more important.

The Xerox personal computer experience provides a good example of this point. Xerox had a significant technological lead in the personal computer business. It developed the first PC for office use as well as the software that proved so important to the ultimate success of Apple. However, it lacked the organizational capabilities to capitalize on its technological core competencies and, as a result, is not in the computer business today.

A Time for Change: Creating Order Out of Chaos

When they are viewed together, the weaknesses and shortfalls of a command-and-control approach to management, the globalization of the economy, information technology, and changes in the work force suggest strongly that a new approach to organizing and managing is a competitive necessity. It is the only way for companies to differentiate themselves from competitors and to develop performance capabilities that are difficult to match and critical to achieving high performance levels. As this point has become widely recognized, there has been an explosion of interest in new management approaches. So much interest exists that the business landscape is littered not just with failed companies but with new management practices, ideas, and terminology. Today, if an organization does not have a total quality management program, if it has not reengineered some of its most important processes, if it has not involved its employees and focused on becoming more of a learning organization that liberates its employees to act as corporate entrepreneurs, it is not in touch with the "latest thinking."

A skeptic might look at the current fascination with new terminology and programs and conclude that there is in fact nothing new except for the language. I see it differently. Many of the new programs and practices are not just micro fine-tunings of traditional systems; they represent pieces or elements of a different paradigm for thinking about management. I believe that many of them have something to contribute to a new management paradigm that is well on the way to replacing the traditional view of how organizations should be managed.

During the construction of a new paradigm and the fall of an old one, it is natural and predictable that there will be considerable confusion, debate, turmoil. And, of course, it is inevitable there will be competition for attention, credit, and financial gain among individuals who champion new programs. When publications from *Business Week* and the *Wall Street Journal* to *Time* and major daily newspapers devote increasing attention to management and organizational issues, when business books are increasingly being ghost written, and when management consulting firms bill large firms millions of dollars a year for change consulting, it is clear that there is a great deal at stake.

Unfortunately, much of the convergence among the approaches is obscured by the use of different language and by each "management guru's" claim to have a new and different approach. It is further obscured by the tendency of some approaches to focus on one "silver bullet" change.

For example, the extensive literature on leadership focuses on how the new leaders need to behave and how they must give direction to the organization and provide meaning. Clearly leadership is one aspect of what needs to change in an organization that is moving away from a classic command-and-control structure, but it is only one.

Other approaches, like reengineering, have focused on work design as the key to the new way to organize. Again, they are concentrating on a significant element of the new logic but are not capturing all of it. As a result, they are adding confusion as well as enlightenment to the discussion.

To be a viable and effective guide to management practice, the new logic has to cover all of the key elements and systems of a complex organization. It is not enough to create a new leadership style, a new reward system, or a new work design. To replace the old command-and-control structure, an organization needs to develop an internally consistent approach to organizing that touches all the major elements of an organization.

One of the reasons that the traditional command-and-control approach has been so effective in the past and is so hard to change in the present is precisely that its elements reinforce each other. Leaders, for example, are trained and selected to behave in a hierarchical manner. Status symbols reinforce their authority, pay plans reward them for moving up hierarchies, and staff support and information flows allow them to coordinate and make decisions more effectively than anyone else. Movement away from this model requires not just a change in their behavior but a change in the whole logic of how the organization is designed, managed, and structured. For a truly new approach to management to be successful, it must provide different—and powerful—answers to three fundamental questions: how will individuals know what to do, how will they be trained and developed to do it, and what will motivate them to do it well?

It is my belief that our understanding of organizations and management effectiveness can be better served at this time by identifying the common elements of the new logic and spelling out the practices and policies that support them than by continuing to develop new language, emphasizing the differences among programs, and marketing new variations on old themes. Although we are not at the point where we can fully and precisely describe the new logic, I believe I can make a meaningful statement of its major principles. I think I can go on to identify the critical management practices new logic organizations can use to create organizations that effectively tell individuals what to do, develop them to do it, and motivate them to do it well.

The first chapter focuses on the core principles of the new management logic and contrasts them with the principles of the old logic. In the chapters that follow, the principles are developed through discussion of how organizations should be structured, how individuals should be rewarded, how performance should be measured, and how an organization's basic approaches to managing human resources should be designed and operated. My goal is to provide readers with a good understanding of how they can use the new logic to create more effective organizations and to manage their careers.

Part One

The New Logic Principles

Chapter One

Changing the Assumptions
The New Logic Principles for Organizing

I got my first hint of the new logic of organizing in 1961 when I read the classic book *The Human Side of Enterprise* by Douglas McGregor.[1] McGregor distinguished between two paradigms of how people can be motivated to perform in organizations. One, which he called Theory X, assumed that people had to be driven by extrinsic rewards (money and other tangibles), punishments, and bureaucratic control systems. The other, which he called Theory Y, argued that individuals can be intrinsically motivated by interesting work and can direct and manage their own behavior. At that time, Theory X guided the design and management of almost all large organizations. McGregor noted that its assumptions were so well accepted that they were rarely explicitly stated and, in fact, were neither debated nor challenged. He argued that a paradigm (or, as I call it, logic) such as Theory X is so fundamental and so critical in determining how an organization is designed that a new logic must replace it in order for new designs to be created and higher performance levels to be achieved.

Although McGregor's statement of Theory Y intrigued me because it was a simple but radical beginning for a new logic of organizing, I also wondered how practical it was. It was not clear how it would play out in the design of such key features of an organization as its financial information system, its control systems, and its formal structure. Still, McGregor's writings, along with those of Chris Argyris and Rensis Likert, opened the door to questioning the old hierarchical model and began the development of the new logic of organizing.[2]

Since McGregor's work on Theory Y, a number of new approaches have been suggested and are competing to replace the old bureaucratic logic. As was mentioned in the Introduction, some of these, such as reengineering and total quality management, have taken on the characteristics of a fad and have been wildly oversold. It would be wrong, though, to conclude that they do not make important points. They do. The problem is that they are not comprehensive. The challenge is to define not just a program or a limited approach to improving organizations but a new complete approach to organizing: one that begins with the statement of a new paradigm that replaces traditional logic principles with new logic principles.

OLD LOGIC PRINCIPLE: Organization is a secondary source of competitive advantage.

NEW LOGIC PRINCIPLE: Organization can be the ultimate competitive advantage.

OLD LOGIC PRINCIPLE: Bureaucracy is the most effective source of control.

NEW LOGIC PRINCIPLE: Involvement is the most effective source of control.

OLD LOGIC PRINCIPLE: Top management and technical experts should add most of the value.

NEW LOGIC PRINCIPLE: All employees must add significant value.

OLD LOGIC PRINCIPLE: Hierarchical processes are the key to organizational effectiveness.

NEW LOGIC PRINCIPLE: Lateral processes are the key to organizational effectiveness.

OLD LOGIC PRINCIPLE: Organizations should be designed around functions.

NEW LOGIC PRINCIPLE: Organizations should be designed around products and customers.

OLD LOGIC PRINCIPLE: Effective managers are the key to organizational effectiveness.

NEW LOGIC PRINCIPLE: Effective leadership is the key to organizational effectiveness.

This chapter outlines and contrasts the most important assumptions and elements of both the traditional logic and the new logic approach. It introduces a new way of organizing and managing based on the new logic principles.

Although they will be discussed separately in this chapter in order to clarify what each means, the six new logic principles represent an integrated approach. Thus they should not be adopted separately. Instead, they need to be taken as a whole and used as the foundation of a comprehensive approach to organizing and managing that involves new approaches to reward systems, structure, work design, communication, measurement, and human resources management—in short, all the systems and practices that are critical to organizational effectiveness. It is precisely for this reason that the first principle argues for organization as a powerful source of competitive advantage.

OLD LOGIC PRINCIPLE: Organization is a secondary source of competitive advantage.

NEW LOGIC PRINCIPLE: Organization can be the ultimate competitive advantage.

The new logic begins with the assumption that management systems, processes, and structures can be the keys to building a competitive advantage if they allow an organization to perform in a way that competitors cannot. With the right kind of organization, new products can be brought to market faster, the quality of products can be higher, and customer needs can be met more swiftly and completely.

This contrasts with the traditional bureaucratic model in which the sources of competitive advantage are assumed to include superior financial, human, and natural resources; market access; and exceptional technology. In some cases, these traditional advantages continue to be powerful. A good supply of cheap crude is still an important competitive advantage in the oil industry, for example. It is still a major advantage for Japanese and French companies to have unencumbered access to their protected domestic markets.

The Japanese domestic distribution system, for example, has long protected its market against U.S. food distribution firms and made it difficult for U.S. car manufacturers to enter the market. But these traditional sources of competitive advantage are becoming less important and less sustainable for a number of reasons.

Because capital now moves freely about the globe, it is difficult for any company to gain a competitive advantage through superior access to financial resources. Similarly, human talent is hard to sustain as a source of competitive advantage when individuals, as we have already discussed, are increasingly willing to move from one company to another, in some cases taking critical knowledge and technology with them.

Equally important is the rising education level around the globe and the new access to highly educated talent in many countries that, until recently, did not participate in the global economy. The fall of communism, the rise of free trade, and the dramatic growth of capitalism have added more than a billion people to the world economy. Many of them are unskilled and willing to work for a few dollars a day, but some are highly skilled. For example, skilled computer programmers are now available in the former Soviet Union, and many Asian countries have skilled engineers and production workers.

Finally, technology is being developed by more and more countries and companies. Japanese and Korean companies, for example, now spend a great deal of money on technology development and have proven to be adept at gaining access to technology developed elsewhere.

A classic example: going into the 1980s, IBM had all the traditional competitive advantages. It had the highest possible financial rating and, as a result, access to low-cost capital; world-class core competencies in the right technologies; research labs that were (and still are) respected for their ability to innovate and make technological breakthroughs; a great global brand name; and international subsidiaries (IBM Europe and IBM Japan) that had access to markets around the globe. Indeed, at the beginning of the 1980s, IBM looked so powerful that the U.S. government was suing it for antitrust violations because they thought no one could compete with them.

However, as the 1980s played out, it became clear that IBM lacked the essential ingredient it needed in order to maintain control over the information- and data-processing marketplace. It lacked a strategy and organizational approach that fit the realities of a rapidly changing, dynamic, and extremely explosive market situation. It was slow to develop and market new products, particularly personal computers. It was a high-cost competitor because of its extensive overhead. And it was not good at focusing on customers and what satisfied them.

Before long, IBM was losing market share to companies that did not even exist at the beginning of the 1980s. Apple, AST, Dell, Compaq, Gateway, and Sun Microsystem all took market share away from IBM, despite the fact that they began the decade with few if any of the traditional sources of competitive advantage. Their one advantage: they understood the market better and were organized to perform in ways that IBM could not.

Realizing this, IBM tried to match its competitors by creating a new personal computer unit in the early 1980s. The leaders of it were told to break the IBM mold and do what was needed to produce a competitive product. They did just that, by changing IBM management practices in many ways, and by starting a new location in Florida. The effort made IBM a major player in the PC business, but a few years later the unit was closed down and the PC business was integrated into the rest of IBM, with a resulting decline in performance. As will be discussed in more detail later, the start of a rogue unit and its eventual shutdown are common events when large bureaucratic organizations try to change.

In one respect, focusing on organization and management in order to gain competitive advantage is not new. Organizations have always tried to do a better job of organizing and managing themselves. However, they have operated within the traditional framework. They have accepted the wisdom of using established management methods such as job descriptions, performance appraisal systems, budgets, and hierarchies and believed that the way to gain an organizational competitive advantage was to use them more skillfully. This, in fact, is precisely what IBM did and did well. It was often recognized as the best-managed company in the world.

No doubt, improving existing practices can lead to some performance improvement, as in the case of streamlining a propeller-driven airplane or giving it higher-powered engines. But it does little to differentiate one organization from another, and it is unlikely to produce dramatic gains in performance. To get those gains, new technology—like jet engines—must be acquired. The new logic argues that a superior and well-executed approach to organizing, one better suited to the realities of today's work force, global competition, and technology than the bureaucratic approach, can provide a significant and sustainable competitive advantage—an advantage that is based not on continuous improvement or incremental improvement but on discontinuous change and dramatic performance improvements.

Convincing evidence that management practices can provide competitive advantages is beginning to accumulate.[3] A study done in 1995 by my Center for Effective Organizations found that companies in the Fortune 1000 which were high users of employee involvement and total quality management had higher returns on equity (22.8 percent versus 16.6 percent), higher returns on sales (10.3 percent versus 6.3 percent), and overall higher productivity than did low users.[4]

There is also considerable evidence from companies that specific management practices make a difference. For example, Motorola data indicate it gets a 30-to-1 return on money it spends on training. Xerox says it has cut manufacturing costs by 30 percent by cooperating with its union. For years, Procter & Gamble has argued that its use of self-managing work teams in its plants has reduced manufacturing costs by 30 percent or more. All told, a growing body of evidence supports the argument that by putting together the right management systems, organizations can gain a significant competitive advantage.

As discussed in the Introduction, organizational capabilities are central to this new way of thinking about organization as a competitive advantage—especially when they are developed to a level that can produce superior performance. A number of studies of the automobile industry from 1970 to 1995 have demonstrated just how important organizational capabilities can be.[5] When the Japanese car companies started successfully exporting cars to the United States, the domestic automobile industry blamed a host of factors for their loss of market share. In the early 1980s, it started to become obvious that Japanese auto firms were winning against U.S. firms largely because they were "better managed." Since that time, study after study has shown that the better quality and productivity in Japanese automobile companies come not from technology or different government regulations but from superior quality management systems, from better employee relations, and from the use of integrated design and production teams to speed up the new-product development process.

Once the U.S. auto companies began to recognize that their lack of organizational capabilities was putting them at a competitive disadvantage, they began to respond and have gone on to close much of the gap between them and their Japanese competitors. Chrysler, Ford, and General Motors have all undergone massive restructurings that have introduced total quality management, eliminated levels of management, and changed their relationship with their unions. As of 1996, though, none of them had yet reached the manufacturing quality and productivity levels of their Japanese competitors. J. D. Power surveys still show Honda, Toyota, and Nissan with fewer manufacturing defects than Chrysler, Ford, and General Motors, clearly demonstrating how management systems can provide a long-term competitive advantage.

Although it took place in 1984, I still remember clearly an interview that I did with a Japanese manager who was restarting the General Motors assembly plant in Fremont, California, that was to become the NUMMI facility. Toyota and General Motors had decided to reopen this formerly unsuccessful plant as a joint venture with Toyota managers in charge because of Toyota's success in running assembly plants with their "lean production" approach.

The manager that I interviewed said that because workers who had worked previously in the GM plant were going to be rehired, they needed to receive twice as much training as Toyota normally would give to workers who had never worked in the auto industry before. When I asked why, he told me that he expected that half of their training would be devoted to unlearning GM habits and the other half to learning the correct habits for the new organization they wanted to create. He went on to add that this would double the cost that would be required for the typical Toyota plant start-up but that it would result in performance levels that no U.S. plant could equal.

So while an organization still needs good human resources, capital, and technology to win in the marketplace, they have become just the ante to get into the game, something all competitors are likely to have. Today, organizational capabilities are the key to winning, because they can provide difficult-to-match performance.

OLD LOGIC PRINCIPLE: Bureaucracy is the most effective source of control.

NEW LOGIC PRINCIPLE: Involvement is the most effective source of control.

In every organization, there must be a way to control and coordinate individual activities; otherwise, individuals cannot accomplish the collective goal that brought them together. The debate in organization theory about control is not about whether it is necessary but about how it is best achieved. The traditional logic (Theory X) argues that control can best be obtained through extrinsic rewards, close supervision, hierarchy, and careful delineation of responsibilities and accountabilities. What Theory X ignores—and what McGregor recognized—is the real-life response of employees to controls. Sometimes workers will be obedient, but they often put as much effort into sabotaging the controls as doing their jobs. Ever since I worked my first summer job in the trucking business, I have been impressed with the ingenuity of the American work force when it comes to defeating management control systems. Somehow, the individuals I worked with always managed to get a daily nap without being caught and were able to manipulate the foreman so they got to work as much overtime as they wanted.

Years later, as a consultant to the auto industry, I saw example after example of how employees eased their work loads by short-cutting work methods and procedures even though they were under close supervision. In other industries with assembly lines, I have seen employees figure out ingenious ways to put the product together incorrectly, simply to prove to themselves that they could do it. They found it much more satisfying to beat the controls than to conform to them and make the product as specified by the company's engineers and work methods experts.

The new logic of organizing has a solution to counterproductive responses by workers. It builds on McGregor's statement of Theory Y by arguing that if individuals are involved in their work and in the business of the organization, they will not only figure out what they should be doing and do it, they will also provide their own controls. It further argues that when people are involved in the business, their energy and creativity will be focused on positive results such as improving production processes and creating better products and services, instead of on beating the system. As a result, much of the costly, bureaucratic control structure in traditional hierarchical organizations becomes unnecessary.

Perhaps the simplest way of expressing how control works in the new logic is to say that it is better to have a customer and the external market controlling an individual's performance than to use a set of bureaucratic rules, procedures, and a supervisor for control. In order to move control into the hands of the market or customer, the entire organization has to be structured so that employees can get feedback from customers about their performance and their responses to customer needs. This can guide performance in ways that a supervisor or a system cannot duplicate, because the customer—not some person or system that is acting as a proxy for the customer—is the ultimate arbiter of success. The customer is more likely to point employees in the right direction and to prompt change as the customer and the competitive environment change.

Admittedly, hierarchy can allow lower-level employees to act quickly with a high degree of precision and conformity through programmed decisions. But the downside of programmed actions is that strict guidelines and controls may prevent employees from acting on their own to meet a demand or to solve a unique or particularly nettlesome problem. The result all too often is slow decision making and poor-quality decisions when it is not business as usual.

I experienced a good example of failed hierarchical decision making when a recent flight that I was scheduled to take was several hours late. Because of the delay, this dinner flight was not going to leave until 10 P.M., and the passengers at the gate wanted to know if they could get a dinner voucher for the airport restaurant. The gate agent responded that he could not make the decision and would have to call his supervisor, which he did. Unfortunately, other flights were late, and the supervisor was busy. By the time the supervisor did arrive, an hour later, most customers had left the gate area angry and hungry. And even though he did give vouchers to the remaining customers, that did not help assuage their negative impressions of the airline, and it did nothing for the customers who had already left to get dinner on their own.

Programmed decisions dictated by hierarchy are particularly problematic when it is difficult to anticipate what decisions need to be made. With the business environment changing rapidly and with more complex situations, products, and services, fewer and fewer of an organization's actions lend themselves to carefully planned, programmed decisions. So unless organizations abandon the bureaucratic approach, they end up with more and more hierarchical "approvals" needed for decisions. As a result, decision makers are overloaded, decision making is slowed (as with my delayed flight), and even simple transactions turn into complicated ones.

Decision quality also can become a problem under a hierarchical approach. Decisions made at higher levels often miss the critical subtleties that the people who are close to the problem and the customers know intimately. Besides, in service situations, telling an irate customer you have to get approval or you are just following the rules does not help to quell anger and dissatisfaction. Customers want immediate action on their requests and problems. They want the first person they encounter to satisfy them. Nordstrom, the department store chain, recognizes this and has given its customer service associates only one rule with respect to refunds and exchanges: satisfy the customer. Ritz-Carlton Hotels has done the same; it too says "satisfy the customer" and gives each employee the power to spend thousands of dollars to do it.

Effective involvement depends on developing an organization structure in which individuals feel that they are accountable for their own and their organization's performance because they have customers that they serve who provide them with feedback. An organization cannot meet this challenge just by grafting customer satisfaction measures onto a hierarchical structure that relies on bureaucratic and supervisory control as well as extrinsic rewards (pay, bonuses, and so on) and punishments (such as firing) in order to coordinate behavior and ensure that customers are satisfied.

The new logic calls for replacing bureaucratic controls with the following four components of effective employee involvement:

- Information about business strategy, processes, quality, customer feedback, events, and business results
- Knowledge of the work, the business, and the total work system
- Power to act and make decisions about the work in all of its aspects
- Rewards tied to business results, individual growth, capability, and contribution

When these four elements are appropriately positioned, involvement can be an effective source of control and organized action.[6]

Involvement requires that the amounts of information, knowledge, power, and rewards that individuals have be balanced and that all employees have significant amounts of them. This does not mean that those at the top have any less knowledge, information, power, and rewards; it does mean that the organization becomes flatter (that is, it has fewer levels) and that the information, power, knowledge, and rewards that were in the middle of the organization are pushed down so that they are spread throughout the organization. This is what makes effective decision making and involvement possible at lower levels in an organization. Figure 1.1 presents this thinking in graphic form.

Figure 1.1. Power, Information, Knowledge, and Rewards.

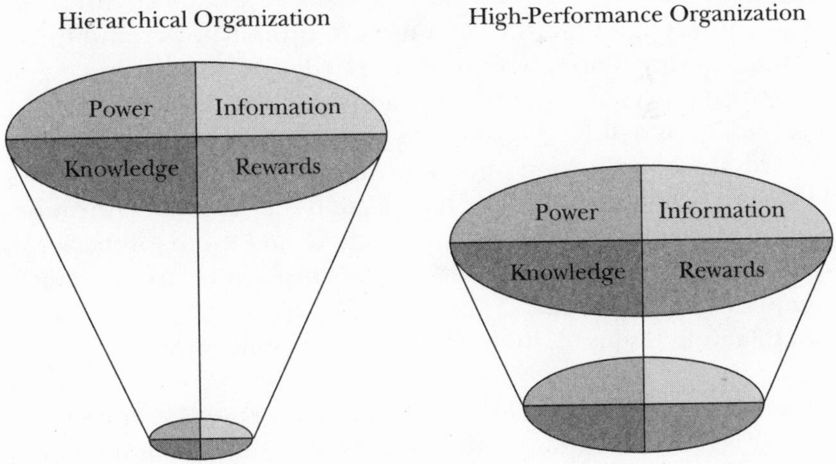

Hierarchical Organization   High-Performance Organization

It shows that involvement-oriented and traditional organizations position these four key elements very differently. In well-designed, traditional, hierarchical organizations, individuals at the lowest levels have little information, power, knowledge, and rewards, while individuals at the top have large amounts of all four. In the involvement approach, individuals at the lowest levels have much larger amounts of these elements.

Recently, as the result of some consulting work that I was doing with General Electric, I saw this flattened, cone-shaped approach to the four elements taken one step further. It showed a cone that was wider at the bottom. I was told this was where GE is heading. Not only don't I think GE is heading there (I cannot see an assembly line operator having more knowledge, information, power, and rewards than the CEO, Jack Welch), I do not think they should be. As will be discussed in Chapter Three, senior management needs to set the direction for the organization, and this requires and warrants a larger amount of these four elements.

Balance among information, power, knowledge, and rewards is critical to effective involvement. In general, they are well managed and balanced when individuals are rewarded based on how effectively they exercise the power that is associated with their position and when they have the information and knowledge to exercise their power effectively. Individuals should not have more power than they can exercise effectively given the amount of information and knowledge they have, nor do they need significantly more knowledge than they can use given their power and information. Having more power than knowledge or information is particularly dangerous, since it can lead to poor decision making.

Finally, as will be discussed in more detail in Chapter Nine, rewards must fit the kind of power individuals exercise, the type of knowledge they have, and the information they receive. Otherwise, individuals will not be correctly motivated, and there will be a lack of accountability for performance because there are no consequences attached to it.

In a well-designed, high-involvement organization:

- Individuals understand the business. They know its strategy, how it is doing, and who their customers and competitors are.

- Individuals are rewarded according to the success of the business. They are owners and share in its performance so that what is good for the business is good for them.
- Employees are able to influence important organizational decisions. They decide on work methods, participate in business strategy decisions, and work with each other in order to coordinate their work.

In summary, the new logic argues that the best control comes from the marketplace and the customer. Through involvement, it creates employees who act like owners and managers, who exercise self-control because they are involved in satisfying the customer and meeting market demands. It rejects the traditional approaches to control as too expensive, ineffective, and in many cases dysfunctional.

OLD LOGIC PRINCIPLE: Top management and technical experts should add most of the value.

NEW LOGIC PRINCIPLE: All employees must add significant value.

The new logic turns the traditional equation of who adds value to the organization's products and services upside down. It constantly pushes for individuals throughout the organization to add more value by

- Doing more complicated tasks
- Managing and controlling themselves
- Coordinating their work with the work of other employees
- Suggesting ideas about better ways to do the work
- Developing new products and ways to serve customers

This is in sharp contrast to the traditional hierarchical organization where individuals at the lower levels carry out prescribed, routine, low-value-added tasks in a controlled manner while senior management adds major value through their work on organizational design, strategy, and the coordination of the work of different groups and functions.

There is little chance for employees to add value to simple repetitive work. Many relatively untrained, low-wage workers in companies and countries around the world can do such work, making the people who do it a commodity. This accounts for the current movement of many industrial jobs out of developed countries.[7] Employees who are doing simple repetitive work in the United States, western Europe, and Japan often are simply overpaid relative to the global value of their skills and the value they add to products. Sometimes the only solution to this problem is to move work to low-wage companies and countries. But this is not always the right or the best answer. The "overpayment" of employees may be the result of organizations following the old logic and as a result not allowing its employees to add all the value that they can.

All too often today, when individuals try to add value through making suggestions or managing themselves, the work systems will not let them. Thus, even though employees earn wages that suggest that they add significant value, the organizational designs and structures—which support top-down decision making and control—do not allow them to add it. This is precisely how companies in developed countries end up with wage levels that are not globally competitive. If they want to compete in a global market, they must create high-valued-added work that requires skills and knowledge. Individuals must have the opportunity to manage themselves and coordinate their work with that of their co-workers.

The relationship between compensation levels and technical knowledge is relatively straightforward and clearly demonstrated. Less straightforward—and perhaps less well established—is the relationship between affordable wage levels and management practices. Simply stated, if work is designed so that employees take on many of the management duties that are typically done by supervisors and staff specialists, then they warrant higher levels of pay. They are in essence adding the value that a highly paid manager or someone in a technical staff role might otherwise contribute.

Information technology as well as advanced automation processes in the manufacturing world can help to transform work. Automation in manufacturing, such as the use of robots, can create work that involves high levels of problem solving, technical complexity, and coordination and can thus make it possible for employees to add considerable value. Employees end up doing programming, skilled maintenance, and machine setup instead of simple routine manual tasks. The downside is that fewer employees are needed. The upside is that those who remain can be paid good wages because they contribute more to organizational effectiveness.

Today, given the realities of a global work force, it is critical to structure organizations so that in high-wage countries employees at all levels add significant value. Organizations can no longer afford the combination of high pay and low value-added work and workers. By making the assumption that individuals at all levels of the organization can add significant value, through new logic approaches to organizing, and through the use of information technology, new logic organizations can be more cost-effective than high-wage old logic ones and in some cases even more effective than low-wage ones. The key is that individuals must know more and do more. If, by following the principles of the new logic, an organization's work can be designed to help create high-value-added jobs, it can be a win-win situation for organizations and for individuals. Organizations can end up with a competitive advantage, and individuals can end up with higher-paid, more rewarding work.

OLD LOGIC PRINCIPLE: Hierarchical processes are the key to organizational effectiveness.
NEW LOGIC PRINCIPLE: Lateral processes are the key to organizational effectiveness.

The new logic puts much less emphasis on hierarchical reporting relationships and much more on lateral, or side-by-side, relationships. It stresses that effective lateral relationships are the key to creating organizations that can perform well on speed, cost, quality, and innovation. Both reengineering and total quality management address this point: they emphasize that when employees at different steps in the work process coordinate their behavior effectively, it can lead to significant gains in organizational performance.

It's not that the traditional logic denies the importance of lateral relationships. Quite to the contrary, it views them as so important that they must be closely controlled and monitored through a hierarchical management and information-system structure. However, there are two problems with the hierarchical approach.

First, individuals tend to compete with each other to move up the hierarchy; thus, employees end up spending their energy and efforts trying to please the boss and the boss's boss rather than concentrating on what is important—that is, relating to customers, vendors, and other employees at their level with whom they need to work in order to produce a successful product or service. This is hardly surprising given that the organization chart shows them reporting to a higher-level manager, not to a peer or customer. Indeed, the only formal connection among peers occurs because they all report to the same level of management.

Second, there is often a lack of accountability for important organizational goals as employees are simply engaged in individual activities, rather than trying to accomplish important objectives. Most hierarchical organizations group employees not by customer or product but by common activities such as sales, production, and accounting. They put those people who do the same things together rather than grouping people who are trying to accomplish the same goals and who are working on the same process.

For example, in the purchasing department of a Ford plant I studied, separate groups communicated with suppliers, checked the price on the bill, matched the purchase order to the bill, wrote the check, determined whether the material had arrived, and so on. A bill passed through ten pairs of hands before it was paid. The result: no one was responsible and no one had an overview of what was happening, mistakes were common, payments were slow, and suppliers could never find out what had happened to their bill.

This is precisely why an organization that operates laterally can have an enormous competitive advantage. When all employees who are working on a product work together and share a common purpose, it increases the chance that the product will be well designed and manufactured. Similarly, when all who serve a particular type of customer work together, they can go beyond their function or step in the service process and grow to know and care about how customers are being served. This can lead to more ownership of both jobs and customers and, thus, to better service and products.

It can also lead to faster decision making and service because information does not need to be moved to someone higher up to integrate it and make a judgment. It can be done at the point of contact with the customer or product—a particularly crucial advantage in rapidly changing businesses.[8] Further, because a laterally focused organization needs fewer control systems than a hierarchy, it can eliminate levels of managers and reduce overall costs.

Only if all of an organization's systems are designed to support it can an organization truly operate in a lateral manner that produces superior performance. This means changing the human resource management systems, the communication systems, and the work structures of vertical organizations to ones that are consistent with a lateral approach. For example:

- Employees need the ability to meet in groups and problem solve together.
- Reward systems must be in place that reflect peer input and reward group and team behavior.
- Team-based work designs are necessary.
- Communication systems must move information and customer data laterally without going through levels of supervisory control.
- Managers need to facilitate lateral interaction and learning.

As will become evident in the discussion of the next principle, organization structure is also crucial to creating lateral relationships that reduce costs, improve quality, and speed decision making.

OLD LOGIC PRINCIPLE: Organizations should be designed around functions.

NEW LOGIC PRINCIPLE: Organizations should be designed around products and customers.

The traditional logic of organizing emphasizes functional excellence and expertise and assumes that good performance grows directly out of these qualities. It further assumes that functional excellence is the result of getting the best possible individuals in each specialty and putting them together. This enables functional specialists to learn from each other as well as get training and development tailored directly for them. The managers, also experts in the specialty, are charged with developing the department's technical competence. In this approach, staff groups in areas such as human resource management, finance, and law typically review the plans and operations of the other parts of the organization and determine whether they are up to their standards. If this all sounds eminently sensible, it is because most organizations have been structured and managed this way for decades.

The main flaw in this approach: no single function—not human resource management, not finance, not marketing, not R&D, and not even manufacturing—can, by itself, make products or serve customers. None alone can create satisfied customers. Only when individually strong areas of expertise are brought together to produce high-quality, innovative products and services that are sold at an attractive price does the organization become effective and satisfy customers.

The new logic does not say that there is little need for strong expertise in particularly critical functions. But it does stress that it is possible to have strong functional expertise and not have a particularly effective organization, because traditional, functionally structured organizations have trouble developing the teamwork and coordination that lead to successful products and services.

The first course I took in organizational design helped establish in my mind the importance of fitting individuals with different skills together in order to form effective teams. Early in the course, Pete Newell, who had just finished coaching the 1960 gold-medal U.S. Olympic team, talked to us about putting together a winning basketball team. His team was an early "dream team" with a number of excellent college players (Jerry Lucas and Oscar Robertson, to mention two of the most famous). The members of the class sat back with an attitude that said, How could anyone lose with a team like that? As Newell pointed out, despite the individual excellence of each of the players, there is a major problem in putting a team of all-stars together. In college, each one of these star players had the ball about 40 percent of the time when their team was on offense. Clearly, there was not enough time, nor enough balls, for each of them to do that on the Olympic team. Newell had to train virtually all of them to play without the ball for the first time in their lives.

The same challenge often exists in large, complex organizations with individuals who are strong in particular functions. They need to be trained to work with other functions and to focus on product and service excellence rather than functional excellence. In short, they and their function can't have the ball all the time.

The new logic argues that you have to organize around units that are focused on products and customers if you want employees with different specialties to work well together. This ties directly to the idea of control coming from customers and the market, the importance of lateral processes, and the need for individuals at all levels to add significant value.

In order for these aspects of the new logic to work, all employees must be part of units in which everyone can see how their behavior affects organizational performance; in other words, they must have a line of sight to the business and its success. Then and only then can individuals feel that they are market driven, that they are responding to a particular customer or managing a specific product. And only when they feel this type of business involvement do the benefits of the new logic occur.

In many cases, applying the new logic means that certain functional specialties will be support services to organizational units focused on making particular products or offering particular services. Functional experts in law, marketing, and finance, for example, will supply knowledge and expertise to other parts of an organization who are their customers. Staff groups will no longer approve or disapprove the actions of a business unit; they will serve more in a consulting or educational role. Alternatively, they may join product development or customer service teams to help those teams to be more effective. The net effect of this repositioning of expertise should be to reduce the amount of corporate overhead in organizations and to create organizations that are primarily structured around customer- or product-focused units.

OLD LOGIC PRINCIPLE: Effective managers are the key to organizational effectiveness.

NEW LOGIC PRINCIPLE: Effective leadership is the key to organizational effectiveness.

Because of the old logic's emphasis on managers, particularly top managers, as the ones who add the most value, their effectiveness is correctly considered to be the critical element in a traditional organization's performance. At the core of the hierarchical approach is the belief that effective management means defining, evaluating, structuring, and coordinating the work of others. At higher levels, management involves setting strategy, making critical business decisions, and defining the accountabilities and responsibilities of others.

The old logic places little emphasis on leadership, because bureaucratic management systems are designed to operate as substitutes for leadership that tell employees what to do and provide the motivation to do it. Leaders are not needed to make an organization successful. Indeed, historically, the senior managers of large companies such as AT&T, Sears, Mobil, and Exxon have not been well known and have not demonstrated great leadership skills. Who, for example, can remember any of the presidents of AT&T from the period when it was the world's largest corporate employer?

In the new logic, leadership, not bureaucratic management, is central. Leadership is not easy to define; it is easier to recognize when you see it. What's the difference between leaders and managers? Managers do things right; leaders do the right thing. Managers influence through bureaucratic systems; leaders influence through vision and challenge. Managers motivate through rewards and punishment; leaders motivate through values and shared goals.

In the new logic, many traditional managerial functions are in essence rendered unnecessary through a combination of organizational design and employee self-management, but leadership is not. It is a critically important substitute for hierarchy and bureaucracy. The old logic emphasizes managerial processes and de-emphasizes leadership processes. The new logic emphasizes leadership behaviors and de-emphasizes managerial processes. It does not, however, advocate turning organizations "upside down" so that senior management is simply there to serve the rest of the organization, as some have suggested. They should not be servant leaders, because they have more important things to do.

The new logic—even more than the old logic—requires that top-level managers create the key organizational systems and processes and that they provide strategic direction. They are almost always in the best position to add value by setting direction and defining the organization's agenda and by sensing conditions and events in the business environment that affect strategy. Finally, they are important role models for others.

In many respects, effective top management leadership is more important in a new logic organization than in a bureaucratic one. A traditional organization can operate without an effective leader at the top and in fact often needs an effective manager, not a leader. Historically, many chief executive officers of large U.S. corporations have been effective because they were good at managing budgets, control systems, and organization restructurings.

In the new logic, effective leaders substitute for bureaucratic controls and structures. They provide a sense of mission, vision, direction, and rationale. Without this kind of leadership, new logic organizations can drift like a ship without a rudder. Herman Miller, the furniture manufacturer, found itself in just this situation when its longtime leader, Max De Pree, retired. An adequate replacement was not found, and for the first time, the organization had performance problems.

In the new logic, it is critically important to have leadership throughout the organization, not only at or near the top. Flatter, more lateral organizational structures and a decrease in the number of traditional means of control call for more, not less leadership from everyone. Teams, for example, rarely operate effectively without someone or some set of individuals who lead by challenging the group, helping it set priorities and addressing performance problems. In traditional organizations, formal systems or hierarchical processes deal with these issues. In the new logic, individuals within the group must take on leadership roles to help the team address them.

In the new logic, all employees need to think of themselves as both managers and leaders. They are managers in the sense that they participate in structuring their work, influencing and coordinating with others and managing themselves. There are times, however, when self-management may not be enough; leadership is needed. Individuals need to motivate and inspire others through words, visions, recognition, and, of course, through modeling the "right behavior" and exhibiting all the leadership acts that encourage others to realize the organization's larger vision.

The new logic does not require an abundance of charismatic leaders, despite the fact that they are currently favored in the leadership literature.[9] Indeed, since there seems to be a scarce supply of charismatic leaders (those who create excitement and inspire commitment as a result of their ability to communicate an attractive vision, who behave in unconventional and symbolically important ways, and who have an extraordinary, almost god-like aura), it is important not to depend on them. Often new logic organizations can benefit from the presence of charismatic leaders, but they need not and probably should not rely on them. In some respects, the ideal leader for a new logic organization is aptly described as the "post-heroic leader" or, as the Chinese proverb says, "The best leader is one who, when he is gone, they will say, we did it ourselves." The heroic leader who commands adulation, respect, and deference and who distances himself or herself is not the type who is needed in a new logic organization.

In their work on what leads to long-term organizational success, Jim Collins and Jerry Porras use the metaphor of a clock for understanding what new logic organization leaders should do.[10] An effective leader, they say, creates an organizational clock that allows people to "tell time for themselves." The leader sets direction for the organization and builds mechanisms to allow people to understand what that direction is and to measure their progress. If the organization is designed properly the leader does not have to spend time reminding everyone of the strategy, telling them how they are doing, and pointing out what customers need. Remember: an effective leader designs an organization so that people know what to do and, at the end of a journey, say they were responsible for completing the trip.

It is particularly difficult for managers who have grown up in traditional bureaucratic organizations to become post-heroic leaders. One of my colleagues, Jim O'Toole, has stated that although 95 percent of American managers understand the logic of the new leadership and can state it, only about 5 percent of them can practice it. I am not sure that O'Toole's numbers are accurate, but I am sure that his overall point is right on. There are clearly many more managers who can profess the new leadership than those who can practice it.

Judging by what I observe in organizations and by the industry that has grown up in the last ten years to identify, train, and develop leaders, it is clear that there is more and more recognition of the importance of leadership. Indeed, there may be an overemphasis on leadership training and development. I am very skeptical about the ability of many of these leadership programs to actually change behavior. Charismatic leadership, in particular, is not easily developed and is unlikely to be influenced by programs that last only a few days and deal with artificially created cases, simulations, and adventure games and exercises (the current favorites of management development programs). Further, the academic literature suggests that the emergence of a charismatic leader is at least partially the result of the situation being right for this to happen.

Given my rather pessimistic assessment of the ability to develop leaders, it is legitimate to ask whether new logic organizations can actually find the quality and quantity of leaders they need to be successful. I believe that they can, but they need to recognize that leadership is a critical commodity and that it is important to develop the leadership skills of the many, not just those of the few who may reach senior management positions. Leadership skills need to be developed over a long period of time through a combination of personal experiences, training programs, and a focus on individual values and skills.[11] They also need to be considered when individuals are hired by new logic organizations.

The six principles of the new logic clearly establish a new paradigm or way of thinking about how to create effective organizations. Together, they can form the basis for developing, from the ground up, organizations that are both different from, and more effective than, the ones that have dominated our lives during the twentieth century. The challenge now is to take these principles and incorporate them into the foundations of an organization.

What types of practices, structures, and systems does an organization need to put in place in order to follow the new logic? To begin answering this question, an overview of the key elements of an organization is presented in the next chapter, along with a discussion of what makes an organization and individuals perform effectively. The chapters that follow focus on applying the six principles to the organizational elements in order to create a high-performance organization.

Chapter Two

Achieving High Performance
Turning Principles into Practice

For years, researchers, companies, and consultants have studied and debated what the key elements or features of an organization are and how they relate to organizational effectiveness. Today there is good agreement on the key features of an organization. Effectiveness is another matter.

The problems with effectiveness begin with its definition. There is a lack of agreement about what constitutes an effective corporation. Some have argued, for example, that effectiveness is only about economic performance and return to shareholders. I do not accept this definition. "Effective" to me means that an organization works well on every level, from achieving its financial and business goals and thereby satisfying its stockholders to building good relationships with its customers by providing the best goods and services. It must also be a "good place to work" for its employees and be a responsible citizen of the communities in which it operates.

Clearly, accomplishing all that an organization needs to in order to be effective is not simple. Sometimes there are conflicts and trade-offs. The best organizational design for productivity or cost-effectiveness, for instance, may not satisfy employees or communities. Nevertheless, I believe we must try to design organizations that perform well for everyone who has a stake in them.

Virtually every study and theory that deals with organizational effectiveness points out that it depends on an organization's ability to deal with its political, social, and economic environment. This simple, somewhat abstract point leads to an important observation: what is effective behavior in one business situation may not be effective in another. The development of the new logic is directly tied to this point: the old logic worked well until dramatic changes in technology, the global economy, and competition made it obsolete. For example, what worked for AT&T in the regulated environment of the 1960s and 1970s simply does not work in the deregulated, highly competitive environment of the 1990s. Witness its breakup into three separate companies in 1996, its third major restructuring in five years.

Saying that organizations need to deal effectively with their environment, of course, does not answer the question of how they should be structured and managed, nor does it tell us how the six principles of the new logic can be used to design high-performance organizations. In order to do this, it is important to first identify the critical elements of an organization and specify how they relate to performance effectiveness.

Critical Elements in Designing High-Performance Organizations

The tool I find most useful in thinking about the critical elements of an organization is the Star Model. It is called the Star Model because, as can be seen in Figure 2.1, it has a pentagonal shape with a five-pointed star inside. It depicts the key features of an organization: strategy, structure, rewards, processes, and people.[1]

The five points of the star are all connected with lines. The interconnections are extremely important because they indicate that organizational effectiveness requires a good alignment or fit among all five. The best test of fit is the performance of the organization. If it matches the strategy, then good fit has been obtained. A second test of fit involves the positioning of information, power, knowledge, and rewards. When they are present in balanced amounts at all levels in the organization, it means that the five points on the star fit with each other.

When you take into account the interconnections in the Star Model, it becomes obvious that if you wish to make a significant change in an organization's performance, all of the five elements must change, because a change in one element of the organization has implications for the rest. Simply changing one or two elements runs the risk of putting the organization out of balance, which is more likely to cause problems than to create better performance.

Figure 2.1. The Star Model.

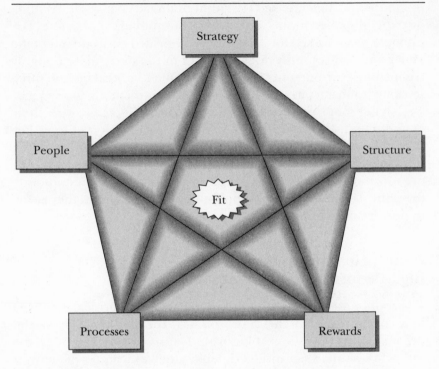

The challenge is to develop an approach to organizing that considers all of the elements and how they fit together to create an organization with the right strategy, competencies, and capabilities to succeed. To provide an introduction to the Star Model, this chapter briefly touches on each of its five points. All five will be discussed in more detail in later chapters. The people point will be discussed in detail here, because a basic knowledge of the performance effectiveness of individuals is critical to an understanding of how the other elements of an organization should be designed. Chapter Eight will consider in more detail the domain of human resource management systems.

Strategy

In the Star Model, business strategy is the cornerstone design element. It needs to define the kind of organizational performance that is needed, the types of organizational capabilities and competencies that are needed, and how an organization intends to respond to its business environment. An organization can do a terrific job of implementing strategy, but unless it offers the right products or services, correctly identifies potential customers, and secures adequate financing, among other factors, it will not succeed.

A clear case of the impact of strategy on organizational effectiveness is IBM's decision to continue to focus on mainframes when the personal computer market and networking were growing. Because of this decision, IBM lost the leadership position in a multi-billion-dollar industry. The opposite was true of Compaq Computer, which recognized that computer users were moving to PCs and quickly established a very successful business that focused on providing individuals and companies with PCs and network servers.

In new organizations, business strategy is usually the first thing to be considered, and it often is addressed somewhat independently of existing practices and structures. In an existing organization, however, the major organizational practices and systems already in place may affect the organization's strategy choices. For example, the reward system often strongly influences the strategy choices organizations make, because it has an impact on management decision making (for example, in the areas of cost cutting and short- versus long-term investing). It is often also important to take an organization's current conditions, resources, competencies, and capabilities into account in formulating strategy. In fact, not to do so runs the risk of generating an entirely unrealistic strategy.

For example, in the early 1980s, United Airlines decided to diversify. They changed their name to Allegis and entered the car rental and hotel businesses in order to offer an integrated travel experience for the business traveler. An interesting and appealing strategy, but United was unable to execute the elements of the strategy because, as a corporation, it lacked the appropriate resources, competencies, and capabilities. It did not, for example, have the information systems to tie the different businesses together. Moreover, all these travel businesses are capital intensive, and United simply did not have access to the cash it needed to fund them.

United is not alone in trying to implement strategies that were far beyond its capabilities. In the 1970s, Exxon correctly identified the business office as a rapidly growing multi-billion-dollar market where enormous profits could be made. As part of its strategy to be a major player in this business, Exxon proceeded to buy one of the first fax companies, an early manufacturer of personal computers, and an emerging semiconductor firm (Zilog). But even though it was one of the first to manufacture and sell these important components of the office of the future, today Exxon has no role in this market.

What happened to this very well financed and apparently well managed company that prevented it from being a leader in a rapidly growing business? The answer is that it lacked the organizational and management capabilities to succeed. Exxon was used to managing businesses that were slow moving, required enormous amounts of capital, and were based on natural resource extraction technologies. In the office equipment world, it found itself in a fast-moving business that required quick decisions and core technological competencies in electronics. Equally important, it relied on getting close to customers and understanding their needs. In the 1970s and 1980s, Exxon, like the other major oil companies, was not particularly good at this.

Structure

The second point on the Star Model is the organization's structure—that is, how people are grouped together, who reports to whom, how tasks are assigned, and the nature of the jobs within the organization. As will be discussed in Chapters Four, Five, and Six, the new logic approach to structure may not include traditional job descriptions and organization charts, but critical decisions still need to be made about how individuals are grouped together, how major decisions are made, how many levels of management are created, and a host of other factors. In many respects, because these decisions are the fundamental building blocks of an organization, they must be closely articulated with the strategy. They are major determinants of how the organization will behave. They also have significant implications for the kinds of people who are needed and the kinds of reward systems that will work best.

Rewards

The third point on the Star Model, reward systems, must fit closely with an organization's strategy so that they reward the correct behaviors. They also need to be closely articulated with the need for human resources since they are critical in attracting and retaining individuals. Further, as will be discussed in Chapter Nine, they are crucial in making all the elements of an organization operate effectively. For example, it does not make sense to develop a strategy that assumes the availability of people with certain capabilities if those people cannot be hired or developed. It also does not make sense to combine a strategy that calls for teamwork with a reward system that rewards individual performance excellence.

Processes

Management processes, the fourth point on the Star Model, are the systems that the organization puts into place to help control, manage, inform, and direct its members' behavior, both individually and collectively, so that they focus on the correct strategic actions. Management processes include information and communication systems, budgeting and financial measurement systems, and the behavior of managers, particularly those involved in decision making and setting direction for the organization.

As with the other points on the star, if the measurement and communication processes are out of alignment or are nonexistent, the organization cannot perform effectively. Some key communication processes—such as meetings and social events—are relatively informal, but most are formal. Budgets, quality controls, and financial information systems are formal means of measuring and communicating performance results. As will be discussed further in Chapter Ten, strategic fit with respect to these systems often means correctly measuring the behaviors that the strategy says are important and that need to be motivated in order for the strategy to be successfully implemented.

People

The final point on the star is people, the organization's human resources. Individual performance is critical to an organization's functioning effectively. In order to ensure it, organizations must have individuals with the right skills and knowledge who are motivated to perform effectively. These will be discussed in more detail after the role of culture in determining organizational effectiveness is considered.

Organizational Culture: The Tangible Intangible

The five-pointed Star Model does not identify a final determinant of organizational performance: corporate culture. It is omitted because it is not a design parameter. Instead, it develops as a result of the influence of all the major elements of an organization.[2] (Some versions of the Star Model put culture in the center of the star to emphasize its importance and indicate that it is influenced by all elements on the star but cannot be directly controlled in the same sense that the major design elements can be.) An organization, for example, is seen as valuing innovation not simply because it says it does but because the reward systems, work design, and information processes all support and encourage those behaviors that lead to innovation.

You can often determine whether an organization is likely to perform in a particular way by looking at its culture, because culture "says" what people in the organization should do and what will be rewarded. For example, in an organization that I studied several years ago, the CEO was concerned about creating a more internally entrepreneurial environment and wondered why there wasn't more innovation and risk taking in the organization. He could have answered his own question had he heard what an individual at the company told me: "The culture here is clear: the rewards for successful innovation are uncertain, and usually minimal. The punishments for failed risk taking are swift, certain, and usually fatal."

The challenge in changing culture, then, is to identify what points on the star give the current culture its characteristics and then to figure out how to change them so that the organization can operate with a new and more functional culture. As will be discussed further in Chapter Eleven, culture is often difficult to change because individuals in the organization have signed up to work there and have continued to work there because they like the existing culture as well as the reward practices and organization design that created it. Thus they are likely to resist change.

Having People with the Skills and Knowledge to Do the Work

No organization can operate successfully if its employees cannot do the work that is assigned to them. Organizations can assure themselves that individuals have the skills, abilities, and capabilities necessary to perform well by selecting and hiring the right people and then developing and training them.

One of the advantages of traditionally structured organizations is that their design principles often define work so that most individuals are asked to do tasks that are relatively easy to perform, as on a traditional assembly line. Until recently, many jobs in automobile assembly plants, for example, could be learned in a few hours or less. Since workers did the same thing every forty-five to fifty seconds, they quickly became proficient. At the upper levels of traditional organizations, of course, the learning and skill requirements are much greater, because that is where the greatest value is added.

My best example of a job that could set an all-time record for low skills was one I saw at a Ford tractor factory. Because the automatic spray equipment occasionally failed to cover an inch-square area on the underside of the tractors, a worker was put under the assembly line to check to see whether the machines had missed the spot. In the cases where it had missed, he used a small paint brush on a stick to touch it up while sitting in a stuffed tilt-back easy chair and listening to the radio. A human had stepped into a breach left by technology—but what a low-value-added job!

In the new logic, employees at all levels of the organization need skills that are not needed in traditional organizations. Thus it is particularly important to pick individuals who have the skills or can develop the skills that the organization needs.

After selection, the key to successfully training and developing employees rests in identifying the skills and capabilities that are needed to perform well in a particular organization design. In very simple, repetitive work, brief on-the-job training may be enough to give individuals the correct skills. In organizations where individuals are expected to participate in teams, do problem solving, and manage themselves, training and development must be an ongoing, intensive process that combines classroom instruction with on-the-job experiences.

Unfortunately, one of the most common errors organizations make is to spend too little time and money on training and development. This is a particularly serious problem in a rapidly changing business environment where individuals need new skills and are expected to direct their own behavior and do extensive problem solving.

As part of a ongoing study that began in 1987, two fellow University of Southern California researchers—Susan Mohrman and Gerald Ledford—and I have been tracking the amount of training that large American companies give their employees.[3] Our data show that, despite some well-publicized exceptions such as Motorola's mandated one week of training for every employee every year, most non-management employees in U.S. companies receive no training during the typical year. There is one encouraging trend: the most recent data show a significant increase in the amount of training that employees received, mostly in statistical analysis, group decision making, and problem solving. Still, the evidence overall suggests that managers are much more likely to be trained than are other employees and that there is still a significant gap between the demands created by the new logic of organizing and the training that employees receive. If, as I believe, we are moving away from the traditional organization design with its simple, stable jobs and tight controls, it is particularly critical that organizations focus on the kinds of skills that are developed.

Some years ago, I had the opportunity to do a study of the best practices of firms in attracting and developing managers.[4] Without question, IBM and AT&T were outstanding. They had extensive, well-validated selection tests. AT&T, for example, developed and pioneered the use of assessment centers to identify high-potential managers. They spent a great deal of money on training and development and were very good at career tracking their high-potential managers. Every two years, they moved them into new jobs that were intended to develop their skills and understanding of the organization.

IBM was particularly impressive because of its focus on careful selection, its heavy investment in training programs, and its especially strong individual performance appraisal system that had well-written job descriptions tied directly to individuals' goals and objectives. In addition to the usual performance factors, managers were evaluated on their ability to attract and retain employees, their impact on work force satisfaction, and their development of subordinates. Overall, I thought IBM was doing the best job of human resource management of any company. It had developed a system that assured a bountiful supply of individuals who would be committed to IBM, would fit their culture, and could do their jobs.

The irony here—which I did not anticipate at the time we did the research—was that this great strength turned into an enormous handicap because IBM was selecting, training, and preparing their work force for the work of yesterday and today, not tomorrow. IBM went from a company that had a lot of people who could do what needed to be done to having few who were ready and able to do what needed to be done in the drastically different, volatile business environment of the 1980s and 1990s. That is one of the reasons IBM ultimately had to go outside its organization in 1993 to hire a new CEO, as well as a number of other senior managers. As the IBM example illustrates, effective people development is not simply a matter of doing things right, it is a matter of doing the right things so that the organization will develop the right capabilities and competencies.

An important element that is often neglected in developing a skilled work force: providing a work environment that is both satisfying and rewarding and likely to attract and retain skilled individuals. Unlike other important resources, employees are mobile and can choose to leave the organization or, for that matter, not join it. As will be seen in the discussion of motivation, using financial and other extrinsic rewards is only one way to make an organization an attractive place to work. Besides providing financial rewards, organizations need to be very concerned with the interest and challenge level of the work, the nature of the social relationships that develop, and the learning opportunities they provide; in combination, they determine whether a corporation is an employer of choice.

Motivating People

The second key to achieving superior individual performance—and in some ways the one that many of us find most mystifying—

is motivating individuals to work effectively. Since my early research in the field of organizational effectiveness focused primarily on motivation, I am often frustrated by the tremendous amount of misinformation about it in the literature on management as well as in the minds of many managers. Admittedly, it is a complicated topic, but the fact is that we do know a great deal about it.[5] Motivation need not be a mystery.

We know that individuals are motivated when they feel that they can do their job well and when they feel that doing it well will be rewarded with something they value. Thus, in understanding motivation, it is important to look at two factors: the rewards individuals value and their perceptions of the behavior that is rewarded.[6]

Important Motivators

One of the best-known motivation theorists, Frederick Herzberg, has argued that extrinsic awards, such as pay, can only be dissatisfiers and cannot be important motivators.[7] Although this argument is accepted by many, it is dangerously misleading. There is an enormous amount of evidence that pay, in fact, can be quite an effective motivator. It is true, as will be discussed in Chapter Nine, that when pay systems are not designed well, they either do not motivate or motivate the wrong behavior. But there are also many examples of successful pay systems.

A classic example of an extremely successful reward system is the one used by Lincoln Electric, a Cleveland, Ohio, manufacturing firm. Employees there have large financial incentives that are tied to their individual performance as well as incentives that are tied to overall corporate profitability.[8] In 1994, factory workers earned an average wage of $19,000, but with bonuses their total compensation came to $55,614. This approach has worked well for Lincoln Electric, at least in part because they have attracted a work force that responds positively to financial rewards.

Abraham Maslow's need hierarchy theory suggests that because individuals vary in their needs, they also value rewards differently. In Maslow's theory, the highest-level needs are for intrinsic rewards such as feelings of growth, development, and competency and are sought only after the needs for extrinsic and social rewards are satisfied.[9] Other key points from Maslow's theory: people are likely to differ in the rewards they value, and the rewards they value are likely to change over time because the needs of individuals change over time, depending upon their satisfaction with the particular rewards they have received.

The critical point that organizations and their managers should remember from Maslow's theory is that human beings are motivated by internal feelings of accomplishment, capability, and competency—not just extrinsic rewards such as food, water, recognition, and financial well-being. Thus organization designs that do not emphasize the role of intrinsic rewards, but instead rely heavily on extrinsic rewards, fail to tap a very powerful source of motivation that can lead individuals to perform at extraordinary levels.

Organizations also need to remember that there is no definitive answer, nor will there ever be, to the question of what rewards are most important to individuals. The results of thousands of attitude surveys have not provided a definitive answer in part because the importance of rewards changes. It is possible to find data (depending on who is surveyed and the way the question is asked) that rate any of several things—the importance of interesting work, high pay, job security, and social relationships—as the reward that people value the most.

In order to motivate individuals, an organization must match the characteristics of its work force to its management system. It is just as foolish to try to use money to motivate employees who are not motivated by financial rewards as it is to try to use interesting and challenging jobs to motivate individuals who are looking for more money. Thus it is important to have individuals who respond effectively to the management systems that an organization uses. This motivational fit is particularly important in the new logic because not everyone responds well to the challenges that are involved in working in a high-performance organization. Thus individuals must be selected for their motivation as well as for their skills and abilities.

Often the selection challenge for traditional organizations is finding individuals who are willing to do low-skill jobs. Turnover in them is often high and expensive. In the 1970s, Ford tried to solve this problem by showing all job applicants a film called *Don't Color It Like Disneyland.*

Ford intended the film to be a realistic preview of work on the assembly line. It stressed Ford's employment contract with its employees (high wages, good benefits, and recreational activities tied to the plant) and showed employees making additions to their houses, talking about their new refrigerators and television sets, and playing in company-sponsored softball games. It also depicted employees on the assembly lines and explained that the work itself was highly repetitive.

It showed one employee who appeared completely frustrated with moving bumpers from a stamping machine to a storage rack over and over again. Finally, he threw a bumper down, walked out of the plant, and, true to the Ford tradition, sped off in a Mustang, never to be heard from again. A voice-over on the film at that point said, "If you do become so frustrated that you cannot work here anymore, be sure to tell the foreman that you are leaving so we will know what has happened to you."

The film actually helped reduce turnover somewhat because it helped individuals decide before they were hired whether or not Ford was a place where they wanted to work. Despite its "positive" impact, Ford ultimately discontinued showing the film because they felt it was a bad public relations practice.

Years later, I saw this same realistic job preview strategy used by Cummins Engine Corporation to be sure that its new hires were a good motivational fit for one of their high-performance manufacturing plants. They showed them a film that was made by the employees. It talked about the challenges and rewards associated with working in the plant.

Perhaps the most important idea to take away from this discussion of the importance of rewards to individuals is that it is futile to argue about the relative importance of rewards to the work force in general. There will never be a definitive study that identifies one type of reward as the most important. The key is to match the characteristics of the work force to the management systems of the organization.

Rewarding Performance

The final motivational challenge is to make sure that employees believe that receiving important rewards depends on good performance. In the case of extrinsic rewards, organizations need systems that clearly and closely tie receiving rewards to performance. A term that I increasingly use to describe this relationship is *line of sight*—that is, how well individuals can see that the extrinsic rewards they receive are a consequence of their performance.

The traditional logic emphasizes individual pay for performance (merit pay and piece work) in order to create a strong line of sight and motivation. The new logic takes a different approach. It argues that such extrinsic reward systems as gain sharing, profit sharing, and stock ownership—which will be discussed in later chapters— should be used to create a line of sight between financial rewards and performance that is more consistent with the new logic.

A crucial aspect of creating a line of sight is the reward policy itself. Organizations need to say that they reward performance, but this is just the first step. Often, a bigger challenge is matching reward policy with actual behavior. People are motivated and act based on their perceptions of a reward situation rather than by what is said about the rewards and in some cases despite what is actually done in reward administration.[10] So-called merit pay plans are a good example. Despite their name and the claim that they reward performance, often employees do not believe that this is true because their results are kept secret and therefore no one is sure what they are based on. Of course, sometimes they are not based on merit, a problem that cannot be resolved by openness.

Given the importance of clear and accurate perceptions of rewards within organizations, it has always seemed a bit odd to me that most companies keep their pay actions secret. The rationale is that secrecy reduces dissatisfaction among employees and makes it easier to administer pay. It may do both, but I question whether secrecy reduces dissatisfaction. In any case, it clearly does not help pay become a motivator because employees cannot readily know the relationship between rewards and performance. What is the point of spending the huge amounts of time and money developing systems that are supposed to reward performance and increase motivation when individuals then have to speculate about the degree to which rewards depend upon performance?

Social and recognition rewards can be created and tied to performance through work designs and workplace layouts that provide opportunities for managers and peers to give praise and acknowledgment. The behavior of managers is important, since they are often in the best position to recognize good performance.

But in the new logic, with its emphasis on teams and lateral processes, peers can also be an important source of praise.

Intrinsic rewards, as will be discussed in Chapters Six and Seven, present a different challenge. Individuals actually give themselves intrinsic rewards, but organizations influence the likelihood of those rewards being tied to performance by addressing such work design considerations as

- How complex the work is
- How challenging the work is
- What kind of feedback individuals receive about their work

Good management of intrinsic rewards can make them potent motivators of both membership behavior and performance. The traditional logic pays little attention to intrinsic rewards, and it calls for jobs that are not likely to produce them. They are, however, a key element in the new logic organization.

Finally, in order to be motivated, individuals have to perceive that they can do what is required in order to receive the rewards. As stated earlier, this essentially means that an organization has to actively manage individuals' capabilities through selection, training, and development so that they can succeed in doing the appropriate work. Then it must administer rewards so that there is a clear connection between behavior and the rewards.

Now that the major elements of an organization and the key determinants of individual effectiveness have been introduced, the next step is to address the key question. How does one convert the new logic from a set of principles to a concrete set of practices and structures that organizations can use to make themselves more effective? Fortunately, there are a number of organizations already utilizing such practices and structures that are consistent with the new logic. Thus it is possible to look at how companies are currently using the new logic to competitive advantage. The next chapter focuses on the first point of the Star Model, strategy, and examines how organizations can set their direction and establish a sense of purpose and mission. This will lay the foundation for discussing the other points on the star and how organizations can be changed to utilize the new logic.

Part Two

Putting the
Principles to Work
Strategy and Structure

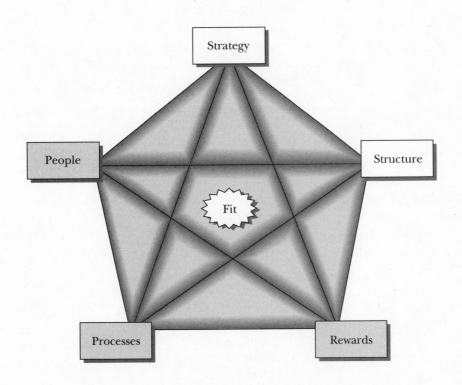

Chapter Three

Business Strategy
Creating the Winning Formula

- Organization can be the ultimate competitive advantage.
- Effective leadership is the key to organizational effectiveness.

An effective business strategy provides the formula an organization needs in order to win. It should state the organization's purpose, direction, goals, and objectives and, in most cases, specify the tasks it must accomplish to succeed.

To be effective, an organization needs to develop the appropriate performance capabilities and to use them to do the right things. The process is not unlike preparing an athlete for the track and field competition of the decathlon, where an athlete must perform effectively in ten events. Athletes cannot work on one event, perform it, and then practice the next event before performing it. All the performance capabilities have to be present simultaneously. That is only possible if the athlete knows what capabilities are needed. In the decathlon, this is rather obvious; the events and the skills needed have been identified for decades. With organizational performance, the necessary capabilities and competencies are not always easily determined, nor is it always clear when different kinds of performance will be needed.

It is up to the leaders in the organization to develop a strategy that identifies the kinds of performance that are needed, to communicate the need for them through mission and values statements, and to develop the competencies and capabilities needed to perform them. They can only do this well if they have a good understanding of the environment the organization faces and how business strategies and performance are related to competencies and capabilities. This relationship is shown in the Diamond Model (Figure 3.1), which shows that organizational effectiveness, and therefore a good strategy, results when there is a fit among four points: mission, competencies, capabilities, and the environment.

This chapter begins with a brief discussion of the way companies have historically developed strategy and why and how strategy development must change in the new logic. The focus will then shift to how mission and values statements, core competencies, and organizational capabilities are the key components of winning business strategies.

The Old Way: Formal Strategic Planning

In the old logic, a large corporate staff of strategic planners and futurists was responsible for developing and communicating corporate strategy to the rest of the organization. These experts, who usually were not involved in producing the organization's services or products, carefully studied them and their positions in the

Figure 3.1. The Diamond Model.

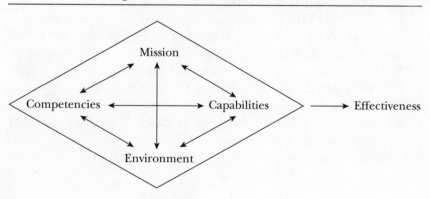

market. They then created one-year and longer-term strategic plans that were regularly updated with new numbers and new planning targets and objectives.

A classic example is General Electric of the 1970s and early 1980s. Once the strategic direction for the corporation was set, managers from the different business units were asked to produce plans for their units that supported the corporate plan. They were also required to produce large amounts of data to support their business plans, to present them to corporate strategic planners, and to convince the planners that their plans should be accepted.

To say that the old logic of strategic planning has fallen on hard times would be an understatement. Henry Mintzberg, a well-known organization theorist and professor, has argued in his book *The Rise and Fall of Strategic Planning* that strategic planning is an oxymoron, because planning is about analysis, and strategy is about synthesis.[1] Planning is about facts, operations, and budgets, whereas strategy requires creative thinking about mission and how to gain competitive advantage.

Recently, organization after organization has decided to abandon traditional strategic planning, because it simply has not produced the kinds of results that justify either the costs of having a central staff or the tremendous amounts of work generated throughout the organization. As Mintzberg notes, there are a number of reasons that strategic planning has delivered disappointing results, but perhaps the primary one is the difficulty of predicting the future in an increasingly turbulent world.

During the period when strategic planning was popular, some organizations spent considerable time and money trying to get good at predicting the future. They hired experts who studied the future through technologies like the delphi approach, which integrates the predictions of many experts. Universities such as my own created centers that focused on predicting future trends in world hunger, oil prices, and other areas. Companies contributed money to these centers in the hope of improving their strategic planning process and gaining an advantage over their competitors.

Unfortunately, most attempts at prediction proved faulty, particularly with respect to long-term trends. In the 1970s, for example, there were predictions that oil would be at $100 a barrel by the early 1990s; none of the experts dreamed that oil prices would fall steadily through the 1980s and stay at around $20 a barrel during the first half of the 1990s.

The demise of strategic planning has led some organizations to say that their strategic objective is simply to make money. Managers are then given annual budgets, financial targets, market share objectives, and new product introduction dates. But this approach goes too far in the opposite direction and is clearly incongruent with the new logic.

The new logic requires much more. It requires that individuals throughout the organization have a sense of purpose and mission as well as values that guide their behavior. Without many of the traditional bureaucratic controls to direct their efforts, employees must understand what the organization is trying to accomplish and what values should guide them. Their understanding is critical to their ability to make decisions and to manage themselves and their work. A simple statement such as "we exist in order to make money for our shareholders" is just not enough to allow the members of an organization to understand what they should be doing, why they should do it, and how they should do it.

James Collins and Jerry Porras present evidence to show that companies that have a strong sense of mission, values, and culture have outperformed their competitors in virtually every instance.[2] They compare what they call built-to-last companies such as Merck, General Electric, and Boeing with companies that lack a sense of mission, such as Bristol-Meyers, Westinghouse, and McDonnell Douglas. The difference in performance between the two types of companies is dramatic. The built-to-last companies clearly have outperformed those that simply emphasize financial returns as their reason for being in business. This supports the new logic argument that organizations and individuals are most effective when they are guided by a sense of mission and values rather than by attention simply to the bottom line and controls.

Westinghouse is a clear example of a company that has had and continues to have difficulty defining its mission. It is one of the oldest and largest corporations in the United States. It was founded in 1886 and has had a number of successes, but it has also been unfavorably compared with General Electric by Collins and Porras as well as others. Incidentally, General Electric was founded about the same time as Westinghouse. General Electric and Westinghouse immediately became competitors, because they both focused on the generation of electricity. Westinghouse has entered and exited many businesses (recently it sold its newly acquired furniture business and its defense electronics business and bought CBS Broadcasting), and its history has been marked by several significant financial crises.

In order to better develop a sense of strategy and mission for the organization, Westinghouse issued a vision statement in 1989. According to this statement, Westinghouse stands for "total quality, market leadership, technology driven, global, focused growth, diversified." Needless to say, this jumble of pop management terms did not get the job done.

Today hardly anyone knows what businesses Westinghouse is in and what it stands for. People remember that they made home appliances, but they have not been in that business for decades. In fact, they own a constantly changing, rather eclectic mix of businesses. This is not necessarily a fatal flaw, if it is part of a well-developed strategy and the organization is managed accordingly. General Electric, for example, also has a diverse set of businesses, but it has managed to create a well-developed and very effective strategy for how to act as a corporation and, as a result, has consistently outperformed Westinghouse.

Today, effective organizational performance depends upon devising and implementing a strategy that fits the new logic. Key to such a strategy is how mission and values statements define purpose and strategic intent, how organizations identify and develop crucial core competencies, and how organizational capabilities support critical business processes. Leadership is also important, both in involving members of an organization in the process of creating strategy and in communicating strategic intent to everyone.

The Mission Statement: What Are Our Goals?

More and more companies are developing mission statements that are designed to be the cornerstone of setting and communicating their corporate purpose. These often brief and very simple statements provide a broad sense of guidance and mission for the organization. Among the more visible ones: Xerox's statement that it is "the document company," and the British Airways' statement that it is in business "to fly and serve."

A new logic mission statement is neither a strategic plan nor a method of controlling the organization, nor does it lay out in any great detail how the company will market and price its products or services or how it will add value. Instead, it provides a broad sense of what the organization does and wants to be.

Of course, mission statements need to go beyond a few simple words if they are to provide meaningful guidance in the creation of an organization design that covers all critical business elements. They must talk about markets to be served, value provided to customers, and the competitive advantages on which the organization hopes to capitalize.

It is very important for organizations to develop and communicate their mission in the form of a statement that management professors Gary Hamel and C. K. Prahalad describe as expressing "strategic intent"—that is, the animating dream or "stretch" goal that energizes a company.[3] For example, British Airways stated in 1987 that its goal was to become "the world's favorite airline," a bold quest given its history. Appleton Papers, a firm with more than four thousand employees that operates throughout North America, has a somewhat more specific strategic intent: "to be a world leader in specialty coated paper technologies, high value-added customer applications and customer focused quality."

Why are goals that represent a sizable stretch for the organization important? Considerable research in psychology on goal setting shows that the highest performance comes when individuals are committed to reaching such goals.[4] It also shows that individuals are more likely to be committed to those goals when there are rewards that are attached to achieving them and when individuals believe that the goals agree with their value systems and contribute to objectives they share.

Hamel and Prahalad suggest that organizations need, in addition to strategic intent, a shared understanding of the future to help them identify what new products they need to pioneer, what alliances they need to make, and what product development programs they should support.[5] This shared understanding needs to focus on such issues as what competitors are likely to do, what new markets exist, and how new markets can be entered and created. Hamel and Prahalad go on to argue that senior management should bear the major responsibility for continually updating this shared corporate perspective on the future.

I cannot agree more. As far as developing corporate strategy is concerned, nothing is so potentially dangerous as today's view of the world because it will soon be outdated. In successful firms it can lead to complacency and doing the old "right thing" long after it ceases to be the right thing.[6] General Motors, for example, committed just this mistake when it failed to recognize the seriousness of the Japanese threat to its dominance of the U.S. car market.

One way to develop a shared understanding of the future is to use scenario planning to help sensitize the organization to the need for change. In scenario planning, a group prepares several possible scenarios (or paths) for the business. Royal Dutch Shell, for example, at a time when industry mavens were forecasting $100-per-barrel oil, outlined an unthinkable scenario: a decline in the price of oil. When the price actually declined, Shell was prepared.

Each scenario should have some leading indicators to identify that it is indeed unfolding. The planning process then provides managers with mental maps to think differently. It prepares them to see facts as they occur in a new light. Scenarios can be great vehicles for preparing for a nontraditional competitor. Shell, for example, still regards Exxon and Mobil as key competitors, but the company is also keeping an eye on Schlumberger, the seismographic tester. After all, who knows more about where oil is?

Mission statements that focus on strategic intent present an interesting contrast to the traditional strategic planning document. They tend to have a much longer life expectancy and require much less maintenance because they are much less specific. As the business environment has become more and more turbulent, strategic intent documents have become a more and more obvious choice. Careful formal strategic planning, even when done well, can rapidly become obsolete with changes in the environment.

Values and Strategy: How Do We Do What We Do?

As part of their effort to provide meaning and direction to their activities, some organizations focus on defining and stating their values—that is, the kinds of activities, behaviors, and performance that are desirable. Such written statements of values are important because they can support a mission statement, guide the day-to-day operations of a company, and help an organization develop a sense of direction and purpose among its employees—all of which are critical to the successful implementation of the new logic principles. They can, in essence, be an effective substitute for the bureaucracy and control systems of traditional organizations because when combined with goals, they specify how individuals should behave and provide meaning to the work that individuals do.

Values statements can cover anything that has to do with how an organization operates—from how it treats customers and employees to what kinds of organizational processes are important. For example, a values statement can stress openness in communication, trust in dealings with internal and external groups, fair treatment for employees, social responsibility, concern for the environment, and consistently high-quality products or services.

Jim O'Toole, who writes about the importance of mission and values, has emphasized that company statements should combine high purpose and high aim.[7] They need to stress critical values that are important to employees and that organizations can use to succeed—values such as community, liberty, fairness, and the dignity of individuals.

One of the most famous values statements—and one that is decades old—belongs to Johnson & Johnson, the large pharmaceutical and personal-care products firm. Johnson & Johnson's first core value in their credo is "Our first responsibility is to our customers." This strong emphasis on serving customers and protecting their health and well-being got a lot of attention during the Tylenol poisoning crisis, when, fearing that their product had been tampered with, they immediately withdrew all of their Tylenol products from store shelves in order to protect their customers.

Johnson & Johnson is not the only company to emphasize values and to work on developing a values-driven culture. Such companies as Patagonia, Herman Miller, and Motorola have, for a long time, emphasized values as an important part of their corporate identity. Years ago, sociologist Philip Selznick argued that organizations become enduring institutions only when they become infused with values that go beyond the bottom line.[8] He further argued that when an organization's values appeal to prospective members, it gives it competitive advantages: greater employee loyalty and more adaptability to a changing environment.

The impact of values and missions on organizational effectiveness has always been evident in volunteer organizations. Individuals work for them simply to contribute to achieving the organizations' missions because they identify with their goals and values. Individuals who do volunteer work at hospitals often will do cleanup and other menial tasks that they do not do around their own home and would never consider doing in any other situation.

Even less glamorous businesses that do not lend themselves to a mission such as improving the environment or reducing hunger can have values statements that include high standards and goals that are motivating, if not inspiring. For example, any company can aspire to be the best at what it does, to offer the highest-quality products, or to treat its customers and employees in a special way.

Levi Strauss is one of the most visible examples of a company that emphasizes the values approach to management. Since 1987 it has had a clearly stated set of values and aspirations concerning diversity, empowerment, communication, and ethical management practices. Its written mission statement is a simple and straightforward one: "To sustain profitable and responsible commercial success by marketing jeans and casual apparel." Not a terribly exciting statement, but when combined with the goals that Levi Strauss sets for itself—profitable return on investment, market leadership, products with superior profitability and service—it begins to take on the sense of a mission that shows not only what the company wants to do but also how it will be measured on what it does.

To me, the most interesting part of the Levi Strauss statement is where it addresses values and aspirations. It states: "We want a company that our people are proud of and committed to, where all employees have an opportunity to contribute, learn, grow, and advance based on merit, not politics or background. We want our people to feel respected, treated fairly, and listened to, and involved. Above all, we want satisfaction from accomplishments and friendships, balanced personal and professional lives, and to have fun in our endeavors." It goes on to talk about the type of leadership that can turn this dream into reality.

CEO Robert Haas, the great-great-nephew of founder Levi Strauss, is clearly committed to implementing the values that the corporation has stated. The mission and values statements, which were crafted by top management in 1987 (not by consultants or the human resource department), are posted on office and factory walls throughout Levi Strauss. Attention to its corporate aspirations has clearly helped Levi Strauss in a number of respects. It has produced loyal employees, and Levi is regularly listed as one of the best companies in the United States to work for.

It has also led Levi Strauss to do some things that have hurt its short-term profitability. For example, it will not do business with countries where the labor conditions are unsatisfactory. Thus it does not use suppliers in mainland China, an expensive decision in a business where manufacturing cost is critical. It has shifted some work to Mexico, however—a shift that has produced charges of hypocrisy and considerable criticism because of the loss of U.S. jobs and the low wage rates in Mexico.

Like most large-scale organizational transformations, Levi's strong emphasis on using values to direct behavior and focus efforts is and always will be a work in process, but it is one that seems to be heading in the right direction. Levi Strauss has reduced its overhead, adapted more rapidly to market changes, and improved its financial performance since it developed its values statement. It thus provides an interesting example of how mission and values statements can play an important role in a new logic corporation.

There is great variation from industry to industry in terms of how easy it is to get individuals to identify with an organization's mission and values. However, as was mentioned earlier, even organizations in industries that do not lend themselves to an appealing mission statement can still state values that will motivate people to work for them and to develop a sense of loyalty and identification with the organization. Levi Strauss provides an example of this, as does another clothing manufacturer, Patagonia, which has strong values about the treatment of employees and the environment.

The Bottom Line: Putting Mission and Values Statements to Work

The sudden popularity of mission and values statements (one estimate is that six out of ten U.S. corporations have one; a recent how-to-do-it book contains 301 mission statements from "America's top companies") has led to the charge that they are a fad and that in many companies they are worthless words on paper. The criticism is not of their content—they usually sound good—but of their lack of impact on organizational behavior. The effectiveness of a mission statement is only as great as the commitment to putting it to work. And quite simply stated, there is good reason to believe that often the commitment is missing.

An ineffective mission and values statement is not just a waste of time and paper. An organization can be worse off because of its values statement. This is very likely if the actual behavior of the people in the organization does not match the values statement. A large discrepancy causes individuals to trust the organization less than if there were no values statement. They are understandably disillusioned when they see that the values statement and the behavior do not agree.

For me the issue is not whether to have a statement of mission and values; it is an important tool that organizations should have. The key question is, how can an organization turn a mission and values statement into a meaningful, realized, living element of an organization's behavior and its systems?

One thing that can be done—which will be discussed in more detail in Chapter Eight—is to wed the corporate values in the mission statement to every human resource management system. Beginning with the hiring process, every job applicant must be treated as the values statement says employees and customers should be.

It is critical that there be a fit between the types of employees who are hired and the values that the organization espouses in its mission and values statement. Southwest Airlines, which says work should be fun, hires employees who have a good sense of humor. Rather than punish employees when they demonstrate a sense of humor on the job, Southwest rewards them. In much the same way, one restaurant that wants employees to help customers have fun has job applicants go on stage and do something "entertaining" as part of its selection process.

Similarly, individuals must be rewarded for the kinds of behavior that the values statement says the organization believes in. At Levi Strauss, one third of an employee's performance evaluation is based on what Levi Strauss calls "aspirational behavior," that is, behavior that supports the mission and values of the company. Employees who ignore values such as diversity and empowerment, for example, do not get a raise. Another example of a company that weds its values statement to its reward system is General Mills, which says it values community involvement and volunteer activity and explicitly recognizes them in its performance appraisal system.

Often what distinguishes a mission statement that works from one that is ineffective is not how it phrases the ideas and the values it espouses but how the leadership develops the mission statement. Senior management must put in place a process that will not only lead to the development of an effective strategy but ensure that it is widely understood and accepted in the organization. Getting this accomplished, particularly getting it accepted, often requires more from senior management than simply preparing a mission and values statement.

All too often I have seen senior managers do just the opposite of what the Levi Strauss executives did in producing their statement. Too many companies send their top managers away for several days to "draft" a mission and values statement. They then present it to the organization, congratulate themselves for having done the necessary activities, declare victory, and go back to their offices. In most cases, when the process is over, everyone in the organization (including top management) simply disregards the statement.

Even worse, some senior management groups hire consultants to produce a mission and values statement for their organization. Indeed, a small cottage industry has grown up around the United States that specializes in developing these statements. They are then printed on wallet-sized cards and posters and liberally distributed throughout the organization. Too often, the implicit assumption is that simply creating them and distributing them will influence behavior. It almost never works. In fact, often all that has happened as a result of this exercise is that the organization has wasted time, money, effort, and paper.

How can the strategic planning process of developing a mission statement and corporate values be made more meaningful? The principles of the new logic provide a clear answer: involvement.

In a relatively small organization, it is possible to get most of the employees in the organization involved in the strategic planning process. Some small organizations have effectively held several day "community meetings" in which the elements of a mission and values statement are hammered out through a process that includes working in small groups, the whole organization debating issues and ultimately fashioning a document.[9] This type of participation is ideal because it captures input from a wide variety of organization members, thereby enriching the final product, and because everyone in the organization develops an understanding and acceptance of what is produced.

In large organizations it may not be possible to have broad-scale participation in developing or updating an organization's strategy. It should be possible, however, to select individuals from different parts of the organization to participate in the process.

In 1984, for example, Eaton Corporation, a fifty-thousand-employee organization that manufactures auto, truck, and electronic parts worldwide, put together a task force representing employees from different levels in the organization to develop a mission statement, known today as "Excellence Through People," that includes a number of important statements about how employees should be treated.

To introduce the philosophy, they did all of the usual things, such as producing a video and passing out brochures that described the philosophy. They did not stop there, however. In 1988, Eaton executive John Wendenhof and Gerry Ledford, a USC colleague of mine, developed an innovative process for monitoring how the philosophy was being implemented throughout the firm.[10] Employee teams composed of a cross-section of managers from throughout the corporation made visits to Eaton locations to help the site employees implement the Eaton philosophy. The implementation teams were trained in organizational diagnosis and given the mandate to gather data from the site. They then gave feedback to the site members on how well the implementation process was going and how it could be improved.

So far this process is working well. Eaton managers who have been on the visiting teams have developed a better understanding of management processes. It also has helped stress to them and the plants they visit the importance of implementing the philosophy. Eaton's commitment to the site visits has also helped demonstrate the importance that it puts on the mission statement.

The Eaton case is just one of many examples that show that involvement is a key to the success of a corporate statement of mission and values. In company after company, the same thing happens: when people throughout the organization are involved in developing the document and in assessing how well it is being used, it has impact.

Involvement can take many forms. After a small group of individuals has done some initial development work, electronic mail can be used to help develop and perfect mission-vision-values statements for companies. A proposed mission and values statement can be put on the computer network with the invitation for all to give their thoughts and reactions. Successive iterations of the work can be edited throughout the organization, thus giving everyone an opportunity to have a say in the final document.

EDS, the large, very successful computer services firm based in Plano, Texas, recently went through a highly involving process in developing their strategic view of the future. Although very successful during the first half of the 1990s, EDS began to be concerned that its market was changing so rapidly that a new strategy was in order. New competitors were appearing, old customers were asking for greater discounts, and whole new markets were appearing, particularly as companies began to outsource their information services activities.

EDS created a corporate change team that used a broad-involvement approach. From across the company, 150 EDS managers who were known to be challenging and bright gathered in Dallas to begin developing their shared view of the future. Five groups of thirty worked on somewhat different issues and gathered data after their initial meeting in Dallas. Other groups, senior management, and the overall change management team analyzed and debated the final outputs from each group. Finally, a team composed of members from all of the groups produced a draft corporate strategy that was debated throughout the company. In all, more than two thousand people participated in the creation of EDS's new strategy.

This process lasted about a year, and it produced both a high level of understanding of the challenges EDS faces and a high level of commitment to the new strategy. That strategy can best be summarized as global and dedicated to giving customer organizations the kinds of information resources they need to gain competitive advantage. It also stresses individualizing information resources to fit the needs of each customer. In many respects, it is a mass-customization approach to information system management. The effects of this effort can only be measured in the long term, but in the short term, it is clear that the process led to a high level of debate, discussion, and, ultimately, commitment to the new strategy.

The challenge in a new logic organization is to make the mission and values of the organization a living piece of the corporate culture that helps to guide and direct behavior. It is also important that the mission and values statement reflect changes in the external environment and the organization's view of the future. Changes in the statement represent a key opportunity for involvement. People throughout the organization can participate in "town meetings" that review and update the mission, and they can work on task forces that help develop the changes and assess the environment.

Core Competencies and Strategy

In their influential 1990 *Harvard Business Review* article, Gary Hamel and C. K. Prahalad emphasized the importance of core competencies—which they define as a combination of technology and production skills that underlie various product lines and services—in the development of a corporate strategy.[11]

For the purpose of developing and implementing strategy, organizations need to know what core competencies are critical to success in their business or businesses. If they succeed in developing the core competencies that support their mission, they can gain a competitive advantage over other organizations because they can produce superior products and services.

Sony's core competency in miniaturization technology allows them to make the Walkman, video cameras, notebook computers, and a host of other products. Honda's ability to produce gasoline motors is critical to their success in selling motorcycles, lawn mowers, outboard motors, and automobiles. 3M Corporation's competency in understanding chemical processes and materials has helped them to develop a vast range of products, from a variety of Scotch tape products and Post-it notes to exotic bonding materials for the aerospace industry.

In the service sector, American Airlines developed a core competency in computer information systems that for a long time gave it a significant advantage over its competitors because it could offer innovative prices and frequent-flier programs that its competitors could not match. Ultimately, American got so good at information management that it created a reservation service for all airlines.

Organizations must ask themselves two questions about their core competencies: Which core competencies do we need in order to reach our goals? How easily can other organizations duplicate our core competencies?

The challenge is to create core competencies that are hard to duplicate or, at the very least, can lead the organization to other competencies that can keep them ahead of the competition. As noted earlier, it is getting easier for organizations all over the world to develop competencies, because technology often moves across international and company boundaries through alliances and a host of other organizational approaches that will be discussed later.

Organizational Capabilities and Strategy

Distinctly different from core competencies—yet, at the same time, very related to them—are organizational capabilities. As was first discussed in the Introduction, they can be a particularly powerful source of competitive advantage because they are difficult to duplicate, and, when combined with appropriate core competencies, they can allow an organization to perform significantly better than its competition. Like core competencies, their development is key to the successful implementation of strategy; thus, they need to be part of the strategy development process.

What distinguishes organizational capabilities from core competencies? Organizational capabilities rest in the systems, culture, and overall design of the organization, not in laboratory research, in the heads of a few technology gurus, or in a set of patents. They are shared knowledge that enables an organization to perform in ways that go beyond the skill of any one individual or set of individuals.

ABB, the Swiss-Swedish manufacturer of rail cars and electrical generating equipment, is a classic example of an organization that has developed the capability to operate both globally and locally simultaneously. Their products such as rail cars need to be sold to a large global market (because of high development costs), but at the same time they need to be built locally and contain some local parts. To achieve this, ABB has a multinational management team that coordinates technological activities in different countries—ensuring that it can develop its corporate core competencies in rail equipment design.

An engineering firm with which I have consulted, CH2M Hill, calls their organizational capabilities "critical success factors." In the late 1980s they identified the following critical success factors as part of a strategic planning effort targeted at understanding what they needed to be good at in order to continue the growth of the company:

- Becoming more client focused
- Devising market-driven strategies
- Integrating strengths
- Fostering creativity and innovation
- Becoming responsive, flexible, and adaptable
- Providing value for clients in all we do

So far, these organizational capabilities have provided a focus for their organizational improvement efforts that seems to be paying off, as the company is continuing to grow and gain market share.

As you may recall, earlier I mentioned 3M's organizational capability to innovate. I believe that its continued growth and success are only partially due to its core competency in the chemical properties of a variety of materials. An important part of its success has to do with its capability to innovate and to develop and market new products.

Norwest, the large Midwestern bank, has developed an outstanding capability in the area of customer focus. They have made it the key to their personal-touch approach to banking. Whereas other large banks have emphasized electronic banking and ATMs, Norwest has decided to emphasize getting close to the customer. They have developed this capability through a number of very specific practices that include cross-training tellers and all branch employees so that they are flexible and can sell many products. They also have developed a number of events to bring people into their branches and encourage interaction with employees. Their strategy is no secret; as one of their executives commented, "I could leave our strategic plan on a plane and it would not make any difference. No one could execute it; our success has nothing to do with planning—it has to do with execution." Execution is made possible because they have the capability to get close to their customers.

A single organizational capability may not be sufficient for success. It may take two or three that are exceptional and a number of others that are at least at the world-class level, because that is the nature of today's competitive environment. The success of Motorola, for example, is only partially based on its organizational capability in quality. As I mentioned earlier, they are also excellent at getting products quickly to market and at technological innovation.

I could go on listing examples, but at this point it is sufficient to repeat that the challenge for any organization is to develop a set of capabilities that support or fit its strategy. It is not enough for an organization to say it will be the world's favorite airline; it must also develop the appropriate capabilities—in this case, those that have to do with giving great service and understanding customers.

Creating a Successful Strategy: The Role of Leadership

The old logic of organizing clearly places the responsibility for developing a business strategy in the hands of senior management. One of their major managerial responsibilities is to design, develop, and communicate the organization's business strategy. Indeed, it is one of the major ways that they are expected to add value to the corporation and to justify their high reward levels. In addition, they are responsible for overseeing the implementation of the strategy and for making strategy changes as the environment evolves.

In the new logic, too, senior management needs to play a leadership role in strategy development and implementation. Note, however, that the emphasis here is on leading rather than on managing. Senior management must lead a process that will not only develop an effective strategy but ensure that it is widely understood and accepted in the organization. Getting this accomplished—particularly, getting it accepted—requires senior management to actively communicate and live the strategy. There are many ways to do it: for example, through personal meetings, videotapes, E-mail, and interactive video broadcasts. But only senior management can do it.

Of all the approaches to communication, I believe personal contact with a charismatic leader is by far the best. I have seen a number of senior managers who are quite skilled at doing this. Among my personal favorites are Bob Galvin of Motorola; Kingman Brewster, the former president of Yale University; and Max De Pree of Herman Miller. They all have the ability to mix high purpose with high aim in their talks and interactions with organization members.

Rich Teerlink, the CEO of Harley-Davidson, is another good example of a CEO who understands how to infuse his company with a sense of direction by making the mission statement an integral part of the organization. Not too many years ago, Harley-Davidson was in serious trouble because of its terrible relationships with its customers, employees, and dealers. Teerlink realized that the company had a tremendous need to improve the quality of its products as well as its stakeholder relationships. He began to continually emphasize the theme of "Creating a Competitive Organization Through People and Processes Centered on Learning." Whenever he talked to managers at Harley, he asked questions focused on learning, the involvement of employees, and the reactions of customers. The business turnaround of Harley has been nothing short of amazing. It is one of the few U.S. organizations to regain market share from its Japanese competitors. Xerox, incidentally, is another, at least in part as a result of the leadership it has received from its last two CEOs, David Kearns and Paul Allaire.

Successful leaders are able to communicate not only strategic intent but also how the goals of the organization are relevant to the personal values and desires of the members of the organization. In short, they communicate what can happen and what it means to individuals if the organization succeeds. This step in the development of the strategic agenda of an organization is without question the most difficult to accomplish. It requires that senior managers act as leaders and motivate and inspire others throughout the organization.

I have a small confession to make at this point. For years I have been a skeptic about the importance of leaders because of the difficulty of defining and describing leadership. All too often, leadership falls into the "I cannot define it, but I know it when I see it" category. Once you get beyond gross generalizations, such as "leaders inspire others" and "leaders define the agenda," there is often very little substance that allows us to identify how successful leaders behave. Further, major change in traditional organizations often occurs not because a leader has galvanized the organization but because the environment threatens the organization's continued existence—which causes the organization, often under the direction of a new group of senior managers, to restructure, change products, or introduce other changes.

Sometimes it seems that the qualities of effective management in a traditional organization are captured in Antoine de Saint-Exupéry's fable of the Little Prince. In this story, the Little Prince points out that he is the absolute ruler of his planet because everyone does exactly what he tells them to do. The secret of his success is simple: he only tells people to do things that they want to do. The Little Prince clearly is a leader who believes in the saying that "a good leader has to hurry to keep ahead of his followers." In an effective traditional organization, of course, individuals head in the direction they do because of well-designed reward systems, job descriptions, organization structures, and so on, not because of leadership.

But as our discussion of leadership in Chapter One suggested, I have come to believe that leadership is a key ingredient in shaping high-performance organizations. I have seen Jack Welch of General Electric, Bob Galvin of Motorola, Larry Bossidy of AlliedSignal, and a host of other leaders produce significant change in the way their very large organizations operate. Thus I am convinced that effective leadership at the top accounts for an important amount of the success of high-performance organizations, because leadership is so critical in defining the agenda of an organization, shaping its values, and determining its competencies and capabilities.

In a high-performance organization, effective leaders need to be able to create strategic goals that people want to head toward. They add enormous value when they get individuals to take new types of actions and move in new directions. And they do this not by creating bureaucratic controls and procedures but by creating a view of what can be and should be that is attractive to individuals and that fits with their values and goals.

Keys to Developing an Effective Strategy

In summary, here is what we have said about the development of an organization strategy:

- Senior managers need to take the lead in developing strategy, but they cannot and should not do it by themselves. The members of the organization need to be involved.
- Strategies should fit the unique situation of the organization; they cannot be copied or borrowed from others.
- Strategies need to set high aspirations for the organization so that members, individually and collectively, will feel that they have challenging but reachable goals.
- Strategies need to focus on how an organization will win in the future, what its outstanding products and services will be, and how those products and services will satisfy the customer.
- Strategies need to reflect the values that will guide how the organization accomplishes its goals and mission.
- Strategies need to appeal to values that will allow employees to identify with the way the organization operates.
- Strategies must communicate a sense of direction and stimulate discovery of what the organization can do and what works in particular business environments.
- Strategies must provide employees at all levels of the organization with a sense of what the company is trying to do and where it is trying to go.
- Strategies need to present a way to the future and provide emotional and intellectual energy for the journey.
- It is up to the leaders in the organization to identify the kinds of capabilities that are needed, communicate them through mission and values statements, and develop commitment to them throughout the organization.

When their strategy is developed, organizations need to create organization structures, reward systems, communication systems, and human resource management systems that support the strategy by creating the right competencies and capabilities and that drive performance effectiveness. This is the clear message of the Star Model and of the new logic principles. The discussion of how this can be done will begin in the next chapter with a look at organization structure.

Chapter Four

Corporate Architecture
Structuring for High Performance

- Organizations should be designed around products and customers.
- Lateral processes are the key to organizational effectiveness.

The structure of an organization—like its strategy—is basic to its ability to achieve high levels of performance. Organizational structure involves how people are grouped together, who reports to whom, who makes decisions, how many levels of management there are, and how work is designed. Just as the architecture of a building defines what it can be used for, structure defines what an organization is, as well as what it does and how effectively it does it.

Mention organizational structure to most people and what comes to their minds are the massive "wiring diagram" organizational charts that large corporations develop. In many organizations, these charts—which often contain twelve or more levels of employees—are drawn and redrawn to reflect changes in thinking and business realities. Levels are added, jobs are redefined, and reporting relationships are altered. Despite the great deal of time, indeed perhaps too much time, spent by senior management deciding what their structures should look like, the basic design in old logic organizations never seems to undergo fundamental change; it remains a hierarchical arrangement of boxes that are connected only by vertical lines. People are still grouped together by function: sales people with sales people, marketing people with marketing people, and production people with production people. At the top of the chart is a single individual—the CEO. Everyone below him—and it is almost always a him—is connected to him by vertical lines indicating that they ultimately report to him.

In essence, the CEO becomes everyone's ultimate customer, because this classic chain-of-command organizational chart indicates that all efforts should be directed toward satisfying him and that he has the power to direct, control, and reward everyone else. It also suggests strongly that a supervisor's main role is to control and to direct the behavior of individuals below him or her and to please managers at higher levels.

In the hierarchical structure of old logic organizations, staff support and service groups such as those in finance and marketing play a key role because they are asked to review proposals and recommendations from individuals throughout the organization. They therefore tend to acquire veto power over what business managers can do with respect to issues ranging from buying new equipment to offering new services. These staff groups, in order to exercise their power, often grow in size to the point where they become a major cost of doing business. First, there is the direct cost of their employees. In addition, there are the indirect costs that result from the extra work in the form of audits and reports, information, and studies that they cause others to do.

In major corporations the corporate staff can be quite large (General Motors, AT&T, General Electric, and IBM at one time had thousands of corporate staff employees) and can create tremendous amounts of work for others to do. It is no wonder, then, that often the response is less than enthusiastic when a member of the corporate staff visits a business unit and says, "I am from corporate staff and I am here to help you."

How do organization structures impact organizational effectiveness? Digital Equipment provides a good example. Whenever my USC colleague Jay Galbraith and I used to discuss Digital—we both did consulting work for them during the 1970s and 1980s—he argued that Digital was bound to get in trouble because its organization structure was poorly developed and potentially inappropriate. I argued back that he was too concerned with developing a "rigid, traditional structure" for Digital. And I took pleasure in pointing out to him how right I was as during the 1980s Digital continued to grow year after year.

From its inception, the organizational structure of Digital Equipment was a bit chaotic and confusing. When I did consulting work with Digital in 1978, most people referred to it as a matrix structure. However, to me, its structure looked much more like a traditional functional structure with a manufacturing function, an engineering function, a sales force, and so on. This seemed like an appropriate structure given the relative size of the company and the fact that it was essentially a single-product company selling mid-range computers and support software services. At the time, Digital did take an interesting position with respect to job design and hiring.

Digital was growing rapidly–30 percent or more a year–and had an enormous need for talented individuals. Thus it often hired people simply because they were talented, even though it did not have a particular job opening for them. New employees were told that if after nine months of employment they had not found a "job," they were in trouble and should probably start looking outside Digital for work. It was also pointed out by some critics that there was no hurry, because even after nine months it took quite a while for Digital to find out that someone was without a real job to do.

As most people know, the wheels came off Digital in the early 1990s. It did not respond effectively to the new competition entering the computer market or to the increasing popularity of personal computers and, as a result, lost hundreds of millions of dollars. It was unable to downsize effectively and reduce its costs. Its confusing structure and loose job descriptions—which I so loved because they let people define their own jobs and figure out how to use their capabilities—suddenly became an enormous handicap. Digital did not know how many people worked for it and consequently had trouble making any systematic change in its operating costs and staffing levels. At one point, it announced a downsizing, but at the end of the program it had more employees than when the downsizing started.

Finally, Galbraith was right and I was wrong. Or, as I like to argue in my discussions with him, I was right for a long time, but when the time came to change to a more appropriate structure, Digital was unable to make the shift. Since its problems began,

Digital has tried to restructure itself several times. Its financial results have improved, but it is not yet clear whether they have developed a structure that will lead to success. The major reason? They are unclear about what their business strategy is. And, as was pointed out in Chapter Three, without a clear business strategy it is hard, if not impossible, to have a clear and effective organization structure.

The new logic principles suggest a much different way of thinking about structure than is captured by the typical hierarchical, multilevel wiring diagram. New logic organization structures are far removed from hierarchical wiring diagram charts; they are built to distribute information, power, knowledge, and rewards more evenly throughout and to encourage lateral processes. This chapter begins an examination of how best to create an organizational structure based on the new logic by using the powerful metaphor of architecture to elucidate some of the key points and concepts. That metaphor helps to convey the notion of the new logic's flatter, more lateral, smaller (either actually or perceptually), less bureaucratically encumbered, and more team-oriented organizations.

How to Build an Organizational Architecture to Last— and to Change

The task of designing a building is a useful metaphor for thinking about designing an organization because both involve dimensional and functional challenges.[1] Indeed, the buildings that organizations inhabit often reflect their organization structures and, in fact, are often built to support them and their management styles.

My favorite example of a building that literally reflects its organization is a German corporate headquarters shaped as a pyramid. Each level of the building contains one level of management. You might say it is a relatively flat organizational structure, since there are just nine levels to the building. In this building, as in the organization, all employees know their exact positions. A promotion truly does mean moving up in the world. The hierarchical orientation in the structures of most organizations is very visible in many corporate high-rise offices, where the top floor is inhabited by senior management who ascend via a private elevator.

Higher Performance with Less Hierarchy

One U.S. executive who has recognized the relationship between physical architecture and organizational structure is Paul O'Neill, chairman of Alcoa. He has abandoned the traditional executive office suite layout that used to exist in Alcoa's high-rise, aluminum-clad headquarters. He and nine other top executives now spend their days in clusters of cockpit offices with L-shaped desks and small tables for impromptu roundtable meetings. According to O'Neill, the layout encourages spontaneous interaction and easy access; executives need only lean over a low wall to confer. There are no long corridors or physical barriers to keep out lower-level employees.

Indeed, Alcoa's offices look a lot like the typical Japanese office where the senior managers simply sit at desks in large open areas. In Japanese companies, the attitude is that all information is public and there is no need for private offices because the only reason for privacy is to keep others from knowing what you are doing— and that is undesirable because it hinders cooperation and trust.

Mars, the large candy and food company; Solectron, a very successful U.S. electronics firm based in Milpitas, California; Intel; and Patagonia are four other examples of U.S. corporations that have structured their offices with a minimum of differentiation. Patagonia has no offices and gives everyone the same size desk. They have a single cafeteria, and everyone is responsible for separating trash and putting it into recycling bins (they are a values-driven organization that cares about the environment).

The advertising agency TBWA Chiat/Day and Tandem Computers in Sunnyvale, California, have taken the redesign of office space one step further. Both have eliminated offices for many of their employees. Employees have access to small cubicles and offices when they need them; they sign up and reserve these spaces through a "hotel manager." Most of the space in their buildings is devoted to common areas where employees can get together to work on projects and exchange information. This common space is critical, because people typically come to the office to work together, not to work by themselves. They can easily work by themselves at home or in their cars since they are equipped with the technology that they need to do independent work.

In some organizations, such an arrangement is called the "virtual office" approach; in others it is perhaps more correctly called the "twenty-four-hour office." Obviously, cost reduction is a factor in this kind of office design, but so, too, is the desire to keep the organization flexible and to help employees become more productive in ways that are essential to high performance.

To many managers, moving away from a traditional office structure can be disconcerting, since acquiring a larger office and its attendant status is an important reward and an indication of one's career progress in a traditional organization. Eliminating offices that clearly indicate status through their size, furnishings, and view is seen by some managers as undermining their authority and much of what they have worked for. Quite frankly, these managers simply need to learn and accept that in the new logic, career progress is different. As will be discussed later, a new perspective is needed as far as an organization's reward and career development system is concerned and in the ways individuals assess their progress. No longer can managers judge their success by how big their office is or by how many promotions they have had in the last five years. Nor, for that matter, can they rely on rank and formal authority for their power and influence. They need to be based on skills, knowledge, and performance.

Creating the Right Seams

As with the architecture of a building, a key issue for the structure of an organization is the number of levels and the way that functions, operations, and tasks are grouped. Groupings and levels create seams in an organization—and despite the popularity of "seamless" organizations, seams are not necessarily bad.[2] Indeed, seams can be quite functional if they encourage the right people to work together (for example, those working on a new product) and if they encourage them to focus on the right processes and issues (for example, customer service).

When the traditional logic is used to design the structure of organizations, the wrong seams are often created, with the result that groups that need to cooperate do not. Particularly problematic are seams that divide functions or different steps in a production or service process. They lead to the need for bureaucratic controls and levels of management that cause individuals to improperly focus on serving and pleasing supervisors. This is a critical point in the explanation by the late W. Edwards Deming (a key originator of total quality management) for the poor-quality performance of many U.S. corporations.[3]

Overall, the challenge is to produce a minimal number of seams so that the organization operates with the same agenda at all levels and within all groups that serve the same customers. The best way to meet this challenge, suggests the new logic, is to group employees around customers and products rather than by functions. This is an essential element of the change process at General Electric. When Jack Welch talks about the importance of a seamless organization, he means a GE where employees work together to focus on customers and products. The intent of this seamlessness is to avoid the all-too-common situation where the customer has to stitch together the internal operations of the company in order to get a good product or service.

Stable Structures That Can Change

If buildings are not well designed, it may be impossible for their inhabitants—when the need arises—to use space differently without very expensive remodeling. The same thing is true with organizations. In today's dynamic environment, the challenge is to put together an organizational structure that can retain its fundamental character but is still flexible, adaptable, and able to handle rapid change.

To meet this challenge, organizations must learn to structure themselves so they can maintain their still-needed, existing organizational capabilities and yet still be able to develop new ones. In other words, organizations must operate so that they are simultaneously stable and changing.

As will be discussed in the next chapter, one way organizations can do this is to organize around business units and encourage the formation of new business units when the environment needs new products and services. This is just what Johnson & Johnson, the health care giant, has done for decades. It is a strategy that has allowed them to maintain both their traditional health care businesses such as Band-Aids and to succeed in marketing new products such as disposable contact lenses.

A structure that allows an organization to be both stable and changing will work only if the key elements of the architecture fit the new logic and individuals can count on them being in place for a considerable period of time. What fundamental elements of an organization must remain stable? One critical group is those that tell individuals what kinds of skills they need to learn, what kinds of career opportunities exist for them, and how they will be rewarded. But, at the same time, individuals must understand that many of the details of the structure will change continuously. That is, they may be asked to work on different projects and in different business units, to do different things, and, of course, to learn new skills and capabilities.

A second group of elements that needs to be stable involves the shape of the organization's structure. In a number of respects, high-performance organizations need to be the structural equivalent of an office building with movable walls and large amounts of open space. While the basic structure of the building does not change, the space inside can be changed, fine-tuned, and reallocated depending on what the occupants want and need. Organization structures need to be able to operate in the same way. They need to have some basic characteristics that are the equivalent of the major architectural features of a building. One of them is the number of levels of management, or the "height" of the structure.

How Many Stories? Levels of Management and Control

In the traditional logic of organizing, "tall" organizations with small spans of control are necessary to provide the close supervision that can direct and motivate job performance, a key principle of the traditional logic. I have always thought it interesting and significant that reporting relationships inside traditional organizations are called *spans of control* rather than simply the number of subordinates that somebody has. The choice of words clearly indicates what old logic organizations consider the main activity of a supervisor: control.

The new logic of organizing argues that it is possible for organizations to have flat (that is, much less vertical) structures. Why? Because individuals can do a considerable amount of self-management if organizations develop horizontal groupings and processes that eliminate the need for hierarchical coordination and control.

The idea of a flat organization structure has intrigued me since I was a graduate student. At that time, I reviewed a large amount of research literature which indicated that flat organizations tend to have more satisfied employees.

I ran into the issue again in 1969 when I did a study with Richard Hackman on job enrichment. We convinced AT&T to enrich the jobs of its telephone operators by giving them new decision-making responsibilities. But when we went back six months later to see how the change was working, we discovered that supervisors had taken back most of the decision making that had been given to the operators. The reason was simple: the supervisors had been left with nothing to do. Thus, to justify their existence, they took the decisions back from the operators.

When we recommended to the AT&T senior management that they remove "several levels of management," they responded in a way that indicated that they were resigned to the inevitability of a tall hierarchical structure. I still remember the president of AT&T at the time telling me that he felt there were at least two management levels too many in AT&T, but since his career was drawing to a close, he had no intention of taking on that challenge. At that point, AT&T was an organization of about one million employees. In many ways it was the ultimate large hierarchical organization. It worked well in its very stable, regulated business environment. AT&T has since eliminated many levels of management, but it still may not be flat enough to be successful in its new competitive environment.

By now you may be asking, According to the new logic, what is the right number of levels of management for an organization? How many individuals should report to a single manager? Unfortunately, there are no simple answers to these questions in the new logic. I have seen some managers work effectively with a hundred individuals reporting to them, and I have seen others for whom twenty is too many. The correct number has a great deal to do with a manager's skills, the complexity of the work, and the organization's ability to develop self-managing teams.

It is easy to point fingers at old logic organizations with fourteen or more levels and identify them as too tall, but it is much harder to be specific about the number of levels they should have.

Much depends on the size of the organization and the diversity of its businesses and activities.

For example, an organization of one thousand individuals rarely needs more than four levels, whereas an organization of ten thousand people or more may need five or perhaps more levels. However, even the largest organizations should have no more than seven levels of management. My experiences in manufacturing plants ranging from a hundred to several thousand employees is that they rarely need more than three levels of management. In some cases, one level of management is adequate. This is in notable contrast to many traditionally managed plants where there are six or seven levels of management for a few hundred employees. In large, old logic corporations, plant managers are four or five levels below the CEO with the result that production employees have ten or more levels between them and the CEO.

AES, a Connecticut-based energy company, has only three levels: worker, manager, and corporate officer. Marriott, Ritz-Carlton, and several other hotel chains that have experimented with employee involvement, empowerment, and moving decisions downward have found that they need both fewer levels of management and fewer managers. They have achieved a manager-to-employee ratio of 1:20 and in some cases 1:30 compared to the traditional ratio of 1:10 in the hotels. Ritz-Carlton seems to have successfully combined a flat structure with outstanding quality and service; they are a winner of the Baldrige National Quality Award, and several of their hotels are regularly rated among the top ten in the United States.

How Big Should Organizations Be? Rethinking Organization Size

As with a building, there are some definite advantages that come from organization size. Size can provide an advantage in such areas as volume purchasing, capital formation, funding of research and development, and developing centralized expertise and services in finance, marketing, engineering, and other functions. In some respects, these are similar advantages to those associated with a large building that has a centralized core of utilities (heating, electricity, water, and elevators, for example).

Yet, as was discussed in earlier chapters, size also creates problems for certain kinds of hierarchical organizations. In some cases, organizations have had to exit entire lines of business because, even though they were big, they lacked the organizational capabilities or core competencies needed for superior performance. This is precisely why much of the diversification by corporations into enterprises that are radically different from their traditional businesses has failed. Previous discussions have touched on Exxon's efforts in office equipment and Xerox's entry into computers. Recently, Anheuser-Busch, the very successful brewer, exited from the Eagle Snack Food business and from its ownership of the Saint Louis Cardinals baseball team. During the 1970s and 1980s the gas utility that supplies southern California acquired and tried to manage drugstores and athletic equipment stores. This diversification, like many others, failed for an obvious reason: the new businesses added mass to an organization in areas where it lacked capabilities and competencies.

The problems of large organizations have led some researchers and consultants to argue that the day of the large organization is over and that small, entrepreneurial, highly adaptive organizations that are specifically structured to fit niche markets will dominate the future.[4] I have no doubt that more highly specialized small firms will continue to emerge and to take business away from large organizations. It is not accidental that Sears has lost out to smaller businesses such as Lands' End, Victoria's Secret, and Eddie Bauer, which have proved to be more market driven and more flexible. But it has also lost out to Wal-Mart, which has over 600,000 employees and is becoming a global business.

The advantage of size is undeniable in certain industries, particularly those that are very capital-intensive and in which an organization must operate globally. Size is an enormous advantage in automobile manufacturing, consumer electronics, and other businesses where products are very expensive to develop and have a relatively short life expectancy. Under such conditions, you need an organization large enough to raise significant amounts of capital and to sell worldwide.

Size is also a definite advantage where brand-name recognition is important and where large-volume purchasing can lead to lower prices. Wal-Mart, for example, has tremendous bargaining power with manufacturers because it can buy enormous quantities of the products its nationwide and, in some cases, worldwide customers want. Thanks to a sophisticated information system that lets them track local buying habits, they can also work with their suppliers to reduce their inventory.

PepsiCo employs nearly one-third million people in its extensive restaurant businesses that include Taco Bell, KFC, and Pizza Hut. Wal-Mart is growing at a rapid rate worldwide and could become the world's largest private employer. But these retail organizations are really aggregations of small businesses that are managed locally and only in part centrally controlled. They are thus simultaneously large and small—large with respect to advertising and purchasing but small when it comes to focusing on customer service.

Despite the success of some large organizations, on balance I believe that the successful large organizations in the next century will be smaller than those that were dominant in the 1950s, 1960s, and 1970s. It is highly unlikely that many organizations will ever reach the size of AT&T or General Motors at their zeniths. They certainly will never have the number of managers and corporate staff employees that GM and AT&T had. The fast-moving business environment of the twenty-first century will simply not allow organizations to become large bureaucracies. What it will allow are some interesting new forms of organization: large organizations that behave like small ones and small ones that develop some of the capabilities of large ones.

Large Can Be Small

Mastering the large/small mix is critical in the new logic; in fact, it can determine success or failure. A case in point: While Sears, Kmart, and Montgomery Ward have tried to control operations centrally, Wal-Mart has focused on giving its stores the power to make important decisions concerning advertising, pricing, and store layout. Wal-Mart's leaders recognize that local knowledge is needed in order to make these decisions well. At the beginning of every week, corporate management visits stores all over the country to learn what is going on. On Saturday, they meet at corporate headquarters to share their findings and decide what they need to do to help their stores be successful. This meeting is open to all employees and is held in a large auditorium. It is also televised to all Wal-Mart locations on WMNT, Wal-Mart's internal television network.

Clearly, a focus on customers and markets is the key to maintaining vitality in large organizations. Jack Welch, the articulate CEO of General Electric, has said that a successful large organization must have the "soul of a small business." His comment nicely captures what the new logic says. A large organization has to be broken down into small units so that employees will care about their products or services and also identify with the success of their business units. Organizing around products or customers can achieve this goal. Keeping the organization relatively flat also helps, because it also allows control to move to small entrepreneurial business units.

Small Can Be Large

A second strategy for dealing with size calls for staying small but capturing the advantages of size through alliances, networks, and partnerships. This has been called everything from the "hollow corporation" to the "virtual corporation." It will be discussed more in the next chapter, but it is worth noting at this point that it is becoming increasingly popular, because organizations are finding that they can't do everything at a world-class level. In order to be successful they need to focus on determining what they can do best with their competencies and capabilities. They can then partner with other organizations who are world-class at what they do (United Parcel Service and Federal Express in distribution, for example).

Staff Support: Putting Experts Where They Belong

The old logic assigns an important role to the centralized staff support and service groups (finance, accounting, marketing, legal affairs, information services, and human resource management). These support and service groups are both a source of expertise and an important part of how strategy is implemented and behavior is controlled in the traditional hierarchical organization. But as was mentioned earlier, they often grow into gatekeepers, decision makers, and controllers of the organization. In the old logic, staff groups are typically part of the corporate headquarters of an organization (they report to and are managed by senior managers). Individuals in these staff groups often spend their careers developing their particular expertise and are dedicated to seeing that the organization operates correctly from the perspective of their specialties. They help assure that the organization has the best accounting, the best marketing, the best finance, and the best human resource management practices possible.

Unfortunately, the corporate staff in old logic organizations all too often behave like the engineers that control the temperature in large buildings. They place a thermostat in every room to regulate the temperature there, but they do not allow the occupants to pick the temperature they like. The thermostat is locked up, and in order to get it adjusted, someone from the staff has to be called to change it. Even after they are called, they tend to be slow to arrive and then disagree with the occupants of the room as to the best temperature setting. This has always struck me as the ultimate in poor service. They end up dictating what the environment will be like, even though they do not have to live in it.

Staff groups that become controllers of the rest of the organization reinforce and contribute to the vertical-decision-making model and to the external control model that are central to the traditional logic of organizing. This is why the new logic calls for staff groups to return to the role they originally had when they were conceived during the Napoleonic era. Napoleon created groups of logistics and intelligence experts to help advise the line officers who were in charge of his troops. The new logic clearly recognizes the importance of staff expertise but looks at staff groups as service providers and business partners rather than controllers or expert advisors to just the senior management. This is particularly true with respect to staff groups that design and manage systems that hopefully will help an organization carry out its strategic plans.

Members of the groups that design reward systems and information systems, for example, must go beyond being experts in their function. They must understand the business and its strategic agenda so they can partner with line managers to create systems that develop the core competencies and organizational capabilities needed for business success.[5]

In order for the support staff to be true business partners, they must be located appropriately in the organization's structure.

Unlike a traditional organization in which most staff is located at the corporate level, the new logic calls for them to be close to the business decisions, that is, to be part of operating units. There still may be a need for a very small corporate staff whose major role is to advise senior management and ensure that others in the organization (in their particular staff functions) have the knowledge they need. But in the new logic approach, staff experts who work in business units should have their main reporting relationship to a business unit head or a line manager, and just a dotted-line or weak reporting relationship to the corporate staff. Continuing with the building metaphor, this is comparable to a series of low-rise buildings, each with its own heating and utilities controlled by the occupants of that building. These separate utilities may be partially controlled and serviced by a central group, but they are primarily under the control of the building occupants.

AlliedSignal, Corning, Amoco, and Levi Strauss take an interesting approach to providing centralized services to different business units. They have created centralized "shared service units" that offer human resource management administrative services as if they are outside suppliers. Employees can call the appropriate group on 800 phone numbers when they have questions on benefits, salary, or the like. The companies collect customer satisfaction and cost data that let them compare the cost and quality of their shared service units with those that are available from outside vendors.

AES, the energy company, has yet another interesting approach. It in-sources staff functions on an as-needed basis. Since it has virtually no permanent staff employees in its team-based approach, it assigns staff functions such as purchasing and finance to employees from all parts of the organization on a part-time basis. In the process, these employees learn a great deal about what it takes to make their business successful. This may sound a bit like empowerment or business involvement gone too far, but the success of the company suggests it is working.

Any staff administrative activity that is primarily transaction oriented can potentially be outsourced. For example, companies such as EDS and Andersen Consulting can help organizations maintain and develop their information processing capabilities. Organizations have, for a long time, used outside service firms to handle payroll administration. They are increasingly outsourcing a wide array of human resource management activities, such as benefits administration, relocation, technical training, and employee counseling.

By skillfully using professional service groups that are dedicated to developing expertise in a particular area, an organization may well be able to spend less and get the latest and best expertise and service. They also can get greater flexibility because it is easier to change the scope of an activity or to reconfigure it when an external vendor provides it. An internal change often involves layoffs and retraining, or hiring and training new employees. A further advantage of outsourcing: sometimes it is easier to develop a customer service relationship between the support group and the organization. When staff groups are employees, it is often difficult to get them to see other employees as customers and to focus on satisfying them.

Some companies are spinning off units as suppliers. IBM has done this with some of its human resource management functions, such as training and employee relocation services. This way the services are still available to the corporation that created them, but the staff is in control of its own small business. In another twist, Pacific Bell has outsourced virtually all of its legal services by getting its existing legal staff to form their own law firm.

Unfortunately, I know of few successful staff spin-offs. All too often they are arrogant about their capabilities and are not prepared for the outside world, where they must market their services and satisfy their customers. Nevertheless, the failure of internal staff groups to be successful as separate businesses should not be taken as an excuse for not treating them as business units. I think it makes the opposite case. Corporate staff groups need to be put in the position of facing a market test regularly and consistently. Otherwise, they are unlikely to produce the kinds and quality of services that organizations need in today's highly competitive business environment. If they cannot compete successfully in the external world, then, in effect, they need to go out of business and be replaced by either higher-performing external units or newly created internal units.

Making the Structure Work: Relationships and Processes in the New Logic Organization

It is one thing to describe an organizational architecture, in this case size and shape; it is quite another to make it work well. As noted at the beginning of this chapter, one of the most striking things about the traditional organization chart is that most of the lines run vertically. This, of course, does not reflect the way most people actually behave in an organization. They talk to and get advice from peers, and in many cases they can do their jobs only because of well-developed lateral relationships. Yet the traditional organization chart does not depict horizontal or team relationships. It tends to picture only vertical ones, upward only for the lowest levels, and up and down for managers. The result is that the primary customer that everyone in the corporation has is his or her boss.

Unfortunately, the vertical orientation of traditional organizations diverts attention from the people who are the company's real customers for its products or services. This may not be highly dysfunctional if the CEO is an extraordinary individual who can operate as an effective proxy for the ultimate customer and can provide the right type of leadership and direction. The problem, of course, is that very few of these exceptional CEOs exist. I do not believe this is because managers are less capable than they used to be; rather it is because the task is extremely challenging in our rapidly changing and increasingly competitive business environment.

This is precisely why the new logic of organizing emphasizes grouping individuals around products, customers, and services. Such an approach reduces much of the need for hierarchical coordination and negates the need for managers and control systems to represent customers and to integrate the work of individuals. It shifts the focus from bosses to customers by making individuals responsible for satisfying customers.

In order for lateral, customer-focused structures to work best, organizations need to make extensive use of teams. In essence, teams substitute for hierarchy and take on many of the duties that are usually reserved for supervisors. Teams can therefore increase the amount of customer focus and the value that employees in non-managerial positions add to the organization's products and services.

As is discussed in Chapters Six and Seven, there are many types of teams. Some teams do not require individuals to sit together and operate as an interacting group. Information technology, for example, can connect individuals laterally, allow them to coordinate their work with each other, and link them to external customers who buy their services or products.

Returning to the architecture metaphor, the new logic argues for locating individuals so that they can interact with other individuals at the same level in the building. The new logic argues against individuals stuck in cubicles and against supervisors in private offices who coordinate the work of individuals and manage the relationship of these individuals with other departments. It argues against people being put together because they do the same thing. Space needs to be open and supportive of many different kinds of activities so that it brings people with different skills and knowledge together to work on common projects, products, and services.

Getting Out of the Box: From Jobs to Tasks and Teams

The boxes on the traditional organizational chart represent jobs that are filled with single individuals, because in the old logic:

- The important thing from an organizational point of view is to carefully specify what individuals do.
- Individuals must be held accountable for their actions.

There is a logical—but for some a difficult to accept—alternative to having boxes on a organization chart that represent jobs filled with single individuals. It is to simply eliminate the idea of jobs and begin to assign work or tasks to collections of individuals or to teams.

This strategy, which suits the new logic perfectly, goes one step beyond the creation of a lateral organization chart in which lateral lines show how individuals are expected to coordinate their steps in the production process. As shown in Figure 4.1, it is both boxless and team based. It reflects the importance of lateral and vertical communication and represents an organization structure—drawn from the work of Sue Mohrman, Monty Mohrman, and Susan Cohen—that better captures the new logic.[6]

It suggests eliminating the boxes that represent individuals and simply representing work areas, projects, or sets of tasks as the basic building blocks of the organization. Individuals or teams are then assigned to collections of tasks. This radical redesign of an organization's basic architecture or structure requires compatible designs

Figure 4.1. Team-Based Organization Design.

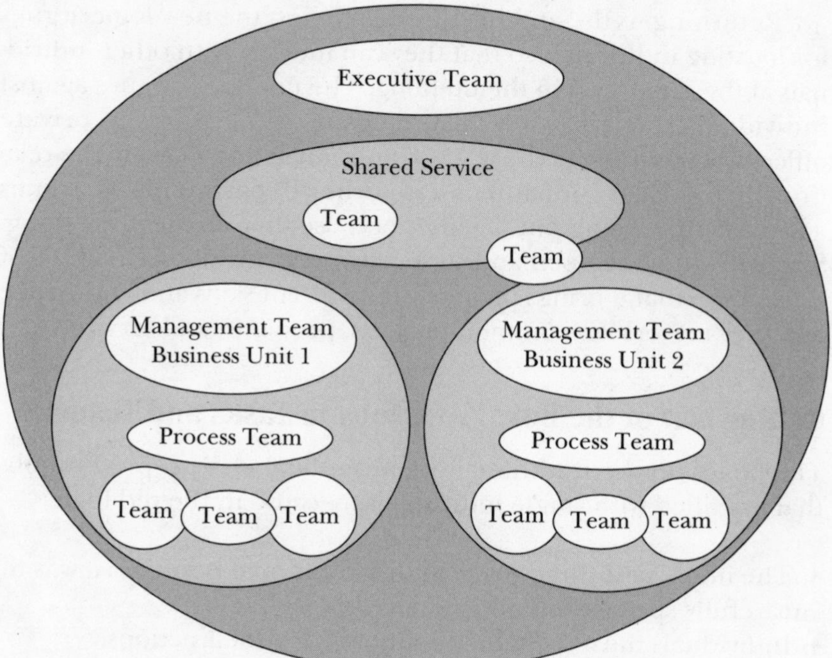

Source: Mohrman, S. A., Cohen, S. G., and Mohrman, A. M. *Designing Team-Based Organizations.* San Francisco: Jossey-Bass, 1995, p. 49. Used by permission.

for all the basic points of the Star Model from Chapter Two in order to be effective. As will be discussed in later chapters, it requires team-based reward systems, new types of information and decision processes, and individuals with different skills and outlooks on performance and accountability. This team-based approach to the fundamental architecture of an organization is well suited to the environment of rapid change and high-performance demands in which business finds itself operating these days.

What the Whole Organization Will Look Like in the New Logic

The overall structure of an organization that fits the new logic has few levels of management relative to its size. It is organized around the customer. It puts as many individuals as possible in direct contact with the customer. It groups individuals to operate laterally by making individuals or teams responsible for an entire product or customer service encounter; thus, groups are no longer formed primarily according to functional areas.

Staff functions have much more of a service or an advisory nature than a decision-making nature. Indeed, these functions may be outsourced, since the services they offer can be purchased on the open market and used as needed. They do not have to represent a fixed-cost commitment for the organization.

Taken together, a flat structure and an emphasis on lateral processes can produce organizations that are simultaneously small and large. People can feel part of and responsible for a small business unit, but they can count on the advantages of a large corporation when it comes to resources and support services.

Completing the architectural metaphor, the new logic approach suggests a series of low-rise buildings that have considerable open space and flexible, movable partitions. The buildings should be grouped together in a campus-like environment or spread around the world and connected by information technology. Individuals should be located in buildings according to the customers they serve or the products they create. At the center should be a building smaller than the others—but similar in layout—to house senior management, leaders of corporate staff groups, and representatives of key core competencies and organizational capabilities.

The next chapter focuses on the types of interior designs that an organization can adopt in order to fit the new logic and broad architectural guidelines laid out so far. The challenge—and it is a significant one—is to create an interior design that develops the right mix of competencies and capabilities so that an organization can be successful in its mission. It is the first of several steps that must be taken to complete the application of the new logic principles to the structure point on the Star Model. When it is completed, I hope you will never again think of structure only in terms of boxes and vertical lines.

Chapter Five

Organization Design
Matching the Organization to the Business

- Organizations should be designed around products and customers.
- Involvement is the most effective source of control.

Now that the basic shape of a high-performance organization has been established, the next step is to determine the details of its interior design. The key parts need to be identified as well as how and in what ways they connect and communicate with each other and the outside world to produce effective performance.

A number of possible designs and structures, each with its own strengths and weaknesses, can fit the new logic principles. New designs are constantly being developed and old ones are being revived and reinvented to produce capabilities that provide competitive advantage. Since organizations have different strategies, there is no single structure that is right for all. Some companies need to use a business unit approach, others are best suited to use a structure called the front-back organization, and still others need to use a network or a project organization.

Where does an organization need to start in choosing a structure? The answer is clear: with its business strategy! It is imperative that companies develop an internal design that can produce the kinds of capabilities and competencies that its strategy demands.

For example, if an organization's strategy focuses on getting products to market quickly, it needs to drive the organization's interior design toward cross-functional teams that can deliver this kind of performance. This is precisely what Hewlett-Packard has done to improve its ability to develop new products rapidly.

As discussed in earlier chapters, often it is simply not enough for the chosen organizational architecture to produce just one capability, such as being customer-focused or a low-cost operator. Companies today need multiple capabilities to succeed. Thus, simple organizational structures are often inadequate—they produce only a limited set of organizational capabilities and limit performance potential. The rapid development of high-quality products, for example, is a complex undertaking that requires multifunctional teams and raises tough questions about who should manage and evaluate these teams as well as how large they should be and how they should relate to other parts of the organization. Sometimes the correct answers to these questions involve relatively complex organizational structures and processes.

Putting Individuals Together

The challenge in the new logic of organizing is not just to eliminate the command-and-control approach to structure; appropriate substitutes for it must be introduced. How people are organized and grouped together—whether in teams, in business units, or in common reporting relationships—is a key. People have to be grouped so that they can have the power, information, knowledge, and rewards that allow them to coordinate their efforts and cause them to feel collectively responsible for their performance.

The discussion of motivation in Chapter Two suggests quite clearly that the best form of organization, in many respects, is the small business that can control its own destiny because it makes its own products and services its own customers. Not only does this approach to grouping fit with a key principle of the new logic— organizing around customers and products—it has the greatest potential to involve people in the business, to motivate them to serve the customer, and to give them a strong sense of ownership.

Although attractive, as noted in Chapter Four, the small-business approach does not fit many modern technologies and global business environments. So organizational structures need to be created to capture the key elements of the simple small-business model and at the same time create an organization that can operate in situations where, for example, extensive research and development is needed, large amounts of capital must be invested, and complex products and services must be delivered or manufactured.

In large organizations, grouping must be done through multiple levels, which inevitably creates both lateral and vertical seams or boundaries in an organization. The challenge is to create the right seams. First, organizations must decide whether to group people at the top by business units or by function. If the top is organized by business units, the levels below need to decide whether to organize themselves into smaller business units based on particular products or customers, on functions, or on some other criterion such as geography (country, for example). There are four organizational designs whose approaches to grouping fit the principles of the new logic. Our discussion of them will begin with the simplest design: the business unit.

Business Units: Being Small in a Large Organization

One principle of the new logic argues that the best approach to grouping workers within organizations is to put all employees who are involved with a product or service together in a business unit that has its own profit-and-loss responsibility. This gives each business unit a particular product or service focus, and all the employees in that unit can concentrate on the unit's success. Historically, many multi-business organizations, including Hanson Trust, Rockwell, Textron, Teledyne, and ITT, as well as companies that are focused on particular industries, such as Johnson & Johnson in health care and Hewlett-Packard in electronics, have been organized this way.

In the most extreme version of the decentralized business unit organization, there may be virtually no corporate staff and only a small executive team that is charged with strategically managing investments in the different business units. In this approach, staff services such as human resources and accounting can be located within the business units or purchased from outside vendors.

Johnson & Johnson provides a particularly intriguing example of how the business unit approach can work for an organization with multiple businesses. It maintains separate names for many of its business units, even though all of them are called Johnson & Johnson companies. McNeil Laboratories, for example, makes Tylenol, while Vistacon makes contact lenses. These business units are not only separate in name. Each unit has its own board of directors as well as its own profit-and-loss statement. But, at the same time, they are all tied to a single set of corporate values and an approach to doing business. What's more, all board members are Johnson & Johnson employees who work in other business units. Thus these separate business units are both integrated with and differentiated from the rest of Johnson & Johnson, giving them the feeling of simultaneously being small businesses and part of a large corporation.

Another interesting example is ABB, the global manufacturer of electrical, rail, and other industrial equipment that has divided its over 200,000 employees into six thousand business units. Each unit has a profit-and-loss statement and is expected to serve its customers and market directly. It is also expected to draw on technology and competencies from other parts of the organization and to share its core competencies with other ABB business units.

Global chemical giant Du Pont is a more recent convert to the business unit approach. During 1991 and 1992, in an attempt to improve its performance, it pared its work force by 25 percent and dramatically shrank its corporate headquarters operation. During 1994 and 1995, Du Pont eliminated management layers and split the company into twenty-one semi-autonomous strategic business units with responsibility for satisfying and dealing with customers. In each operating unit, managers have the freedom to make deals and invest capital. This is in sharp contrast to the Du Pont of the 1970s and 1980s, which had huge civil service–like bureaucracies in Wilmington, Delaware, and Geneva, Switzerland, and epitomized all that was staid and sluggish about corporate America.

Creating an Effective Business Unit Design

Despite the strengths of the business unit approach, organizations that are structured around multiple small business units do not automatically become high-performance organizations. To be effective, the units must be designed and managed well, the amount and type of corporate overhead that is created must be appropriate, and inter-unit issues—that is, how units coordinate their activities when different business units deal with the same customers and suppliers—must be well managed.[1]

Design and management are the first keys to successful business units. Organizing by units does not guarantee that an organization will be flat and focused on particular products and customers. The business units themselves may be organized in a traditional way—around functions, with extensive hierarchy—and therefore not have the kind of involvement and lateral relationships that are the basis of a high-performance organization. Often the best approach is to create mini business units within major business units.

Even making a relatively small number of individuals responsible for a product or service does not ensure that they will have a line of sight to the customer. Measurement and communication processes need to be introduced that give people the information they need to develop a line of sight.

The structure and nature of the corporate organization can also strongly influence the effectiveness of small business units within multi-business corporations. To work properly, the multiple business unit model requires an extremely flat hierarchy above the business units, with minimal corporate staff to oversee them. All too often, organizations with multiple business units create an extensive hierarchy above them and develop large staff groups to direct their work.

Often the corporate executives to whom the business units report do not—and cannot—understand the business as well as members of the unit do, because it is only one of many businesses that the executives deal with. Unfortunately, in many cases, this lack of understanding does not prevent corporate executives from making key decisions and trying to manage the operations of the business units that report to them.

What's more, members of the business units often have to spend a considerable amount of time providing regular reports and data to the corporate organization in order to show how they are performing and how they are conforming to corporate mandates. They also must justify any changes they want to make in their operations. Thus the corporate hierarchy becomes as much a customer of the business units as those who buy its products. When this happens, individuals in the business units feel as though they are part of a carefully controlled and orchestrated large corporation and do not feel that they control and run their own business.

A final issue with the multiple business unit design involves the coordination—or the lack of it—across business units, particularly when the units are in diverse businesses. In such cases, it is difficult for the corporate executives to add value, instead of just overhead costs, to these units. This is one reason why the stock market often devalues companies that are made up of many independent business units. Another reason is that sometimes one unit may make it more difficult for another unit to do business with some customers. This often occurs when one unit is a business competitor of a firm and another unit is trying to be a supplier of that firm.

Two good examples of the way the investment community values multiple-business companies are provided by ITT and AT&T. When ITT announced in 1995 that it was splitting into three separate companies—one focusing on hotels, one focusing on financial services, and one focusing on a variety of manufacturing businesses—the stock market responded by increasing the value of ITT stock by almost 10 percent. It was almost a videotape replay six months later when AT&T said it would split into three separate companies—one for communications services, one for communications equipment, one for computers. Its stock also rose about 10 percent. The investment community clearly voted with its dollars that the corporate levels of ITT and AT&T did not add value to their multiple business units by indicating that the parts are worth more without them. Indeed, given the large increases in the value of the companies, they were sending an even stronger message: the corporate level actually decreased the effectiveness of the parts of ITT and AT&T, presumably because it added costs and took control away from the business units.

An interesting example of a successful organization that does little to add costs or controls to the business units that are part of it is Berkshire Hathaway, which is headed by Warren Buffett, one of the world's richest and most successful businessmen. Berkshire Hathaway invests its capital in its independent business units and tries to outsmart the market by using its information about how its businesses are performing and their prospects for the future (its units are in furniture, investment banking, insurance, and ten or more other businesses). It allows its different, mostly unrelated units to operate independently so that they can focus on their particular businesses. Berkshire Hathaway may intervene, at times, in decisions about the allocation of capital and the appointment of senior managers, but it does not get involved in controlling and directing the businesses. If it becomes dissatisfied with a business and its prospects, Berkshire Hathaway simply sells it and moves on to a better investment opportunity.

Hanson Trust operates in a somewhat similar fashion. At the moment it owns a wide variety of businesses that operate primarily in the United States and Europe, including a cigarette business in Ireland and a chemical business and a coal business in the United States. They have a very small corporate staff in England that operates essentially to help the organization measure the financial returns of its business units and to support the goal-setting process that the corporate-level managers go through with the heads of each of their businesses. The company regularly buys and sells business units as it changes its view of what businesses it thinks represent the best investments. Recently, for example, it sold its cookware, forest products, and golf businesses in an effort to simplify its structure.

Rockwell International is a good example of a successful, technology-based, multiple business organization. It is in a variety of businesses ranging from auto parts to consumer electronics (it is the leading maker of computer modems). Each of its units operates as a stand-alone business, but CEO Don Beall and the corporate staff do try to achieve limited synergies across the business units. They work hard on technology core competency transfer and on organizational capability development and transfer.

Overall, operating with unrelated multiple business units can be a viable form of organization if senior managers act like Warren Buffett and Don Beall of Rockwell. They need to use their superior knowledge of their businesses to outperform the investment community by making key strategic investments for the corporation, to keep corporate overhead to a minimum, and to allow the members of business units to operate their businesses.

Profiting from Coordination

So far in this chapter I have argued that a series of small business units can be a useful organizational structure if the organization is characterized by a flat structure, minimal staff, and a high level of autonomy for each unit. But what if coordinated activity can provide some advantages? Is it possible to be simultaneously autonomous and coordinated? I believe the answer is yes, particularly if the business units are in related businesses, producing a number of different auto parts or a number of health care products, for example. In this situation a corporation may be in a position to have separate business units and have the corporate level add value to the businesses.

TRW and Honeywell provide interesting examples of how to do this. They have sold off some of their unrelated businesses and are therefore better positioned and focused at the corporate level to add value to the activities of their remaining business units. They now have businesses that can profit from coordination, if that coordination can be done in a relatively cost-efficient manner and without building a large corporate group.

The key lies in deciding where it is desirable for business units to be independent and where coordination can be an advantage. Economies of scale are often the greatest in purchasing, raising capital, doing research and development, and perhaps in marketing, advertising, and sales. But in the new logic of organizing, keep in mind that the role of a corporate function is not to control the activities of business units but to coordinate certain activities so business units can have the advantage of a large corporation without sacrificing the benefits of an autonomous business unit.

There are two ways to do this. One method of coordination that fits the new logic is to use overlay teams made up of representatives from the different business units who are collectively responsible for coordinating their activities in such areas as purchasing and marketing.[2] These groups can be led either by someone who represents the corporate level or by a business unit member who is designated as the lead person for this particular activity. In a multiple business unit organization, it is often desirable to have individual business units take the lead in different areas that require coordination. One unit, for example, may take the lead in advertising, while another takes the lead in purchasing. This creates a reciprocal relationship in which the units all depend on each other to coordinate different functions and types of activities.

A disadvantage to the use of overlay teams to coordinate the activities of different business units is that they have limited authority and often must rely on persuasion and shared mutual interest to get work done. But their effectiveness can be strengthened by giving them considerable decision-making authority. For example, if they are coordinating advertising, they can be given the final say on how corporate and individual business unit dollars are spent.

A second way to coordinate key activities is to assign the responsibility for them to different business units. The business unit that is responsible for a function takes leadership for the entire corporation by providing the resource itself or getting the best deal for the other business units from an outside supplier. Just as with overlay teams, it is critical that these business units have both lead and follow positions in different activities. This reciprocity gives them bargaining power with each other and prevents some business units from gaining excessive power.

When decision making for key activities is vested in the business units, they are unlikely to develop the corporate hierarchy disease of not understanding the implications of decisions and having no sense of urgency. In short, regardless of which business unit they come from, individuals are much more likely to feel what it is like to both be in a business unit and have overall corporate responsibility for a particular issue.

I have not seen very many organizations use the approach of making business units responsible for providing corporation-wide services and expertise. AlliedSignal has done this to a degree by making some of its divisions centers of excellence for particular functions or activities. One division, for example, is a center of excellence with respect to organizational effectiveness and organizational design.

An Irish firm that I have consulted with had some of its U.S. business units identified as centers of excellence and providers of shared services to the rest of the business units. For example, one of them developed the financial systems for the other business units. They got these roles because when they were acquired they had expertise in particular areas, and it seemed natural to capitalize on their expertise.

The Front-Back Organization: Serving Internal and External Markets

An interesting alternative to the business unit organization is a structure called the front-back organization.[3] It creates an internal and external market structure to produce coordination where it is desirable and independence where it is desirable.

In front-back structure, one part of the organization (the back) is responsible for developing and delivering the products or services that the organization offers. For example, if the organization makes computer equipment, there may be one back-end unit dedicated to software, one to printers, one to personal computers, and so on across its array of products. In financial services, each back-end unit may be responsible for developing different types of investment vehicles.

The other half of the organization—the front end—is responsible for delivering the organization's products or services to particular customer groups. The front end is usually organized around customers with common interests who are likely to buy related sets of products or services. It may also be organized around a particular geographical area.

The front-back approach is consistent with the business process reengineering movement because it, too, emphasizes organizing around the critical processes in the organization rather than around functions.[4] The front-back approach fits businesses that want to focus simultaneously on multiple products/services and multiple customers. Examples here include Fidelity, the large financial services firm, and a number of computer companies that want to sell solutions to particular markets (financial service firms and hotels, for example) rather than offer just hardware or software.

Harley-Davidson, the motorcycle company, has created this type of organization but with only one unit in the back, manufacturing and delivering the product, and one unit in the front, creating demand. This is in noticeable contrast to AT&T, GTE, and the American Express-owned financial services firm IDS—all of which have ended up with multiple units in the back and front of their organizations. In the case of IDS, the back end consists of a number of financial product units, and the front end consists of a number of market-focused units that serve different types of customers. Nonetheless, the design thinking is similar. These front-back organizations all stress the importance of focusing individuals on processes that they can control and understand, and that have identifiable outputs and customers.

One strength of the front-back organization is that it can grow easily in an almost amoeba-like way, adding different pieces or business units to either the back or front as new products and market segments appear. This approach to growth avoids extensive bureaucracy and large-scale reorganizations and keeps more individuals in direct contact with the marketplace.

A second advantage is that each piece of the organization has its own customers and bottom-line profitability requirements. This creates a line of sight for everyone in the organization that goes from costs to customer satisfaction and revenue. In most organizations, the back can sell only to the front, and the front can buy only from the back. But the ideal twenty-first-century approach may be to allow the back to sell outside and to allow the front to buy from other suppliers. For example, in Sun Microsystems, the computer company, the back end can sell integrated circuits to other customers while the front end can buy from other vendors in order to satisfy its customers. This fits particularly well with the new logic of organizing because it creates true external customers for the major products of the organization and keeps the back as well as the front very much in touch with the market.

The front-back approach is in sharp contrast to the classic business unit model where each division has its own sales force and may even compete with its own company for sales. This was a common occurrence at Digital during its chaotic growth years. A corporation may choose to accept this scenario, leaving it up to the customer to sort out its offerings and in some cases to coordinate what the supplying company has chosen not to coordinate. It is as if the company were serving customers a buffet from which they can choose what they want.

The buffet approach often fails to capture the full value that can be added through coordination. It leaves it up to the customer to add this value. Thus there is less revenue for the seller. In addition, the customer may not use the full range of products and services the company offers, choosing instead a mix of products and services from different companies.

Although some customers like buffets, the number is shrinking. Customers frequently lack skill at integrating products and, as a result, end up with indigestion. They do not want to deal with multiple suppliers for a variety of reasons that include the extra effort, skill, and costs associated with doing it that way. Further, in some cases, the parts and services gathered from different suppliers do not work well together as a system. Thus, more and more, companies want to buy integrated product offerings and systems.

In the automobile industry, for example, Ford, General Motors, and Chrysler have found it more effective to deal with a relatively small number of suppliers who produce systems rather than parts. That is, they prefer to buy suspension systems from a single company rather than buy shock absorbers and the other pieces of a suspension system from a variety of suppliers. In order to meet the auto companies' demands, auto parts suppliers such as TRW and Rockwell have had to both broaden the range of products they make and get better at integrating them into systems that in turn can be integrated into car designs.

Challenges in the Front-Back Organization

There are many challenges in operating a front-back organization. It is not a simple organizational form. There are tough pricing issues in selling from the back to the front, as well as difficult decisions about dividing customer segments and the markets in designing in the front end (by geography or by business type). All the points on the organizational star need to be designed to fit it. If you shift to the front-back approach—as Digital tried to do at one point—it requires a radical change in the skills of many employees as well as new measurement systems. For example, in Digital, sales representatives, who previously needed to know about only a few products, had to learn to understand the customer's business and learn how to work in teams in order to be able to choose the right mix of products for the customer.

The front-back approach permits an organization to focus on what it does best by letting it develop alliances, partnerships, or both to do those things that it doesn't want to do. However, this can raise difficult questions about which outside companies are competitors and which are partners. What if, for example, the back end of the organization partners with one of the front end's competitors? The front end might feel that the back end should not give its competitors the best technology or the best prices. The back, on the other hand, may feel it needs to do so in order to prevent its competitors from getting the business.

Managing multiple competitor/partner relationships can be complicated. For example, Motorola, a front-back organization, recently found that it had thirteen different relationships—some cooperative and some highly competitive—with another large company. They had to create a coordination group just to manage those relationships.

My guess is that the long-term viability of the front-back approach in a corporation ultimately depends on the back-end units having the freedom to go to the market and the front end of the organization being able to buy from other suppliers. Without these options, there is likely to be too much debate inside the company about internal pricing and product quality. It is too easy for the back end to claim it is producing great products but the front end does not know how to sell them, and for the front end to claim that the back end is a supplier of poor, overpriced products. Allowing outside relationships for both parts of the organization is the only way to provide objective evidence and data upon which to manage the relationship between the two.

Even though the front-back approach has limitations and is extremely complex, it does have some significant advantages for organizations that are trying to be both large and small and trying to focus on both products and customers. Like the business unit model, the front-back approach creates a series of small businesses within a large organization. It is particularly appropriate for organizations that have a number of related products and services to offer to a diverse set of customers and markets. It also seems particularly appropriate for organizations that are trying to manage global businesses and need to focus very strongly on particular countries or particular market segments within countries while at the same time maintaining a strong product or service orientation.

So far, the discussion has centered on organizational approaches that apply primarily to situations that require relatively stable, long-term structures to support ongoing work and coordination among continuing business units. But in industries such as entertainment, fashion, software, and consulting, the situation is very different, and as a result network and project structures are more appropriate.

The Network Organization: Partnerships and Alliances

Network organizations have been around for decades, but only recently has the network structure been recognized by organization theorists as an important approach.[5] The network approach fits the new logic because it is based on small business units with clear customer and bottom-line accountabilities. In network organizations, separate companies come together to produce and sell particular services or products. One way to think of network organizations is to view them as front-back organizations in which the back and the front—instead of being part of the same corporation—are made up of separate companies (from two or three to hundreds). They can also be thought of as process-driven organizations in which the processes are performed by different companies.

In essence, a network organization is the ultimate move away from an integrated organization that tries to add value by managing, owning, and coordinating all steps in the production or service process. Each organization in the network does only what it does best and focuses on that. Thus it needs fewer capabilities and competencies and can often get a higher percentage of its work force involved in the business.

An organization that is part of a network may perform a single function, produce only a single part or component of the final product, or do more; there are many possible approaches. In the entertainment business, network members are often very specialized, doing only lighting or catering, for example, whereas in the manufacturing businesses they may supply complete systems and do design and marketing, not just manufacturing.

The advantage of a network organization is that every company that joins it is, in a true sense, constantly subject to market pressures and demands. Thus the line of sight to business performance for individuals in these units is potentially much stronger than if they were part of a large organization. The network organization, in essence, substitutes an interconnected web of markets among its members for the layers of hierarchy and the many control systems that coordinate the activities of different functions and different pieces of a large, hierarchical, vertically integrated organization.

A crucial advantage of network organizations is that they are highly flexible and adaptable and can shift to new configurations as needed. All it takes to add a new product, or improve manufacturing, is to add a new company to the network and/or drop one of its current members.

Network organizations are frequently used to make motion pictures, produce athletic shoes and fashion-related products, and handle large construction projects. There is usually a network coordinator that assembles the pieces of the organization (the individual companies) into a network that will handle every phase of the business, from acquisition or preparation of raw material to the delivery of a product or service to a customer base. Often the network coordinator controls and carries out a key process such as product design or marketing.

Calvin Klein, for example, is a network coordinator that does not manufacture but controls the design and marketing of its products. Nike is a network coordinator that controls the design of its athletic shoes and clothing but employs many companies to do its manufacturing and still others to handle its shipping, distribution, and selling. Similarly, in clothing, Benetton has been very effective as a network coordinator. It controls some manufacturing technology and its brand name but neither manufactures nor sells most of its products. It has a few of its own stores just to keep in touch with the market.

Solectron, the company mentioned earlier that specializes in assembling electronic boards for other companies, is an interesting example of a specialized network organization that is not a network coordinator. Instead, it is part of a number of networks, since it makes electronic circuit boards for such companies as Motorola, Hewlett-Packard, and Apple. Its competitive advantage is that it is better at its core competency—the technology of board manufacturing—than the organizations it supplies. Thus the companies who buy from Solectron do not need to invest a tremendous amount of capital to start up their own board manufacturing operations, nor do they need to develop technical knowledge in board design. They can rely on Solectron for the latest technology and for its world-class core competency.

Customers tell Solectron the characteristics of the board they want to buy and Solectron supplies the board. Solectron, in turn, gains economies of scale through focusing exclusively on board manufacturing. Participation in multiple networks allows Solectron to develop organizational capabilities in quality and low-cost manufacturing. It is essentially a focused business that through networks is part of many large businesses. Because it is focused, Solectron does not have a need for some functions and organizational capabilities, but it does have a need for one unusual capability: partnering.

Solectron has grown so much as a result of its success that in order for it to continue to grow, it must increasingly think of itself as a series of small business units that develop different boards for different customers. If it fails to keep a small business focus, it runs the risk of becoming a slow, bureaucratic organization—much like the internal parts of the organizations that it often competes with for business.

One interesting way to evolve from a classic front-back organization to a network organization is by spinning off internal business units and making them into suppliers. IBM has done this successfully with its Lexmark printer division. Thermo Electron has done it with a number of its internal units. In this approach, once a part of an organization gains a particular capability, it is spun off as a separate corporate entity rather than put into a front-back structure. Typically, the organization that spins it off keeps a partial equity interest in the new organization and retains it as a supplier or service provider to the network it coordinates.

The Project Organization: Coming Together for the Short Term

Project organizations are becoming much more common. The reason for this is clear: work is becoming more knowledge-based and short-term. In order to perform it, knowledgeable individuals need to be brought together for a relatively short time—often days or weeks, not years—to work on the development and delivery of products or services.

From an organization design point of view, project work represents some interesting challenges, because individuals must be developed and managed as important assets. At the same time, they must be available for assignment to a continuous stream of new projects.

One type of project organization is the "virtual organization," in which individuals who are not employees come together only to work on a project.[6] This is similar to a network organization, except that it usually lacks the formality, contracts, and agreements that exist in a such a network. Often it is a collection of individuals rather than companies. In the entertainment business, where short-term projects are common, virtual organizations are quite common and may last a day or less (just long enough to record a song!).

A radical attempt to create a virtual organization—but within a single business organization—is being tried by Oticon, a Danish hearing-aid company. In 1991 it eliminated all departments and managers' titles. In the place of desks, each employee now has a cart that holds his or her possessions. In this ultimate self-designing organization, employees are responsible for finding work for themselves. They create their own project teams and gather where they wish in an environment that is full of workstations. Once they have decided what project they intend to work on, they create an electronic record of the project and their responsibilities that is available to everyone throughout the organization. The CEO calls this the Spaghetti Model.

To facilitate the operation of this spaghetti organization, the physical layout of Oticon was changed. Sprinkled throughout the building are coffee bars with counters for fast stand-up meetings. In addition, dialogue rooms scattered around the facility vary from large to small and often have a tiny table just big enough for a few cups of coffee. The idea is to remind employees that it is much more important to talk to colleagues about what to do than to protect themselves behind a paper or a table. Copiers and other equipment are positioned in the corners of the building to encourage employees to walk about to get from one piece of equipment to another and engage in more casual interaction. The Oticon approach probably does not fit most organizations, but it makes a key point: organizations need to design internal structures that fit the kind of project work they do. The possibilities are many, and the opportunity for gaining competitive advantage is real.

The virtual organization approach to project management is not the answer for all project work. Sometimes it is advantageous to use more structured approaches and to create project teams from a single firm to serve a particular client. This is often true in accounting and other businesses where firms need to stand behind their services and develop continuing relationships with customers. It is also often true in building custom, one-of-a-kind, complex products, such as communication satellites.

Often the best way to organize a firm for project work is to use some form of the classic—and often discredited—matrix organization. In the matrix approach, individuals report both to a long-term manager who is responsible for their professional development and technical skills and to someone who is responsible for the particular project or projects on which they are working.[7] The key to the success of the matrix organization: make sure that the project managers have the appropriate authority to operate as a small business in acquiring talent and in rewarding and controlling the individuals who work on their projects. If they don't, there is a risk that the project and the customer will get lost in the bureaucracy.

Matrix structures have worked well in the aerospace industry, where TRW, Hughes, Rockwell, and others have developed world-class project management capabilities. In consulting organizations, such as McKinsey, it has also worked well because it gives individuals a strong focus on a project or projects but does not neglect their technical and professional development.

When matrix management fails, it is usually for one of two reasons. One reason is that the matrix approach was not the right way to organize, given the work that needed to be done. For it to be effective, there must be work that requires high levels of specialized expertise and work that is constantly changing as the organization moves from one assignment or project to another. The other reason for failure: poor implementation—that is, employees are not trained, and reward, measurement, and information systems are not changed, to support a matrix structure. In essence, the organization does not spend the time and effort needed to develop matrix management as an organizational capability by changing all the points on the Star Model.

Clearly it is not simple to install or operate a matrix structure. I regularly encounter organizations in which matrix management is referred to with a four-letter word, as "the M word," or in other derogatory terms. When I ask why it is so poorly regarded, I usually find that the organization tried it in the 1970s or early 1980s and found it confusing and hard to operate. Further investigation usually reveals that it often created additional hierarchy and that many employees found it uncomfortable to report to two bosses, a functional boss and a project boss.

To be effective, a matrix organization needs to tilt strongly toward the project side. Because there are external customers, the project must be an integrating force that controls behavior and that runs as a business, even if it is a temporary one. The part of the organization that supplies talent to the project side must be able to run as a small business that provides expert labor and resources to its internal customers, that is, the project managers and the project-based organization. For example, at Fluor Corporation, the large engineering and construction firm, project managers control their own budgets and use them to get skilled help from global expertise centers. (Fluor has engineers in Holland, Asia, and the United States.)

The challenges in structuring an organization according to the new logic are clear. Corporations need to be like small businesses in how they involve individuals in the success of the business, and they need to be large when there is an advantage to being large. In most cases, this can be done by using a business unit, network, front-back, or project approach to structure, because they all make business units their primary grouping. Small business units are critical to providing individuals with a line of sight from their activities to the market and customer.

As will be seen in later chapters, the success of these small business units requires that the work design, rewards, processes, and human resource management practices all be aligned with the organizational structure. Individuals must obtain the information, knowledge, power, and rewards that are relevant to their business and its success. This is needed to create the feelings of ownership and control that are so difficult to achieve in a large, traditionally structured business.

Chapter Six

Work Design
Moving Beyond the Limits of Jobs to Work and Involvement

- Involvement is the most effective source of control.
- All employees must add significant value.

In my research on organizational effectiveness, I have interviewed literally thousands of employees and discussed everything from their reactions to their pay to how they feel about the effectiveness of their senior managers. Regardless of the focus of the interviews, one topic always comes up: the nature of the work that individuals do. CEOs talk about it. Telephone operators talk about it. Insurance salespeople talk about it. This is hardly surprising, since work is a key determinant of how individuals feel about themselves and their organization. It is the one thing that constantly occupies individuals in the workplace. Thus how they react to the work they do determines how well individuals perform and how well organizations perform.

The importance of work to all individuals leads to an obvious question: Are there predictable reactions that employees have to the nature of their work? The answer is definitely yes, and these reactions will be the major focus of this chapter.

One consistent finding of the research on work design is that there are significant individual differences in how people react to work. What is interesting to one person often is boring to another.

I am often surprised by what some individuals find interesting about work. For example, several years ago I was interviewing a woman who put the serial numbers on skis at the end of a production line. When I asked her how she felt about her work, she reported that she liked it because of the variety. When I asked her what variety there was in putting numbers on skis every minute or so, she gave me what to her was an obvious answer: "Each ski is different because it gets a different number." Clearly, one person's variety is another person's repetition.

Most employees, when asked, say that they want more power and influence in the workplace. Yet I have interviewed more than just a few production line workers who want to be mentally absent from their jobs and live their lives during their non-work hours. They not only don't want more responsibility, they want less. In truth, some employees simply don't have a tremendous desire to be challenged by their jobs and prefer simple, predictable work. Quite likely, years of working in repetitive jobs has led them to focus their energies elsewhere. Would these individuals change their minds if they were given more interesting work? Perhaps, but I believe there are some people who simply do not see work as that important and do not want to change. They, however, represent a minority of the work force.

Most employees want to work in challenging jobs. Often, they are trapped in old logic jobs, are frustrated by them, and are forced to do counterproductive things in order to experience interesting work. I remember interviewing an electric coffee pot assembly-line worker who had a very simple task that she repeated approximately every twenty seconds. For her, the "challenge" came not from finding ways to do things more efficiently but from figuring out a way to put the coffee pot together incorrectly. Why? Industrial engineers in the plant had worked for many years to make the assembly process "worker-proof," but because her work was so monotonous she worked just as hard to figure out ways to beat the engineers. At the time I interviewed her, the engineers had just redesigned the pot again, and she was thinking about how to overcome the new design as she correctly assembled the pots that went by her in a never-ending stream.

Employees who do not want challenge in their jobs are a poor fit with the ideal work design in the new logic, which is one that involves each employee. The new logic principles call for work situations in which individuals are challenged because they are responsible for designing, making, and selling a product or service. The new logic argues that if organizations can make work challenging and give individuals control over how the work is done, employees will not have to create their own challenges, as the coffee pot assembler had to do. They can also add value by coordinating, managing, and improving how they do their work.

As discussed in the last chapter, grouping individuals by products and services from the top down—a key principle of the new logic—is the first step in creating an organization in which individuals throughout the organization have the power, information, knowledge, and rewards that will ensure their involvement in their business. Also crucial to the involvement and high performance of individuals is the way work is designed.

It is worth noting at this point that I am avoiding using the term *jobs* in discussing the structure of the work of individuals. There is a good reason for this. In the new logic approach, the word is obsolete, at least with respect to its traditional meaning of a fixed set of tasks that are assigned to individuals and recorded through a job description. Instead of performing jobs, individuals increasingly need to perform a continuously changing series of tasks. There are two primary reasons why this change needs to occur. First, the environment constantly forces organizations to change what they do, and thus individuals must change. Second, the new logic argues for individuals to expand their activities constantly, to work outside of what might be encompassed in a traditional job description, and to do more of their work in teams.

Before beginning a discussion of what work should look like in a new logic organization, it is important to look at how work has evolved, so it is clear why the traditional approach to work design—assembly lines and standardized work—has lost favor.

The Old Logic of Work Design: Assembly Lines and Standardized Work

Early in the twentieth century, the scientific management approach to work design argued that jobs should be specialized, standardized, and simplified. Individuals were trained to do simple tasks in a standardized "best way"—as on Henry Ford's automobile assembly line. With this approach, little power, information, and knowledge was needed or existed among the individuals who actually made the cars. This allowed companies to use relatively cheap and easily replaceable labor.

The only kind of motivation that mattered in the logic of scientific management was extrinsic. Jobs were designed so that individual job performance was easy to observe and measure and thus to reward or punish. This was probably for the best, because the work was easy to do and there was little sense of self-esteem and personal satisfaction to be gained from doing it well, and, as a result, it was not intrinsically motivating.[1]

Ignoring intrinsic motivation created a number of problems for those who adopted scientific management. Some of the historical problems with product quality in the auto industry are the result of workers not caring and of their sabotaging the products in order to experience a sense of self-esteem and competency. It may seem strange that individuals would feel good about doing their jobs only when they perform them in a counterproductive way, but as the example of the coffee pot assembler illustrates, this is exactly what happens. When doing a job correctly is so easy that anyone can do it, but doing it incorrectly requires intelligence to avoid being caught, it is more challenging and satisfying to do it incorrectly. It also, of course, introduces an element of variety in what is often a monotonous work situation.

When I consulted with the U.S. auto companies in the 1960s and 1970s, I saw many examples of creative sabotage. Employees would weld cans of bolts into cars so that the cars would forever rattle. They would tighten bolts in order that automatic transmissions would begin to leak after a few thousand miles, and they would leave Coke bottles and other parts in car doors.

One employee who objected to the odor in his workplace brought in an incense pot and burned it regularly for several days until the company demanded that he stop. He filed a union grievance over the company's restriction of his right to enjoy a pleasant odor while working. For him, the incense and the grievance were ways to add some variety and excitement and, of course, to torment management, who was responsible for his boring, repetitive work in the first place. Actions such as this often lead management to escalate controls through new rules and more supervision, all of which, of course, create new challenges for the employee who wants to experience variety and control.

Although the manufacturing assembly line is the most frequently used example of highly repetitive and boring work, it is just one of many. Service work such as the telephone operator's job, the check encoder's job in banks (they type the bar codes on the bottom of checks at the rate of more than a thousand checks an hour), the mail sorter's job, and many telephone sales jobs are typically even more repetitive and mind-numbing.

Old logic jobs are often expensive to set up and control and, if the product or service is complex, difficult to coordinate. For example, enormous amounts of engineering and research time are needed to set up automobile assembly lines so that they are balanced with respect to the amount of work each individual is assigned to do. Inevitably, some employees are not fully utilized because the line is not exactly balanced. It is also difficult to set up the lines to allow the car to be assembled in the correct sequence.

Another serious disadvantage of repetitive, simplified jobs is that they can result in high levels of employee turnover, because individuals become bored and dissatisfied with their work.[2] If they are not locked in by extrinsic rewards such as retirement systems or high levels of pay, employees will often change jobs simply to find a new situation. For example, when jobs are plentiful, fast-food firms experience turnover rates as high as 200 to 300 percent per year.

Trying to avoid turnover leads some organizations to raise pay levels to the point where individuals cannot afford to quit once they get a "good job" on an assembly line. That's what the U.S. automobile and steel industries did during the 1950s and 1960s. Even so, in the 1960s, Ford, Volvo, and other auto manufacturers often had 30 to 40 percent turnover in their factories. And, as discussed in earlier chapters, nothing is more fatal for a company than to end up with highly paid employees who add little value. For example, during the 1960s and 1970s, as the U.S. auto and steel companies raised wages to combat turnover and to try and provide extrinsic incentives for employees, they actually made themselves less competitive. In an increasingly global market, companies in other countries began producing the same products more cheaply due to lower labor costs and, in some cases, better work designs.

The Beginnings of the New Logic: Individual Job Enrichment

Even though many of the problems associated with standardized work began to become apparent in the 1930s, the first clearly stated alternative—called "job enlargement" because it involved adding variety to work by such methods as rotating jobs on an assembly line every few hours—did not develop until the 1950s. It proved to be of minimal value. Although job enlargement helped reduce boredom, it did little to increase motivation and to enable employees to add value.

The first significant alternative developed in the 1960s, when a series of research findings suggested an entirely new approach: that of creating enriched work that is intrinsically motivating because it is interesting, challenging, and involving.[3] This approach broke from the traditional logic with its emphasis on self-control and involvement in the job instead of on managerial direction and machine-like performance.

The enrichment approach—which provides the foundation for much of today's thinking about employee involvement and team-based work. It suggested that, if work is to be truly enriched, there are three requirements: work must be meaningful, its design must allow individuals to control how it is done, and employees need to have feedback on how well they are performing.[4]

Of these characteristics, the most difficult to establish is meaningfulness. To achieve it, a work design is needed that allows an individual to perform a complete task. The more an individual can take a piece of work from beginning to end—that is, produce a whole product or deliver a whole service to a customer—the more meaningful the work is. The work design should also enable employees to use a variety of skills that they value and to perform tasks that have an important impact on others.

Meeting these requirements usually means an organization has to expand the work of individuals both horizontally, to include more tasks, and vertically, so that an individual does things that supervisors customarily have done.

Our research at the Center for Effective Organization indicates that job enrichment continues to be a rather popular approach to work design in most large companies: 80 percent of the Fortune

1000 companies reported using it in 1993.[5] This is hardly surprising, because job enrichment has some clear advantages. Further, computers and information technology, by providing much more information for people to use in doing their jobs, are facilitating engagement in a wider variety of work activities. A job design strategy that is based on individual job enrichment and information technology can lead to an organization in which some individuals have the kind of independent jobs that allow them to work virtually anywhere at any time. This in turn can lead to the elimination of offices and to telecommuting.

Telecommuting, by the way, has grown slowly in the United States, partially because supervisors fear the loss of control that is inherent when someone works at home. Extensive electronic control over the work that people do at home is one solution, but a more realistic approach is to give the work the characteristics of an enriched job. That is, make individuals responsible for a whole or complete piece of work that challenges them and gives them meaningful feedback. When work is enriched in this way, individuals are likely to perform well out of intrinsic motivation and as a result work effectively at home, saving money for both themselves and the organization.

Conditions for Success

Doing an enriched job obviously requires substantially more skills than doing a simplified, standardized job. More skills make workers more costly, but since individuals handle some of the coordination and control themselves, they also add more value by reducing the need for management overhead. Enriched work also requires employees who want challenge and involvement, a factor that needs to be considered when employees are selected to work in new logic organizations. As was mentioned at the beginning of this chapter, not all employees want challenging work.

For job enrichment to be truly effective, it must be consistent with the organization's architecture and design—which is why it does not always achieve its potential in traditional organizations. Just altering the nature of the jobs within a particular work area or department of an organization will not produce all the positive results that can come from job enrichment.[6]

When organizations are designed functionally, it is hard to give individuals a large piece of work to do because, often, part of the work that they need to be given is in another department. In manufacturing, individuals must be given whole products to assemble and be made responsible for sending them directly to customers. In customer service, individuals must have their own customers and be responsible for answering all inquiries and making all service calls. Nordstrom, which is well known for its service, takes this approach. Their sales representatives send thank-you letters to "their" customers. Recently, I was in the office of a manager in a utility company when a Nordstrom sales representative called to tell her she had reduced the price on a ski parka the manager had purchased several days earlier, because it was going on sale and the representative did not want "her" customer to feel badly about buying it just before the sale started.

In Mary Kay Cosmetics and Tupperware, individual customer sales and service representatives in effect run their own small businesses. They buy products from the vendor (the manufacturing part of Mary Kay) and sell them directly to their own set of customers. Customers tell them what they want and don't want. The representatives have tremendous autonomy in how they handle their sales activities. For the Mary Kay representatives, the organization structure has been designed to enrich their jobs by making them highly autonomous and responsible. In many respects, Mary Kay (and other companies like it) are front-back organizations with multiple products (the back) that are sold to sales representatives (the front) who have their own territories and customer bases.

One of the most interesting examples of job enrichment I have seen involved a Motorola plant in Florida. Originally, pagers were made on a production line with more than thirty steps; it made pagers relatively rapidly but with a high defect rate. It was often difficult to identify who was responsible for the defects, so people on the assembly line had little chance to learn and correct their errors. Motorola decided to try a competing assembly operation where individuals went to an inventory parts location and picked up all the parts needed to build a pager. Then they sat at a workstation and built a pager from beginning to end. Once the task was completed, they took the pager to a test station where they tested it and then to a shipping area. At the shipping area, they labeled the package and signed a note stating they had personally produced the pager. The note had their telephone number and indicated that the customer should call them if they had any questions about the operation of the pager.

Motorola also tried producing pagers in work teams. In these teams, individuals were cross-trained, but they rarely produced a whole pager from beginning to end. Instead, each individual worked on multiple steps in the production process before passing it on to another member of the team. Overall, the work team approach seemed to produce the best results in the Florida plant, and today it is Motorola's predominant approach to making pagers. However, I was recently in Singapore and found that the Motorola facility there still produces pagers on an assembly line. Apparently they have decided that this is the most cost-efficient method of producing pagers given their situation in Singapore. Once again it is important to note that choosing the best work design requires consideration of the environment, the employees, and the business conditions that an organization faces.

The nature of supervision is a key factor that needs to change in order for job enrichment to be successful. Research evidence shows that the lack of decision-making power eliminates the possibility of intrinsic motivation and the kind of involvement that is critical to the new logic.[7] For employees to feel good about performing well and to be involved in their jobs, they need to be in control. In many cases, giving individuals control means that supervisors have to give up substantial amounts of moment-to-moment control over how the work is done. As I noted earlier, this is often difficult for supervisors to accept. Their job security rests in their control of their subordinates' performance, so they may be inclined to prevent employees from making decisions.

The Limits of Job Enrichment

My work with job enrichment has convinced me that its core ideas about the power of intrinsic motivation and greater involvement are important and valid. However, many businesses simply cannot be structured in ways that create individually enriched jobs, because many products and services are just too complex and too difficult for an individual to produce or provide. In other cases, the technology that must be used to create products and services dictates work that needs to be done by a number of people. Examples here include autos, steel, chemicals, electronics, software—indeed, most of the products and services that involve complex knowledge work. It is simply impossible for one person to produce a whole or meaningful part of an automobile, a gallon of gasoline, a complex software program, and so forth. These complex products require a different concept of work and organization. As will be discussed later in this chapter, they can often be effectively produced by team-based organizations that are built on the principles of the new logic and that create their own forms of enriched work.

Clearly, not all work can be enriched by using either the individual or team approach. Sometimes it is not technologically possible to design enriched jobs that allow individuals or teams to add significant value by managing themselves and doing complex tasks. That's why, even today, there are some products that are best produced on highly repetitive assembly lines. High-volume assembly of electronic parts, for example, is difficult to make into complex, challenging work and as a result is often best done where the cost of labor can be matched to the demands of the work process. In a global economy, high-cost labor must add value beyond what is added by low-skilled, manual work.

Similarly, in the service sector, jobs such as those of toll collectors, telephone operators, telephone sales representatives, and reservation agents, where duties are tied to repetitive customer contact or to technology that partially automates the work, rarely allow individuals to add much value. Some of these jobs, such as that of the telephone operator, will be completely automated in the near term, but technology has not yet advanced to this point. In other cases, such as in banking, some customers do not want to or are unable to interact with a machine (an automated teller), so a human being is needed. In any case, because the individuals doing these jobs are prevented by the technology from doing more complicated work or managing themselves, there is little opportunity to use the new logic.

When technology can be designed to help create high-value-added jobs, it can be a win-win for organizations and for employees. Information technology as well as advanced automation processes in the manufacturing world can transform some work. Automation in manufacturing, such as the use of robots, can create work that involves high levels of problem solving, technical complexity, and coordination and can thus make it possible for employees to add considerable value. Employees end up doing programming, skilled maintenance, and machine setup instead of routine manual tasks. The downside is that fewer employees are needed, but those who remain can be paid good wages because they contribute more. The key is that they know more and work in new logic organizations where they can do more.

The New Logic Alternative: Teams, Teams, and More Teams

Teams offer the possibility of doing complex, value-added work in a way that combines innovation, speed, quality, and low cost. Thus it is not surprising that our research at USC on the Fortune 1000 U.S. corporations shows that teams are the fastest growing of the new logic work practices and are used by virtually every major U.S. corporation.[8]

Teams are increasingly popular despite the fact that they can be extremely complex, both in their design and in the way they work. Teams do not take one form or purpose or style in organizations. Teams in the total quality management approach, for example, are substantially different from those that are installed as part of reengineering programs. Nevertheless, these different approaches do converge on some important points. They all emphasize that groups can do things that individuals cannot. They recognize that teams are an important way to allow employees to add more value to products and services. And they understand that teams can eliminate some of the hierarchy in organizations.

There are five particularly important types of teams: problem-solving teams, work teams, project teams, overlay teams, and management teams. They differ in purpose, duration, and membership, and each type is suited to a particular set of organizational circumstances and goals. The next sections introduce these types of teams, setting a foundation for the discussion in Chapter Seven of how to use teams and make them effective.

Problem-Solving Teams: Finding Ways to Work Better and Smarter

Problem-solving teams are usually formed to work on a particular problem, such as a high defect rate in a manufacturing process or the slow processing of orders. I often refer to them as *parallel participation structures,* because they are extra creations that operate outside of, and do not directly alter, an organization's normal way of operating.[9]

Problem-solving teams are based on the assumption that individuals can add value when they are part of such teams because they can use their superior knowledge of their work area to improve work methods. In order for these teams to be effective, employees do not have to add skills, except perhaps for some basic skills in group process and problem analysis. They do not need to understand their corporation's business strategy because they are not supposed to be self-directing.

The problem-solving team is without question the most popular type of team in the United States. Our USC study of the Fortune 1000 found that the use of problem-solving teams grew by over 30 percent from 1987 to 1993 and that almost all organizations use them. Yet membership in them is not widespread within corporations; typically fewer than 20 percent of an organization's employees are on problem-solving teams at any point in time.[10] Little research information is available on the presence of these teams in other parts of the world, so we can only guess how much they are used. They are probably most popular in Japan, where the total quality movement makes extensive use of them as part of their continuous improvement approach.

There are several types of problem-solving teams. The best known is the very structured quality circle that is designed to examine the way work is done and to continuously improve work methods and processes. In the typical quality circle, the members identify the issue they want to work on, then meet a few hours a week for at least several months. Circle members get the opportunity to use their knowledge of the work to contribute ideas on how it can be done more effectively; thus they add value beyond what they add when they perform their regular work.

Quality circles, both in Japan and the United States, typically have little or no authority to actually make decisions; they can only make recommendations. It is management that ultimately decides whether to accept and implement all ideas. The relationship of quality circles to the formal organization is pictured in Figure 6.1, which shows the quality circle as a parallel organization that, in essence, borrows people from the work organization and returns ideas to it. In Japanese companies and some American companies, there are staff groups that support quality circles. These include trainers, meeting conveners, and technical experts who are available to help the quality circle organization perform effectively.

Years ago, I had a chance to interview the president of Fuji Xerox in Japan regarding their very successful quality circle program (they have won the Deming Award, the highest Japanese quality award). Asked what his role was in supporting quality circles, he stated he spent about a quarter of his time listening to recommendations from quality circles and supporting their work activities. The CEOs of Xerox, Motorola, and other companies in the United States have also been very supportive of their quality circles. However, I know of none that commit as much as 20 percent of their time and energy to the success of their quality circle activities.

Figure 6.1. The Quality Circle Approach.

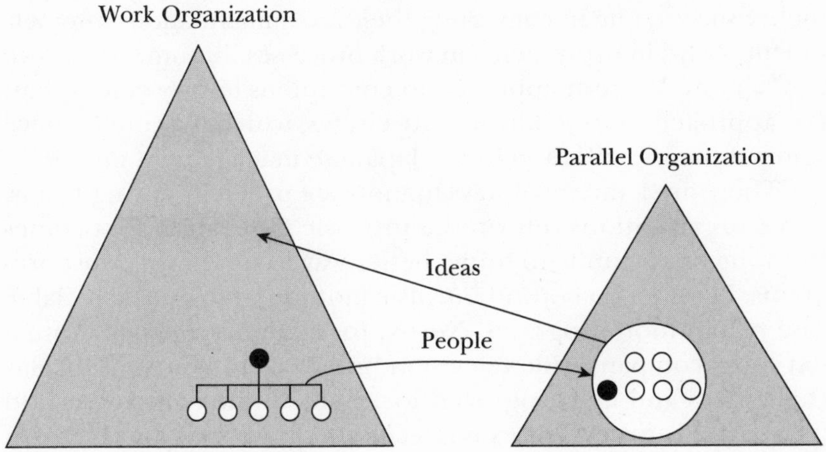

Work Organization

Parallel Organization

Ideas

People

The extensive research literature on quality circles presents a mixed picture with respect to their success.[11] I first began studying them in the early 1970s and quickly became intrigued by the members' high level of involvement and the many ideas the groups generated. However, I also saw that because quality circles have relatively little authority and power to implement their ideas, many of their suggestions are not implemented. There are other reasons for this as well, including resistance from managers who are threatened by the ideas, lack of funds, and, of course, the fact that some ideas that sound good are based on incomplete or inaccurate information. Finally, since only a few individuals are typically in quality circles at any point in time, the organization is using the problem-solving talents of its total work force to a very limited extent.

As a result of the problems with quality circles, many organizations now use problem-solving or improvement teams that are assigned to work on particular issues and that have the authority to make decisions. They usually get a budget as well as a sponsor to provide them with support and advocacy. They are often given a completion date for their work, which helps to hold them accountable for their activities.

This variation from the original quality circle concept seems to be an improvement, at least in the U.S. companies I have seen adopt it. Because they are given specific mandates, these groups understand what is expected of them and they often perform better. They tend to be more efficient than quality circles and have a higher success rate in converting their recommendations into new practices and improvements in work processes. In some ways, they take a more Western approach to continuous improvement than the approach followed by quality circles, which, of course, have some of their foundation in the Japanese management model.

There are a variety of ways to motivate problem-solving teams. Some organizations rely on the intrinsic motivation that comes from the opportunity to find a better way to do things. Most programs, however, go beyond intrinsic motivation to establish elaborate recognition programs. Xerox, for example, uses an annual day-long, company-wide television broadcast to let teams display their ideas and be recognized for them. Some companies add financial incentives. For example, Donnelly Mirrors and Herman

Miller use a company-wide bonus plan. Teams that significantly improve work methods and operations can earn a pay bonus for the entire organization, which creates a win/win relationship for all employees and the organization.

It is important to emphasize that problem-solving teams are not a radical departure from the old hierarchical approach to organizing. Their logic is based on a view that individuals can add additional value because they know their work better than anyone else. The teams are designed to capture this knowledge and convert it into improved methods. They do not require employees to add a great number of additional skills or to make important decisions. Employees are not expected to make managers, controls, or overhead costs unnecessary. They are only expected to behave differently a few hours a week; the rest of the time it is business as usual.

Work Teams: The Basic Unit for Getting Work Done

Work teams or, as they are sometimes called, *high-performance teams,* are driven by a significantly different logic than the logic of problem-solving teams. Instead of being brought together periodically to solve a problem or improve a process, work teams, in organizations based on new logic principles, are actually the basic unit for getting work done. Work teams are typically given responsibility for producing either a major part of a product or a whole product or for carrying out an entire process (such as order fulfillment). Work teams are often self-managing because they make important decisions not only about how the work is done but also about how they will organize and manage themselves to do it. This is a dramatic step away from the individual job design approach that is so characteristic of traditional management thought. Just how far away is illustrated by an experience I had at IBM.

When I gave a speech at IBM in the late 1980s, I suggested that they needed to hold teams accountable for some of their complex software development and manufacturing processes. The senior managers in the audience responded very negatively, saying that teams cannot be held accountable because only individuals, not teams, do work.

IBM stubbornly clung to that "individuals only" approach to work until the early 1990s, when they finally issued a policy statement indicating that there are some conditions under which it is reasonable to create work teams. Yet even that assertion was made with great reluctance, as the policy also stressed that IBM was in no way abandoning its view that the primary relationship at IBM is an employee's relationship to his or her manager. This traditional boss-subordinate view of management runs counter to new logic thinking about what it takes to create, reward, and develop effective teams. As will be discussed in the next chapter, to be effective, teams must be managed as performing units or entities, not as a group of individuals.

The logic underlying work teams suggests that when individuals are put in teams, they can add value beyond simply solving problems and improving work processes. Because work teams can ultimately become self-managing and coordinate their work with that of others, they can make layers of supervision and extensive staff support largely unnecessary. Indeed, this is perhaps the most significant way in which they can add value.

The earliest efforts to form work teams focused on creating relatively stable teams to run entire production and service processes. Individuals were typically members of a team that might, for example, run a paper machine or operate a chemical plant. Work teams have proven to be one of the most important building blocks of the "greenfield" or new high-involvement plants that were first built in the 1960s and have been built in great numbers since then.[12]

High-involvement plants combine the use of work teams with a number of other new logic practices in order to increase the effectiveness of plants. In fact, as was mentioned earlier, studies done by Procter & Gamble, one of the leading practitioners of the work team approach, suggest that its team-based plants tend to be 30 to 40 percent more effective than its traditional manufacturing operations. Work teams have also proven to be a good way, in service organizations, to do work that involves interdependent tasks and well-developed skills, such as processing insurance claims, managing accounts for financial services firms, and processing mortgages.

As far back as 1954, research by Stan Seashore found that the best work teams are significantly better than a collection of individuals working independently.[13] But by the same token, the worst teams are significantly worse than a collection of individuals. The reason:

putting people together in teams, particularly self-managing teams, tends to magnify the best and worst relationships within them.

Unlike problem-solving teams that are brought together for their existing expertise, work teams—particularly self-managing work teams—often require a considerable amount of skill development and learning. In addition to learning how to do the variety of tasks assigned to them, they need to learn how to operate as a team and how to manage themselves while they do their work.

Intrinsic motivation is supremely important in work team design. It depends on making the team members feel collectively responsible for a whole product or service and for performing meaningful tasks that are under their control and that provide performance feedback. Peer pressure is also needed to motivate team members and encourage them to work toward team goals.

Finally, as will be discussed more fully in the next chapter, work teams are not easy to build and operate effectively. It is critical that organizations do the things that are needed in order to make them successful. One of my colleagues, Tom Cummings, likes to refer to self-managing work teams as the "Ferraris of work design." Why? Quite simply, they are expensive to build (training costs are high; reward and information systems need to be changed to support them) and they often have high operating costs (they require time to meet, and replacing members can be complex).

Project Teams: Work Teams with a Temporary Task

Project teams are similar to work teams except that they only last for a limited period of time. They are typically formed to manufacture a particular product or deliver a service that has a known limited life expectancy. Project teams are also frequently created to develop new products or to redesign existing ones. As noted in the discussion of project-based organizations in Chapter Five, project teams are particularly common in businesses that emphasize new or custom product development.

Chrysler has used the project team approach to gain competitive advantage by bringing new cars to market in a fast and cost-effective manner. Boeing successfully used multiple project teams in the development of its 777 aircraft; they used customer and component teams that were focused on particular sections of the aircraft, as well as teams devoted to integrating the activities of the many different component teams.

In addition to their life expectancy, there is a second key difference between work teams and project teams. Individuals on work teams are usually full-time members of the team, which when combined with the team's permanence allows them to develop a high level of cohesiveness and to build their team skills and capabilities. Individuals often have membership in several project teams at the same time. One recent study of high-tech teams by three of my colleagues, Sue Mohrman, Monty Mohrman, and Susan Cohen, found that many employees were on six or more teams at any point in time.[14]

It is not unusual for project teams to change their membership as the project goes through different phases. This, of course, means that it is more difficult to develop a high degree of cohesiveness and that team members may require some special skills. For example, individuals who join a team in midstream must have the skill to quickly become productive in teams that are already formed and performing. From a motivational standpoint, it is important that organizations develop reward systems that focus on the project team's success and on how quickly individuals can get up to speed and contribute to the project teams they join.

Obviously project teams are very different from self-managing work teams which often stay together for years, with only minimal changes in their membership. Because of this, as will be discussed in the next chapter, the use of project teams requires different thinking about the management of team skills and about the management systems that an organization needs to have.

Overlay Teams: Coordinating the Work of Others

Overlay teams are created by organizations to coordinate group and individual activities. They are usually made up of representatives from different teams or parts of an organization. Just as with project teams, membership in an overlay team is not necessarily full-time. What's more, being on an overlay team may be secondary to the time spent on a team that has responsibility for making, selling, or marketing a particular product.

An overlay team typically has both a relatively permanent position in the organization and a stable membership, since the work of coordinating the activities of different divisions and product lines is a long-term need. In essence, the job of an overlay team, in most cases, is to set strategy and settle disagreements among the parts of an organization that need to act together to deliver a service or sell a product. As was mentioned in Chapter Five, their effectiveness is often a critical determinant of organizational effectiveness when organizations are structured around separate business units.

A typical overlay team might coordinate a corporation's sales activities with respect to a particular large customer that buys multiple products and services. For example, Wal-Mart buys such a wide variety of products from Procter & Gamble—across all of P & G's product categories—and accounts for so much of P & G's sales that it gets very special treatment in purchasing, shipping, and account management. Procter & Gamble has also created a special team to coordinate all its Wal-Mart business. The responsibility of the overlay team in this case is to coordinate the actions of the different product lines so that P & G presents "one face to the customer."

Overlay groups are sometimes organized around geography. For example, when an organization needs to act in unison in dealing with the government of a country where it operates, it may create a country coordinating team to deal with government officials.

A major advantage of assigning work to overlay teams rests in the team's ability to make several levels of management unnecessary. Because the team brings together representatives from different areas, from different products, and from different functions into a group that is given the power to resolve conflicts and make policy, it can be a substitute for hierarchy and replace levels of management.

Overlay teams can often be more effective than a single individual because of the members' combined expertise and power. They are usually much closer to the customers and to the key decisions that need to be made. As will be discussed in the next chapter, it is critical that they be held collectively accountable for their decision making and, of course, their ability to deal effectively with the relevent parts of the organization.

Management Teams: Shared Leadership

Management teams are relatively rare. But there is reason to believe that they will become more popular, because they offer some of the advantages of work teams. In a sense, they are a specialized version of a work team. Their responsibility is the management of other teams or of individuals rather than the direct creation of a product or delivery of a service.

When management teams are collectively responsible for the operation of a particular area or business, they have a strong motivation to resolve cross-functional issues. This can help solve some of the integration issues that organizations with multiple teams often encounter. Management teams can often resolve some of the conflicts between functions, such as manufacturing and engineering, that occur within teams and between teams.

In addition, if work teams report to management teams, it is possible to reduce the number of managers that are needed to oversee the teams and to have greater flexibility in where managers are assigned and how their expertise is used. When members of managerial teams have different skills, they are in a good position to provide a variety of help to the teams or individuals who report to them.

One of the best early examples I saw of management teams was at Xerox. During the restructuring of its field sales and service organization, Xerox removed the district manager level of management, a position that historically had coordinated the administrative, sales, and service activities in a district of 100 to 250 or more employees. A team made up of sales, administration, and service managers replaced the district managers, collectively supervised the work force, and managed itself as well.

One of the most intriguing places to use a management team is at the top of an organization, where the work load is often too heavy for a single individual. As organizations realize this fact, some are creating an "office of the president" or "office of the chief executive officer." Motorola, GTE, and other companies have moved to this model over the last few years. Although, in the typical corporate model, members of this team are not of equal status, they do, in many cases, share decision making and rotate some of the duties according to work load demands and the skills of the individuals on the team.

Nordstrom recently developed an interesting team-based approach for its senior managers. They created a two-person Office of the Chairman and a six-person Office of the President. The members of these two offices operate as teams and share all the duties that are normally performed by the chairman and the president. Already a leader in customer service, Nordstrom has seemingly broken new ground with respect to structuring senior management teams.

A possible future approach to the use of teams at the top of a global corporation calls for an office of the CEO that consists of a virtual team that has its members in different locations and links them electronically. One approach would be to put a member of the CEO team in the United States, another in Europe, and another in Asia. This would help to give an organization twenty-four-hour coverage of the world and place a CEO in each of the major business arenas. The key, of course, would be for the three CEOs to be extremely effective in relating to each other and for them to be well connected electronically. Of course, they would also need to meet with some regularity so that their relationship would be more than just electronic.

As organizations operate more and more on a global basis, my guess is that variations of the team management model will become prevalent. It is a potentially effective way to deal with the time demands on executives and the growing complexity of the senior management role. Today, the typical global corporation operates twenty-four hours a day, seven days a week, and has major operations on at least two and more likely three or more continents. This places incredible time demands on the CEO. Just visiting all the locations of a company once a year can use up all of an individual's time. Besides, there are an increasing number of governments to deal with, not to mention customers.

Team-Based Organizations: The New Logic of Work Design

As was suggested in Chapter Five, using the right combination of project teams, problem-solving teams, work teams, overlay teams, and management teams, it is possible to develop organizations that are entirely team-based. In team-based organizations, individuals might well be part of several teams. On one team, they might be a leader or a manager, and on another team they might make technical contributions. This type of flexibility is critical to creating a team-based organization, but it is quite contrary to traditional concepts of supervisor-subordinate relationships and to the idea that some individuals are managers while others are workers and still others are technical experts. It definitely represents a new logic of work and organization design.

Teams can be the basic building blocks of an organization that is built on the new logic. They provide an important way to create an involvement-oriented approach to control and to allow organizations to operate with a flat, lateral organization structure. Effective teams can help to solve problems of coordination, overhead, and motivation, because with them an individual can receive feedback and have a considerable amount of autonomy and accountability.

Teams are not appropriate everywhere in every high-performance organizations, nor are they right for everyone. The job enrichment approach to work design has a role when independent enriched jobs can be developed. However, at least one kind of team is needed in virtually every type of organization design in order to create a high-performance organization. The challenge is to utilize the right types of teams and, as detailed in the next chapter, to put in place the practices that make them effective.

Chapter Seven

Teams
Keys to Making Them Successful

> - Lateral processes are the key to organizational effectiveness.
> - Involvement is the most effective source of control.

Recently I received a call from the vice president of human resources for a major international chemical company. He had a problem. His CEO had fallen in love with the idea of teams and had asked him to create team-based organizations throughout their corporation. He, too, believed in the advantages of teams and was eager to take on the task. Two consulting firms were hired that professed to have expertise in team development, and they set about developing a massive program to form teams and to train managers and employees to operate more effectively in teams.

When the teams first started, everything went very well. But when the company conducted one of its regular attitude surveys a year after the teams were established, the results indicated that many employees were dissatisfied with their teams. What's more, many of the teams were having problems matching the productivity levels that the traditional approach to organizing had produced. Of course, there were exceptions. Some teams were highly effective and breaking production records. The question from the human resources vice president was a simple one: "How can this happen? Why are some teams working so effectively and others causing us such great problems?"

Unfortunately, his situation is not unique. Remember, the research by Stan Seashore on work teams found that time after time that effective teams perform significantly better than groups of individuals, but poor teams perform much less effectively than groups of individuals.[1] Still, there was no simple answer I could give the frustrated vice president except this: my research indicates that when most organizations install teams, they simply don't make the many changes that are needed in order to create effective teams, whether they be problem-solving teams, self-managing work teams, project teams, overlay teams, or management teams. Quite often, human resource management systems and information systems are an initial—and deadly—problem.

In order for work teams to be effective, organizations need to use new types of training, different employee selection processes, and new performance measures. To put these in place, most organizations have to go through a major learning and change process so that their managers and their management systems can shift from an individual focus to a team-based approach.

Studies by my colleagues at the University of Southern California, Sue Mohrman, Susan Cohen, and Monty Mohrman,[2] show that in order to be effective,

• Teams must know what they are supposed to do and be given a clear set of tasks to accomplish.
• Teams must have work that is meaningful enough to motivate the team members to perform effectively.
• Teams must have the skills necessary to function as a team and to do the work well.

This chapter discusses how an organization can put in place the right structures and supporting practices to create these three conditions.

Team-Based Work Design in the New Logic

In designing work teams, the first and most crucial issue is the creation of a task or set of tasks for the team to perform. The tasks need to motivate individual members and support the organization's goals and objectives. Remember: in order to be motivational, the tasks need to be meaningful, provide feedback about performance, and allow individuals or teams discretion in how they are carried out. Meaningful work comes from its wholeness or completeness, as well as from the sense of challenge and complexity it provides. It does not come from assigning teams tasks that are simplified, standardized, specialized, and machine-controlled.

The ideal design for a work team lets it take a product through the entire production process. It begins with an external vendor (from whom it buys raw material) and ends with an external customer (to whom it delivers the finished product or service). In this scenario, a team gets to manage an entire mini-business. The team gets feedback from the most important source, the customer. And the team has the discretion to control the way it works to meet the customer's demands. Taken to its extreme, as it is in Shell's Sarnia chemical plant in Ontario, Canada, this can lead to a single team running an entire facility.

The socio-tech and reengineering approaches are the most frequently used approaches to designing work for teams. The socio-tech approach, which dates back to the 1940s, had its origins in team-based manufacturing plants in Europe.[3] It was also the conceptual foundation for many of the early team-based manufacturing facilities in the United States, such as the greenfield Procter & Gamble plants mentioned earlier. The reengineering approach is a product of the 1980s and the efforts of large corporations to reduce their costs and better use information technology.

The socio-tech and reengineering approaches use different language and have tended to focus on different areas (production for socio-tech and order fulfillment for reengineering). The leading proponents of reengineering argue that it is new and different.[4] Nevertheless, there is little disagreement in the kinds of recommendations both approaches make with respect to actual work design. Much of reengineering is simply an updated statement of the socio-tech approach that pays much less attention to the human issues, such as motivation and social interaction, in work design. Both strongly recommend combining work that is part of the same work process in an organization and making a single team or individual accountable for what used to be done as separate jobs, often in different departments. This very important point is clearly one key to making teams effective and, as was mentioned earlier, to designing high-performance organizations.

Organizing Around Key Processes

One of the best examples of the difference between a team-based design and a traditional functional approach to designing work is a five-hundred-employee cookie and cracker bakery that I had the opportunity to help redesign. Before the bakery instituted a work team design, receiving employees handled raw materials, shipping employees handled finished products, separate groups of employees ran the batch mixers and the ovens, and there was a group of packers at the end of the six production lines. Different supervisors managed each step in the production process; staff specialists took care of human resources, finance, and scheduling; and four layers of management above them directed and integrated the work. The plant manager was responsible for quality, costs, and productivity; no single person or team below the plant manager level had responsibility for all the steps it took to convert raw materials into a packaged product.

An analysis of the interdependencies among mixing, baking, and packing indicated that they were highly interrelated because they all involved the transformation of flour and other raw materials into a packaged cookie or cracker. Thus it called for creating production work teams to take products from their raw material through the entire baking and packing process. It also called for making the work teams accountable for cost, quality, and rate of production. To add a further level of accountability and even more identification with their work, teams were given responsibility for a specific cookie or cracker product.

Service businesses and companies with knowledge work can also create work teams to offer an entire service or deal with their customers from beginning to end. As was mentioned earlier, IDS has teams that perform all the activities necessary to serve customers from a particular region.

The team approach has also become popular in order administration, where a team of employees becomes responsible for order entry, pricing, shipping, payment, collection, and credit checking for a particular set of customers. The team approach is in sharp contrast to the traditional approach in which different departments may handle each of these and where it can take days to get an order processed, and five to ten different individuals to tell a customer the status of an order or the condition of their account. With a team handling the entire relationship, customers can often call one person to get any information they need or assistance they want with their account. Gone are the days when a customer is switched from one person to another in order to get questions answered.

A team-based design can lead to dramatic performance improvements in cost, speed, and quality. For example, lenders have been able to reduce approval time for home mortgages from weeks to hours by reorganizing work so that a processing team takes an application through all the steps rather than move it from department to department for different approvals (or rejections). In the same way, one life insurance company reduced the time to issue a new policy from six weeks to one day. The total work time did not change greatly, but because work no longer sat in in-boxes waiting for someone to deal with it, the customer got a much faster response.

Effective Problem-Solving Teams

Work design is just as important for problem-solving teams as it is for work teams. These teams need a clear statement of what their task is and what constraints or limitations exist. They also need to know who their customer is. Organizations often make the common mistake of not making these teams aware of the constraints on the solutions they might propose. Time after time, I have seen situations where problem-solving teams are told that there are no boundaries on what they can propose. As a result, they come up with solutions that are unrealistic for any number of reasons, most often because of the amount of capital investment that they require.

Problem-solving teams may also fail to discover "acceptable" solutions for a much more basic reason: management has narrowed the list of acceptable options to two or three but does not tell the team what it has already decided. So groups end up making one suggestion after another until they hit on the one that management had in mind all along. This kind of scenario is a real exercise in pseudo-participation that management justifies as a way of getting employees to commit to a solution. It may work once, but as soon as employees recognize it for what it is, they become cynical and often wait for management to tell them what the "correct" answer is.

New-Product Development Teams

Advocates of concurrent engineering stress the importance of putting together empowered project teams to carry out the new product development process from beginning to end. These project teams typically include representatives from a cross-section of the organization: manufacturing, engineering, marketing, research and development, and, in some cases, the vendors who will provide parts for the products.

With project teams, the auto industry has cut the development time for new vehicles from six years to less than three years. A good guess is that soon the world-class standard will be less than two years. As mentioned earlier, Chrysler has led the way among American auto manufacturers, but Ford and General Motors are also changing in order to be able to compete in an industry where new products have to be developed in less and less time. For example, to design its 1996 Taurus and Sable cars, Ford put all its engineers and designers in the same space and had them work in teams. They also involved factory employees who tested the designs and made hundreds of suggestions that helped make the cars easier to manufacture.

The airline industry has done the same thing. As noted in Chapter Six, Boeing used cross-functional project teams to dramatically cut the development time for its 777 aircraft. The teams at Boeing included not only representatives from the different functions in the company but customers as well to make sure that their wishes and needs were considered in the plane's design. Computer networks allowed people working on different parts of the airplane to coordinate their actions and allowed teams from different geographic locations and companies to easily shift data among themselves.

Boeing estimates that the use of cross-functional teams in the design process of the 777 cut the typical development time in half. In fact, Boeing management has made it clear that without the use of teams, the development of the 777 simply would have been too time consuming and expensive—and never would have happened. When Boeing first started assembling parts from its various suppliers, another advantage of the new design process became apparent. For the first time in the history of Boeing, parts from different suppliers needed little reworking. The fits from different suppliers had an unprecedented level of precision. Because of this and other factors, Boeing has gotten the fastest flight certifications ever for a new commercial aircraft.

Teams and Customers: Making the Critical Connection

Throughout this discussion of work design, emphasis has been placed on the important connection between a work team and its customers. Feedback from customers is critical not only to the team's motivation but also to the team's ability to know what to do and whether it is doing its work well. As a result, how an organization defines its customers, both internally and externally, is crucial to a team's effectiveness.

The total quality management literature has helped to legitimize the idea of internal customers as an important and valid source of feedback. However, its emphasis on internal customers may have done a disservice to the idea of customer feedback and satisfaction. There is no disputing that sometimes internal customers are an important and valid source of feedback. Indeed, the complexity of some products (automobiles and aircraft, for example) makes such internal "customers" necessary in some situations. But all too often, the feedback from internal customers is limited and biased. Too often it is based on whether another group in the organization is making their work easier to do. And easier work, of course, is not the critical issue in organizational effectiveness—it is external customer satisfaction.

Wherever possible, teams should interact directly with the external customers who make buying decisions about their services and products. Self-managing work teams in service and manufacturing can have this interaction most easily, but it is also important for problem-solving teams. Although the beneficiaries of problem-solving teams will most likely be their co-workers in the organization (because their mandate is usually to improve internal operations), the teams should still use external customers to gather data on what actually constitutes an improvement in the product or service.

Limits to the Use of Teams: Is the Work Right?

All the publicity about teams has led organizations like the chemical company mentioned at the beginning of this chapter to believe they are appropriate for any work situation. Despite many examples of highly effective teams in the manufacturing and service world, the use of work teams is simply not always possible—or desirable. In fact, organizations can actually create significant problems by using self-managing work teams when individually designed jobs are more appropriate. The reason: self-managing work teams can only add the type of value that will justify their costs if they have relatively complex, interdependent tasks to perform. This often is not true for problem-solving teams or quality circles. They are more robust and can be of value in almost any situation where work methods can be improved.

The telephone companies that have tried to create work teams for their operators inevitably report that their managers complain about wasting time in team meetings. A quick look at the operators' work explains why. Their major relationships are with the customer and the technology that they use. They do not have to interact with each other to do their jobs. In fact, the major things they share with their fellow operators are physical space and a supervisor. When they get together in team meetings, they talk about what they have in common—the supervisor, the parking lot, the air conditioning, the cafeteria, and so on. Not surprisingly, many supervisors consider this conversation a waste of time; the operators tend to agree, but sometimes enjoy the chance to talk to each other. The simple fact is that work teams are just not a good organizational design for telephone operators.

Another example of an organization forcing work into teams when the situation wasn't right for it: the management of a medical products company had read literature on teams and wanted to have a team-based production process in a new plant that it was building to manufacture sutures (the needle and thread that doctors use to close wounds and incisions). When I looked at the work that needed to be done, I had serious misgivings about the usefulness of work teams. A single operator could do much of the work involved in assembling and packaging a suture, because most of the tasks were self-contained and repetitive, and required a high level of manual skill. In addition, because the individuals worked alone, there was little opportunity for a group to set and enforce productivity or quality norms.

Nevertheless, despite these misgivings, my colleagues and I—at the request of management—went ahead and helped them install "high-performance" work teams. It soon became obvious that this was a poor move. Team meetings were often seen as boring and not terribly productive. In the end, after months of failed efforts to create effective work teams, the company decided to abandon them and rely instead on individually enriched work. Employees did the basic work on their own and were measured and rewarded as individual contributors. It used some problem-solving teams to deal with issues of scheduling, machine maintenance, and important issues in the physical environment.

I could continue to cite numerous examples of the misuse of work teams, but the point is clear: teams pay off when there are critical interdependencies that a team can manage, thereby adding value to the organization. But when work does not require high levels of interdependence, a work design that encourages *individuals* to perform well is best.

Integrating Work Teams and Technology

An organization often determines whether it has interdependent team-oriented work when it decides how it will produce its products or services. Certain production and service technologies create work that is appropriate for teams, while others do not. As noted earlier, in some industries (gasoline, glass, and chemicals, for example), there is little choice in technology because there is only one way to successfully manufacture products. The service sector often enjoys much more flexibility, because the work is less controlled by technology and more dependent on personal contact. Still, even in the service sector, technology dictates the nature of the work for telephone operators, toll collectors, and mail sorters, to mention just a few previously cited examples.

Sometimes new technology can create new work design options. For example, as noted earlier, the rapid development of information and computer technology and computer networks has made it possible to bring together all the data about a customer and put them in the hands of a single service representative or a team of representatives. Not only has this made the use of teams for one-stop customer service possible, it has made it a competitive necessity.

Before computer-based information technology was utilized, individuals in financial services, airline reservations, and many other service jobs simply could not respond quickly to a customer's requests. Work had to be distributed among different individuals in an assembly-line type of arrangement. But information and computer technology has allowed for entirely new work designs and in many cases has made teams and group work possible for the first time.[5]

When a large packaged goods company that I worked with put in a new computer system for order administration and product delivery a few years ago, it meant every customer service representative had access to all the information about a customer's account. That ended years of frustration for customers who often had to talk to several individuals, each of them trained in a single step and none of whom were sure about the overall status of an account or order.

The strength of the relationship between work design and technology can be seen by looking at some examples from the automobile industry. Volvo's efforts to change its production approach to allow for a team-based work design are particularly heroic. In the late 1960s, they recognized that the traditional production line made it extremely difficult to create meaningful, motivating work. They began searching for alternative approaches to the assembly-line process that would allow for more meaningful team-based jobs. Eventually, they built two "new design" plants.

In the first plant (Kalmar), teams assembled part of a car. The cars were mounted on pallets and moved from team to team when each team decided their work was finished. In the second plant, Uddevalla, Volvo went even further. Teams of fourteen to twenty people assembled an entire car. Volvo added an element of customer contact in this plant. When customers came into Volvo showrooms to order a car, they were put in contact with an assembly team. The team then invited the customers to see their car being built. In some cases, the team then delivered the car to the customer and maintained contact to keep track of defects and possible improvements for future versions of the car. Although Volvo's team-based plants have been praised and have produced some positive results, both have been closed. The reasons for their closing remain in some dispute. Supporters argue that the plants were more effective than traditional plants, while critics claim they were a misguided social experiment.[6]

My conclusion is that self-managing teams that assemble entire cars are not the right answer to providing more meaningful work in the mass production segment of the automobile industry. There are simply too many advantages to automation, mechanical assistance, and specialization. Still, over the last twenty years there has been a welcome shift in auto production away from the classic machine-paced lines, with their highly individualized jobs, to a work environment where individual teams have responsibility for parts of the line. They often have some control over the pace of the work and continuously improve their assembly methods.[7]

Even Toyota, which is famous for its "lean production system," with its machine-paced assembly lines and strong emphasis on robotics, has apparently begun to move away from automation toward plants based more on the team concept. In an old plant south of Tokyo that produces a new four-wheel drive vehicle, Toyota has broken down the assembly line into five subsections. Likewise, the Saturn division of General Motors has teams that take responsibility for sections of the assembly process, even though the cars still move on a production line through the plant.

The need for human input in automobile assembly makes it unlikely that in the foreseeable future there will be completely automated production lines with robots. Robots have major weaknesses with respect to flexibility and understanding. Robots cannot understand customer feedback about product quality and satisfaction. And robots cannot make suggestions about how to improve parts, products, or assembly methods. Their lack of flexibility is becoming a bigger issue because the world is increasingly demanding "custom mass production": products that are customized to customers' needs and preferences, but with the quality and low cost that come with high-volume production.

Stories of automation gone wrong still surround the highly automated plant that General Motors created to produce Cadillacs in Hamtramck, Michigan. One widely circulated story tells about the automated painting system that painted everything except the cars. Part of the problem: workers were not trained to run the equipment, and managers did not know how to manage the technically skilled employees who were needed to program and maintain robots.

Conclusion: organizations should carefully consider work and organization design when they choose the technology they will use to do their manufacturing or service work. All too often, in my experience, they make the mistake of thinking technology first and work design second. It is impossible to separate work design from technology. When a technology has been chosen, it limits the available work design options.

Work teams are inappropriate in certain situations because the technology does not create a favorable setting for using them. Faced with this situation, it is clearly unwise for organizations to force a team-based design into place. They have only two options: the first is to simply go with an alternative approach to organizing, and the second is to change their technology to one that permits a team-based design. The latter option may give them the opportunity to follow the new logic principles and create a high-performance work organization. Despite the attractiveness of this option, it may not be right if it means choosing a technology that has disadvantages in areas such as speed, material handling, and cost. The advantages associated with the high-performance model may not be sufficient to tip the scales in its favor. However, if organizations do their homework well and consider technology and work design simultaneously, they may very well find that the best technology is the one that leads to work teams and high-performance organizations.

Team Size: What's the Right Number of Members?

There is little question that as teams get bigger, they become more difficult to manage because they are much more complex. Psychologists suggest that teams should have between five and nine members and certainly never more than fifteen. This applies equally to work teams, project teams, overlay teams, and problem-solving teams.

Although such guidelines are useful, it is also necessary to consider the task or tasks that the team is performing and the team's access to feedback about its performance. If a team is going to be completely responsive to its customers, its members need to have contact with their customers and control over what it takes to satisfy them. Because this is so important, the preference to create a small team should take a back seat to the nature of the task; it is simply more important for a team to control an entire process or make an entire product than it is to limit its size.

I have found that teams of twenty-five to thirty can work effectively, particularly in manufacturing plants. Chemical plants, glass plants, and oil refineries, for example, often require large teams because of their complex, interrelated production processes. In some cases, large teams can be divided into subgroups that take responsibility for particular parts of a production process or take over specific work hours if it is necessary to operate more than forty hours a week. Further, if members of a subgroup are trained in all of the production tasks and are able to move freely from one to another, they can complement the larger team structure and reduce the amount of communication that it needs.

Authority: Decision Making in Teams

The amount of authority that organizations give to teams is critical to their success and to the amount of value that they can add to a product or service. The more decisions that teams are allowed to make, the fewer managers organizations need to direct activities and the fewer staff services they need to employ to help teams with complex problems and coordination issues.

As already discussed, for work to be motivating, people must feel that they can control how work is done. In that respect, work teams are no different than individuals. Only when they manage their work and many of their own internal issues will they be highly motivated. Teams need to be able to assign work, hire, fire, and decide on the pay increases that members of the team receive. Making these decisions creates teams that feel they are responsible for how effectively they perform. If teams are not allowed to be self-managing and make major decisions, they tend not to "own" the product of their work. They also hesitate to do the things that can make the work process more effective and through which they add value to the organization. For example, they are unlikely to discipline each other, or encourage each other to perform well, or do the daily management tasks that allow them to operate with relatively little supervision.

How much authority teams must have to be effective depends upon the type of team and its situation. Work teams in high-performance organizations often need the most authority; in fact, their success relies on their being highly motivated by the work to be done, since they typically operate without a great deal of direct supervision. Since work teams are permanent, ongoing organizational units, their decision-making capabilities can be built up over a period of time.

Work teams are often ineffective at making decisions about work assignments and pay when they are first formed. But after a year or more of working together, they can gain the ability to make decisions effectively. Teams do not easily get to the point where they are self-managing. They need substantial up-front investment in technical support, training, and learning. This is why it can take months, if not years, before they become relatively self-managing. Thus, unless the situation is such that it allows teams to be together for substantial periods of time, self-management may not be cost-effective because of the start-up costs involved.

Some of the most effective work teams I have studied were in a TRW plant in Kansas that supplied the oil industry. After five years, the teams had matured to the point where they were truly self-managing. Their ultimate test came when volume fell so sharply that they were faced with a layoff. Management asked the teams to recommend which of their members should be laid off. Instead of using a strict seniority criteria, the teams decided to look at the value of the team members to the organization and to lay off those that were judged to be least valuable.

Since decision making goes hand in hand with motivation on teams, it is not surprising that problem-solving teams are often the most difficult to motivate. Most organizations let problem-solving teams only recommend changes in work practices. This limited authority is a major reason why they do not survive in many organizations. However, as previously discussed, an organization can make problem-solving teams more effective by giving them a clear charter about what kinds of recommendations will be acceptable. It can also designate a specific individual to be responsible for reacting to their suggestions and set aside budget money that can be used to ensure that the problem-solving teams have the opportunity to develop and implement their ideas.

The General Electric "workout process," for example, has problem-solving teams present their recommendations to a senior manager, who immediately makes a decision.[8] This is a good way to ensure that problem-solving teams get feedback and that their recommendations have at least a reasonable chance of being favorably received and quickly acted on.

As will be discussed in Chapter Nine, extrinsic and financial rewards can partially substitute for the lack of power by helping to motivate employees to participate in problem-solving groups. For example, gain-sharing plans that involve sharing the financial savings that result from team recommendations are a popular way to reward problem-solving groups. Unlike individual suggestion-award programs, they spread the savings among all employees, not just the team that thinks of the idea. The rationale behind this is simple: it takes commitment from an entire organization to make most ideas work. Not only does someone have to think of the idea, someone has to develop it, budget for it, and oversee its implementation. In addition, often many people in the organization have to change their behavior in order to put the idea into practice. A reward system that shares the gains with everyone reinforces the point that everyone needs to work together in order to produce meaningful improvements in organizational performance.

Our research at the Center for Effective Organizations indicates that project teams need a considerable amount of autonomy and authority to be effective.[9] A project team developing a new product, for example, must be able to make important decisions about the features of the product and how it will be produced and marketed. The reason? Having to check with managers and higher-level executives who are not part of the team leads to less-than-desirable decisions, slows the product design process dramatically, and, in some cases, destroys the team's ability to make trade-off decisions about what is good for manufacturing, what is good for marketing, and so forth.

Project teams that have the power to make decisions and that can focus on satisfying the customer can often make excellent trade-off decisions. For example, they can make the tough decision that even though it is more difficult for manufacturing, it makes sense to add an extra feature to a product or to give a customer a choice among different features, because it will mean more sales. The alternative to having project teams make these decisions: cross-functional management teams that manage conflicts among different interest groups.

Overlay teams present the most difficult issues in terms of authority. Because their purpose is to coordinate the activities of other teams and individuals, giving them too much authority may diminish the effectiveness of the other teams. On the other hand, giving overlay teams too little authority may make them useless. Often, the solution to this dilemma is to put people who are good deal makers—and who are well respected—in charge of overlay teams. We all know that some individuals simply have the ability to organize things and make deals even if they don't have great amounts of formal authority. These are often the same people who, as children, organized pickup games, sports events, and parties. They develop personal relationships with key individuals and, as a result, are often able to get agreements and favors that other people in an organization cannot. In matrix structures, they often end up as project managers. In the world of manufacturing, they are often "expediters."

Training and Developing Effective Teams

The saying that a camel is a horse designed by a committee, although a bit unkind to camels, is an all-too-accurate characterization of teams whose individual members do not have the skills to work in a new logic organization. Quite simply, individuals on teams need to have skills that are different from those needed in an organization built around individual jobs. Members of teams need skills in group decision making, problem solving, interpersonal relationships, and group process. These skills are critical to a self-managing team's ability to make fair and reasonable decisions, to hold open and frank discussions of issues, to confront each other about performance problems, to handle technical and interpersonal conflicts, and to develop an efficient approach to decision making. In the absence of these skills, a team is likely to use inefficient ways to get work done. The result: too much time will be spent in unproductive group meetings trying to get decisions made and work done.

Building the skills that individuals need in order to operate as a team is partially an individual-training issue and partially a team-building issue. Team members can certainly learn feedback skills, discussion skills, and presentation skills outside of the team in which they use them. But having individuals with these skills is not the same as having teams with the capabilities that are needed for high performance.

Teams need to be able to integrate the skills of their members and develop habits and decision-making methods appropriate for their particular work situations. When quick decisions are needed, a team may need to delegate certain decisions to individuals so that they can be expedited. In other situations, a team may need to get input from all team members and reach a consensus before any action is taken. A team's members, therefore, need to be trained together so they can determine how the team will make decisions and how they will deal with each other. In essence, a team must develop its own culture and capabilities, not just independent competencies. They are critical factors in a team's ability to know what it has to do and its ability to do it.

Cross-Training: Spreading Expertise in Teams

Team effectiveness typically requires that team members be able to perform several of the tasks the group has to perform.[10] In production teams, for example, individuals need to be cross-trained so they can work throughout the production process. In financial services such as mortgage processing, individuals must be able to both take applications for mortgages and assemble the necessary data in order to make a funding decision. In paper and chemical manufacturing it is important that individuals be able to work at different workstations. On product development teams, it is critical to have individuals who understand production as well as design. Often this means career moves for engineers from production to design and vice versa. Such cross-training is a good way to give individuals insight into both of these aspects of new product development.

Lack of cross-training is one reason the solutions from quality circles and problem-solving teams all too often conflict with the realities of the situation. These teams rarely have members with knowledge of all of the elements that need to be considered in addressing complex issues. They may not know, for example, that the planned purchase of new equipment will make some of the steps in a production process unnecessary, or they may not be familiar with customer demands. Further, individuals who are very knowledgeable about only one area often try to get a team to make decisions that most benefit that particular area. This can be disastrous in problem-solving and new-product development teams. By contrast, individuals who have worked in different areas and in multiple functions can often come up with integrative solutions that effectively meet the demands of several functions or areas.

The amount of cross-training that is possible and desirable depends upon the difficulties of mastering the different steps in a team's work process. For some manufacturing teams, it is reasonable to expect that most individuals can do every step in the entire production process. At Shell's Sarnia plant mentioned earlier, every member of the team is expected to know every step of the production process. As a result, each individual is highly flexible and can understand and participate in all discussions and decisions concerning production. It helps individuals identify with the product. It helps them make a commitment to the success of the plant. And it improves their ability to make decisions that take the entire work process into account.

Complete cross-training is not practical in complex work such as that done by surgery teams or by product development teams in the automobile industry. Nevertheless, in these cases it is still critical that some of the people on teams be cross-trained. They need to be able to represent and understand several functions and areas of expertise in team discussions and push toward win-win integrative solutions.

In service situations, an individual must be cross-trained in order to be an effective single point of contact between a customer and the organization. Even though information technology has made one-stop customer service feasible, it is only possible if individuals are cross-trained so that they understand the different services that can be offered and the steps it takes to deliver each one.[11] Cross-training can be particularly advantageous where the demand for services and expertise is irregular.

A classic example is the airline industry, where customer check-in people, baggage loaders, and flight attendants in a traditional organization may work only a few hours in an eight-hour day; the rest of the time they are "waiting" for their skills to be needed. In a study we did with an air freight carrier, we found that out of an eight-hour day, people who loaded planes worked only two to three hours, because that was the only time period in which planes were being loaded. Cross-training can solve this problem. Employees who are not tied to limited job descriptions and skills can load baggage, clean planes, or check in customers or freight when each of these services is needed.

Southwest is one airline that understands the advantages of cross-training. It uses cross-training to produce a flexible work force that can better respond to customer needs. One of the things I always notice when flying Southwest is that there are rarely employees standing around waiting to do work. When there is a long check-in line at the counter, flight attendants simply jump behind the counter and help out by checking in passengers. This is just one example of what a flexible, committed work force can do to improve customer service and control costs.

Management of Teams: Formal and Informal Leaders

An important difference between a team and a group of individual workers concerns how they need to be managed. A supervisor can effectively manage a group of individuals one by one, directing each as needed in order to increase the performance of the whole group. Most managers are trained to manage individual employees and to organize their work in a way that coordinates their efforts. But an organization built on the six principles of the new logic and composed of self-managing work teams must be managed quite differently. A manager must interact with the members of a team in a group setting—that is, treat the team as if it were an individual.

For example, typical management activities—goal setting, giving credit for a job well done, and developing and nurturing competencies—must be done with the entire team. Managers must also provide teams with a sense of mission, direction, and purpose. They need to get team members to collectively accept certain performance goals and to work together to achieve them. This means managers need to be skilled at

- Recognizing the team for its good performance
- Challenging the team when it needs to perform better
- Critiquing the team when it has performed poorly
- Helping the team improve its decision processes and self-examination skills

When work teams are created, the number and the kinds of managers that are needed change dramatically. There may be only one manager for three or more teams, in contrast to the situation in a traditional organization where each group of individuals has its own supervisor who monitors performance and coordinates activities. This can reduce supervisory overhead by more than 50 percent or more and eliminate one, two, or more levels of management.

The elimination of management levels and traditional supervisors does not mean that there won't be individuals within teams who act as leaders and who assume responsibility for some of the traditional management activities. In self-managing teams, members spend part of their time recruiting new members, training people, monitoring safety, and running group meetings. In effect, they become part-time managers. In many self-managing teams, the management roles rotate so that members are cross-trained and flexible in handling management activities. This has the dual advantages of building management competencies in a number of individuals and building a sense of performance accountability in the team as a whole.

Most teams develop informal leaders who are particularly influential in determining how the group operates. Effective team performance in an organization depends upon each team having the right individuals emerge as informal leaders. This is something that the formal organization has little direct influence over once the team is formed. But it can have an influence at the stage of assigning members to a team, by identifying and carefully assigning individuals who are likely to emerge as informal leaders.

It is a bit of an oversimplification, but it is still true that organizations get the kinds of informal leaders and teams they deserve. If the organization has a positive culture with the right practices and team designs, then the informal leaders that emerge tend to align their leadership efforts with the organization's goals and objectives and make positive contributions to the team's performance. However, if the organization has not created the right culture or right team structure, then dysfunctional leaders can develop. Often this can only be fixed through a broad organizational change effort that includes removing dysfunctional leaders.

Supporting Team Activities

Chartering and structuring effective teams is not a simple matter. In most cases it should not and cannot be an initiative from a single supervisor or even from a group of supervisors. In fact, because teams always exist within the broader context of the organization, organizational practices, particularly those concerned with human resources management, are crucial to team effectiveness. As will be discussed in Chapters Eight and Nine, the employee selection process and the reward system have a particularly powerful impact on team effectiveness. In addition, information systems must be structured to deliver information in ways that support a team-based organization design.

I have been involved in a number of situations where teams were inserted into organizations that were not designed to support team activities. The result: there were almost always conflicts between the team and the rest of the organization. Many of the conflicts were small and petty, such as complaints about work teams scheduling their own breaks. Others were more significant, such as dissatisfaction over who represents the team, how to contact and communicate with the team, and how to measure and reward its performance.

This is not to say that stand-alone teams cannot be successful. They can, particularly where technology supports them and where local managers can protect them from the rest of the organization. In my experience, however, these conditions are rare. Much more typical is the experience of General Electric in the 1960s. Senior human resource executives at GE had heard about how effective self-managing teams had been in Europe and decided to test them in their manufacturing operations. GE's in-house staff of Ph.D. psychologists convinced the executives to put one or two self-managing teams in each of fifty different locations. Two years later, all the teams had been eliminated.

When the researchers followed up to see what happened, they found the same thing in factory after factory. The teams had shown initial promise, and, in most cases, they had outperformed the parts of the organization that did not use teams. But they also caused so many "problems" that the plant managers were faced with a tough choice: either eliminate these "effective" teams or convert the entire organization to teams so that everyone would "be treated the same."

What were the "problems" these teams created? It appears that other employees in the organization were envious of them because they scheduled their own breaks, worked and communicated differently, and needed less supervision. Further, the rest of the organization did not know how to work with them because they lacked a traditional supervisor.

In every case, local management decided to eliminate the teams because they were not prepared to convert their overall organization to a team-based operation. This choice was hardly surprising given the lack of corporate-level support for creating a team-based organization and the lack of knowledge about how to create such an organization.

In the 1970s, I studied a large corporation that took a different approach to introducing teams. It created one team-based plant in an otherwise traditional organization. One afternoon, I was in the office of the manager of the team-based plant when the phone rang. He politely told the caller—the corporate vice president of manufacturing—that if he would call such and such a number, a representative of the blue team (the work group currently running the plant) would update him on the plant's production information. Because the plant manager was not involved in the day-to-day management of production, he did not have the information. The production team did, so it made sense for the team to provide the information. However, at the time I wondered if the vice president understood this difference and could accept the status issues involved in his being told to call a production team member.

Just a few weeks later, when I was in a traditionally run plant of the same company, a similar call came in. The plant manager immediately provided all the production data needed from a computer printout he had been eyeing while we talked. After giving the data, the plant manager sat back and relaxed; he seemed to be through with his work for the day.

A month or two later, the plant manager who knew the production data was promoted while the plant manager in the team-based plant was told that his opportunities in the corporation were very limited and he should look elsewhere for employment. When I inquired about what the manager of the team-based plant had done wrong, I was informed that he just did not understand the culture and did not know how to deal with the rest of the organization.

Unfortunately, the problems of the manager in this team-based plant are not unique. I have seen the same problems occur time after time when team-based organizations are placed in the middle of traditional organizations. Teams require different leadership, different information, different reward systems, and different training—in short, an entirely different set of support structures and systems. It is very difficult to be a partially team-based organization. In my experience, being partially team-based works only if the organization is clearly divided into very independent business units which are either team-based or not.

Space and Location: Bringing Teams Together

The correct layout of the physical space in which teams operate can be critical to their success. Putting team members in the same physical space tends to promote more cohesive and more effective teams.[12] Organizations can also use meetings to bring their members together or use information technology to create virtual teams. "Groupware" software programs, for example, have been developed to support group work among individuals in different places.[13]

Even though virtual teams have been successful in some of the organizations I have worked with, I am convinced there is no substitute for face-to-face contact. How much actual in-person contact is needed depends upon the type of team. Self-managing work teams seem to require both interaction time and common physical space—members may be spread out over a large facility, but they definitely need dedicated meeting and gathering spaces to allow them to operate as a team.

Common space and high levels of personal interaction are also critical for most project teams, because their members come from quite different backgrounds and are often together only for a short period of time. Thus they need activities and structures that cause them to talk to each other. For example, when Ford decided to reorganize in 1994, it devoted an entire floor of its corporate office building to the project team working on the reorganization. The physical togetherness made it easier for the project team to work together, and it even influenced the kind of reorganization that they recommended because they saw the advantages of having cross-functional teams and processes located together.

Research evidence also shows that casual and incidental contact is particularly useful in research and development, where it supports innovation by encouraging the exchange of research and ideas.[14] As I mentioned earlier, I am impressed by workplace designs that have virtually no offices and that create spaces where people naturally bump into and talk to each other. Chrysler has used this concept in its multi-million-dollar car design center. Representatives of different functions who are working on a new design are located with others working on the product.

The Oticon example mentioned earlier is another good illustration of using space to support teams and interaction. As you may remember, instead of desks, each employee has a cart that holds his or her possessions. Coffee bars and dialogue rooms are scattered throughout the building. All of this is to encourage interaction and discussion among colleagues.

Overlay teams probably have the best chance of succeeding if they are not located together, but they can also benefit from interpersonal interaction. It is often helpful to bring them together—at least when they are formed, and periodically thereafter—so that they can socialize, learn from each other, and get to know each other as people.

Overlay teams are one case where, when they start, it is often worthwhile to do team-building exercises that involve doing physical or community service activities. Providing a personal context often makes it easier for individuals to understand the comments and input they get through voice mail and E-mail. Often it can help to break down some of the functional barriers that are particularly severe with overlay teams.

One of my colleagues likes to remind me that teams that are not teams are not teams. It is hard to argue this point, because teams differ in their purposes, their structures, and their characteristics. Nevertheless, I believe that the following points are useful when thinking about how to make virtually all types of teams effective:

- The work to be done by the team must be interdependent and relatively complex.
- Teams must have leaders who understand group process and provide a sense of direction.
- Human resource management, reward, and information systems need to be designed to provide the right kinds of training, feedback, and recognition for teams.
- The location of the members of a team and the size of a team are crucial to its effectiveness.
- Teams should have the responsibility for satisfying their customers.

These general points, of course, must be adapted to individual situations to account for the differences among team designs and the kinds of performance they must demonstrate. But unless these basic issues are dealt with, it is unreasonable to expect teams to outperform individuals; indeed, it may be more realistic to expect them to underperform individuals.

Part Three

Putting the Principles to Work

People, Rewards,
Communication,
and Measurement

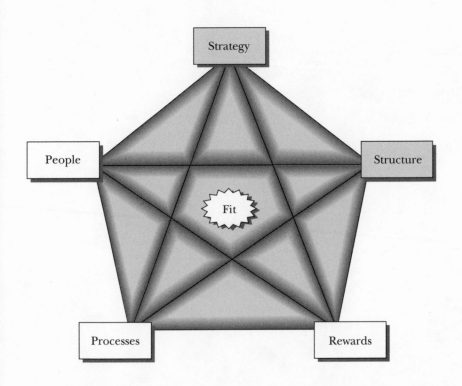

Chapter Eight

Human Resources
Managing People in New Logic Corporations

- Involvement is the most effective source of control.
- All employees must add significant value.

During the first course I took in graduate school, the professor pointed out that human resource management systems are designed to find and develop correctly skilled people to fit the job openings in organizations. He added that even when organizations start out trying to select the proverbial round peg for a round hole, they end up all too often with a square, rectangular, or pentagonal peg. When this happens, companies resort to training activities to round off the peg so that it fits reasonably well into the round hole, and then they offer rewards to motivate the now somewhat rounded peg to perform well in the round hole.

When I first heard of this approach, it sounded reasonable and was appealing because it suggested that an organization could be designed and managed with the same precision that is used to engineer a piece of equipment. Today I know better. I realize that it incorrectly assumes that it is better not to change the round hole to fit the person. I also realize that it incorrectly assumes that the round hole (the job) will be a relatively permanent feature of the organization—which is how it justifies the time and effort spent to create a better fit between the individual and the job. This is just not a valid assumption in today's fast-changing global business environment. Nor is it a valid assumption that individuals always can be or should be shaped to fit available openings.

As pointed out in Chapter Two, and as the Star Model illustrates, individuals and the other elements of an organization have to mesh for an organization to be effective. The challenge, therefore, is to create human resource management systems that can find, develop, and motivate people to work well in high-performance organizations. As will be seen in the rest of this chapter and in the next chapter—which focuses on reward systems—developing these new systems requires practices and approaches that are different from those that are typically used by traditional logic organizations. The systems development work must start from the assumption that both work and people are constantly changing and that change needs to be managed.

The Old Logic of Jobs Meets the New World of Competencies

For decades, human resource management systems have focused on jobs—specifying their accountabilities, responsibilities, and activities—as the basic building blocks of an organization's structure.[1] It is an approach that can be traced back to the early 1900s and the era of scientific management, when Frederick Winslow Taylor showed that jobs can be specified and that work methods can be improved and rationalized through careful study and scientific analysis. From that old logic came job descriptions, job evaluation methods, selection testing, supervisor training, assignments to work groups, merit pay, and a host of management practices that focus on seeing that individuals do their jobs correctly.

In the old logic, jobs are the tools that organizations use to assure themselves that their employees know what to do, know how to do it, and are motivated to do it. Inherent in the old logic is the assumption that the best way to improve organizational performance is to increase the skills of the work force and to motivate workers to perform their jobs more effectively through pay and other rewards. In the traditional approach, the value that an individual adds to the organization depends on how he or she fits the organization's jobs. Thus employee selection tests are used to identify people who fit existing jobs; training programs are used to develop employees' skills for specific jobs.

The new logic questions the usefulness of focusing on jobs and job-related human resource management systems. It argues for taking an approach that is 180 degrees different in order to give organizations greater flexibility in both their structures and their performance. It argues that it is time to move toward a focus on people and their skills and competencies, just as it is important to focus on core competencies and organizational capabilities.

The rapidly changing business environment demands that organizations have individuals who regularly change what they do and who constantly develop new skills to support the development of their organization's competencies and capabilities. It is no longer appropriate for organizations to think of people as having a job with a particular set of activities. Nor does an individual's worth necessarily rest in his or her ability to do a particular job, nor should individuals be paid according to the worth of the job they do. It is more appropriate and more effective to think of people as resources whose knowledge and skill contribute to the organization's competencies and capabilities.

It is not news to anyone who reads business magazines that organizations have become flatter to reduce their costs and increase their competitiveness. In fact, three-fourths of the Fortune 1000 reduced the number of their management layers during the 1980s, while two-thirds of the Fortune 1000 both downsized and reduced layers.[2] The new logic argues that when organizations flatten, individuals must take more responsibility for managing themselves and for their performance. Even more important, individuals must be able to identify what needs to be done without being told and directed.

Individuals are simply not encouraged to take initiative by a system that uses job descriptions. Job descriptions both specify—and limit—an individual's activities, and make them reluctant to do things that are not in their job descriptions. Time after time, I have seen individuals refuse to do a task that a supervisor has asked them to do because "it's not in their job description." In other situations they carry out the task, but they then want their job description changed to include the "new responsibilities and duties"—and they want a pay increase as well.

The flatter organizational structures used in the new logic also pose interesting challenges for career development. Quite simply, there are not as many opportunities for individuals to be promoted and to move up the hierarchy as there are in old logic organizations. In fact, in some cases, individuals may have to stay at the same organizational level for five to ten years before an opportunity for a promotion opens up. In a traditional career, that is an eternity.

If an individual is going to continue to learn, to grow, and to progress in a new logic organization, organizations must create other channels of career development, such as lateral moves and development assignments. The job-based systems of the old logic do not facilitate such alternatives. Neither do their reward systems. In fact, pay systems in traditional job-based organizations sometimes punish individuals when they make horizontal moves or broaden their skills by doing a greater variety of things.

To sum up, the need for organizations to be more adaptable, to have all employees add significant value to their products and services, and to rely on capabilities as a source of competitive advantage fundamentally challenges the idea of using jobs as a basis for managing individuals and organizations. A job-based approach runs the risk of underusing employees and not developing the kinds of capabilities that are necessary for high performance. The development and management of individuals is a secondary concern in the traditional, job-centered approach. What is needed in organizations built on the six principles of the new logic is an approach that has as its primary focus the development and motivation of individuals and teams.

The New Logic: Strategies Focused on Skills and Competencies

The alternative to a job-based approach to human resource management is a system that focuses on the skills and competencies of individuals. The focus needs to shift from developing detailed job descriptions to developing skill and "person" descriptions that indicate what an individual needs to know in order to be effective in his or her particular work area, department, or team. To be effective, this focus must permeate every human resource management practice, from employee selection to career development.

As was mentioned in the discussion of teams in Chapters Six and Seven, a skill-based approach is particularly appropriate when the work teams are highly interdependent and rapidly changing. In many cases, because work teams rotate the tasks they assign to individuals, no member has a permanent work assignment. Instead, teams take responsibility for a specific work or production process and/or set of customers. Within the work team, individuals must be developed so that they can contribute critical skills and knowledge. Effective human resource management means identifying those skills and developing a learning program so that individuals can contribute to their team's effectiveness.

In production teams, for example, this process is relatively straightforward. The tasks that a team needs to perform are identified. Depending upon the complexity of the work, there may be anywhere from five or six up to twenty or thirty tasks to be performed. A decision then needs to be made concerning how many individuals need to be able to perform each task. As discussed in the previous chapter, in some cases everyone should be able to perform all tasks, while in other cases only a few people need to be able to do all of them. Usually, just a few members need to develop in-depth knowledge of particular specialties and certain management tasks, such as facilitating group meetings. But keep in mind that within the work team, each member must continue to develop the skills that the organization needs so that he or she can contribute to the critical organizational capabilities.

Clearly, where the work is dynamic and where the tasks that a team performs change rapidly, learning activities can be complex to manage. It requires supportive human resource practices with regard to employee selection, training and development, skills assessment, career management, and employment stability. We will turn to these issues here, then discuss reward systems in the next chapter.

The New Logic of Selection: No More Pegs, No More Holes

In the new skill-based logic, the employee selection process needs to emphasize finding people who fit the organization's skill needs and its learning environment, rather than people who fit specific job openings. In essence, the task is to select individuals for organizational membership, not for a particular job.[3] Thus organizations must develop an employee selection process that will allow them to identify people who can learn the kinds of skills the organization needs (for example, statistical analysis and problem solving for those organizations that want a high level of capability in total quality management) and who can work well with the management approach of the new logic organizations. It is one thing to be a good follower in a traditional bureaucratic organization; it is quite another to manage oneself, lead others, and operate as an effective team member in a new logic organization.

The employee selection process must also identify individuals who either have or can develop the skills and knowledge that enhance the organization's key core competencies. For example, if understanding certain chemical processes is a key core competency, there is no substitute for hiring people who are the best at that. This is precisely what 3M has done. Similarly, Sun Microsystems and Microsoft have focused on hiring the best software engineers from MIT, Stanford, and other leading schools.

Historically, management style has not drawn a great deal of attention in the employee selection process even though, as the Ford film example mentioned earlier showed, it perhaps should have. Finding individuals who fit the management style may well be the most important part of the employee selection process for new logic organizations.

An individual's fit with the organization's structure and management approach is as critical as his or her technical proficiency and knowledge base. Members need to know how to work effectively in a self-managing team and how to manage themselves, and they must be willing to make lateral career moves. Individuals who value rapid upward career movement are unlikely to fit well in a new logic organization. People who need specific job descriptions with clear accountabilities may also be uncomfortable in a new logic organization. Likewise, a manager who is used to getting things done by commanding individuals and using extrinsic rewards such as promotion and firing to motivate individuals may be unable to operate effectively in a new logic corporation.

It is one thing to say that the employee selection processes need to be changed. It is quite another to specify what they should look like. So far, it is possible to identify three key aspects of the right selection system for new logic organizations that differentiate it from the process used by traditional organizations: realistic work previews, employee participation in the selection process, and the thoroughness of the selection process.

Work Previews: Road Testing the Work and the Organization

An effective way to improve the employee selection process is to give applicants the opportunity to experience the nature of the work that they will do and to expose them to the culture, values, and management practices of the organization.[4] Work previews give individuals a chance not only to learn what will be expected of them but to make an informed judgment about the organization as a place to work.

Realistic previews are especially important in new logic organizations because the work environment is dramatically different from the traditional workplaces with which most job applicants are familiar. Thus one key to effective work previews is to take the necessary time to make them truly realistic. In some cases, a realistic preview can take days or even weeks as an individual does work in a simulated situation or does the actual work. It is important that realistic previews establish what an individual's relationship with the organization will be like and communicate the new logic values of open communication, mutual decision making, self-management, and teamwork. Remember: people differ; not everyone wants challenging work and likes teamwork.

An interesting example of a realistic preview was mentioned in Chapter Two: the preview video used by the Cummins Engine plant in upstate New York that makes diesel engines for trucks. When it interviewed potential workers, Cummins found that many people who applied for a "job" had no idea what it would be like to work in a plant that operated with self-managing work teams, where individuals had to learn multiple skills and function as a team member. The video debunked the idea that working in teams was easy and fun and that the Cummins plant was a country club kind of environment, a common impression in the community because the workers there seemed to enjoy their work so much.

Two of my colleagues at USC's Center for Effective Organizations, Gerry Ledford and Dave Bowen, worked with a plate-glass maker that used another work preview approach when it opened a plant in California. Individuals were asked to actually do the jobs for a while before they decided if they wanted to be employees. During this process they learned what the job was really like—having plate glass shatter during the production process, for example—and had the chance to get feedback from others on their performance.

Clearly, realistic work previews give individuals the opportunity to make an informed decision about whether they want to work in a particular organization. But keep in mind that the work preview approach is not mistake-free. Sometimes individuals may need a job so much that they fool themselves and the organization about whether they represent a good fit. They will delude themselves about their skills and motivations and take a job that is a poor match. Thus, as will be discussed next, it is important that the organization do a good job of selecting the best people.

Full Participation:
Bringing Co-Workers into the Selection Process

In selecting employees for high-performance organizations, it is vital that the people who will work with a new employee have an active say in the selection process. Work teams should interview job applicants and assess their fit with the team. This provides the applicant with a realistic sense of how a work team acts and the team members with an opportunity to assess the individual who wants to join them. In most situations, team members can then veto or approve new members of their team. In many situations, the use of a realistic work preview allows team members to participate in the selection decision because they administer and run the job preview.

Aside from the fact there is considerable evidence to show that work teams are often good predictors of who will be successful as a new team member, the advantages of having team members participate in the selection process are twofold. First, they can see things that managers and human resource specialists may miss during the interview process. Second, once a team interviews someone and says that an individual will be successful, it significantly increases the probability that the individual will fit into the team. When team members say they can work with the individual, it creates a self-fulfilling prophecy. The team members put in extra effort to work with that person to help him or her succeed.

Conducting a Thorough Selection Process

In assessing prospective employees for a new logic organization, the employee selection process needs to be extensive and thorough. It must consider all the many relevant factors and assess individuals on their current skills and capabilities as well as their ability to learn in ways that are important to an organization's capabilities.

Motorola, for example, tests the ability of job applicants to participate in problem-solving groups. It shows them a video of a problem-solving situation and then asks them how they would behave if they were a member of this team. Would they speak up? Ask for more data? Job candidates are then scored on their knowledge of how to participate in a team process.

An extensive selection process can serve as the basis for a greater mutual commitment than exists when an individual is hired who knows little about the job and when the organization knows little about the applicant. The psychological literature clearly shows that the thoroughness and length of a selection process significantly affect how an individual feels about an organization. The more thorough the process and the more informed the decision, the more likely an individual is to stay with the organization and develop a high level of commitment to its goals. The reasoning of employees goes something like this: "If this organization is so tough to get into, it must be terrific. And I must be terrific because I was able to make the grade."

For example: I consulted with several Japanese firms when they were establishing U.S. production operations during the 1970s. They put applicants through weeks of selection activities. This rigorous testing helped introduce individuals to the idea that every employee is important and that everyone is expected to make a major contribution to the success of the organization. It also drove home to them that their skills and capabilities are important and that they needed to do a considerable amount of learning and development in order to be successful.

Honda literally spent weeks interviewing and testing people before they hired them. To Honda, hiring an employee was as important as deciding where to locate the plant and what types of manufacturing systems to use. They followed up this initial commitment with an equally extraordinary commitment to training and development. Months before production was scheduled to begin in the United States, Honda sent newly hired employees to work in one of its factories in Japan. Not only did these employees gain extensive technical knowledge and familiarity with Honda's high-performance standards, all the employees I talked to were extremely impressed by Honda's serious commitment to their training and development. Toyota and Nissan have used similar practices in starting their U.S. operations, and it seems to have paid off. Their cars made in the United States are generally equal in quality to those produced in Japan.

I cannot help but contrast these extensive selection processes with the process frequently used by U.S. companies. All too often, individuals are interviewed by a few managers and given a short test, after which a hiring decision is made—an approach that research indicates is invalid and unlikely to predict future job success.[5]

Companies that use the principles of the new logic can also benefit from using rigorous review processes when individuals seek to move from one work area to another within the organization. This gives the organization the opportunity to assess individuals as if they are outside applicants and to give them feedback about their skill development. It also gives new logic organizations a chance to once again show the importance they place on skill development and competencies. Some organizations, such as Texas Instruments, even ask individuals to prepare a resume. They treat internal job applicants as if they are applying for a job with another organization. This gives them experience in marketing themselves and in becoming more career self-sufficient, a topic that will be discussed in more detail later.

Management Selection in the New Logic: Looking for Leadership

The importance of leadership skills in high-performance organizations makes the selection of managers a particularly critical task. Leaders in the new logic need to be more participative than directive, and able to build consensus and generate alignment among the systems and individuals in an organization. As a result, managers from traditional organizations often perform inadequately in a new logic organization because they are used to taking charge, directing others, and operating effectively in a command-and-control environment.

In my consulting on organizational change, I have found that over half of the managers from traditional organizations are unsuccessful when they are given managerial roles in a high-performance work organization. Even when old-style managers want to learn the new management approach and receive training and support to help them change, the failure rate is usually this high.

One company I studied used a "Three R Rule" (re-educate, rotate, and remove) for managers as it changed the management of its organization from the old logic to the new. It first provided training in new leadership behaviors for all of its managers. If this did not change the behavior of a manager schooled in the old logic, it rotated him or her to a new work environment and provided more training. If that too failed, as it often did, the company would give him or her the chance to remain with the organization as an individual contributor but would remove the person from a managerial position. In sum, they helped their managers try to change but would not tolerate someone who did not.

General Electric uses an interesting approach in order to change the leadership behavior of its top managers. They use a 360-degree assessment process, which gathers data on managerial behaviors from customers, subordinates, peers, and bosses—that is, everyone who interacts with an executive. These data are then used to develop an overall profile of the management styles of its top six hundred executives. These executives are then counseled on how they need to change their behavior.

How serious is GE about this? In one of GE's recent annual reports, CEO Jack Welch made it clear that even managers whose units are performing well will be dismissed if they are managing inappropriately. If they are managing appropriately but getting bad results, they are given some slack and time to improve their performance.

Such a policy is remarkable, since in most organizations performance is all that counts: high-performing managers can behave any way they want. I strongly support Jack Welch's view that good results obtained the wrong way are not acceptable, and that managers who are working to learn new leadership behavior and showing promise deserve every opportunity to be successful. It is an important part of running a new logic company that is driven by its mission and values.

Often, the best candidates to fill leadership positions in new logic organizations are individuals within the organization who know the technology and have critical core competencies. But it is still important that they be treated just like applicants from the outside and be required, through simulations and other methods, to demonstrate their ability to perform as leaders. Paper-and-pencil tests often do an inadequate job of measuring leadership ability. One reason for this is that the ability to lead varies depending on the situation; someone who may be an effective leader in one situation is not necessarily an effective leader in another. Another reason is that some individuals know the right thing to say about leadership, but they do not know how to behave correctly.

In simulations, job candidates can be put into groups to discuss a particular issue or solve a particular problem and can be scored on their behavior during this group activity. Although these exercises often start out as just that—exercises—they become very real for the participants. Often the frustration of not being able to get the task accomplished brings out the true character of an individual and provides great insight into their underlying leadership abilities.

The power of simulated leadership situations has prompted a number of organizations to offer them as a commercial product. For example, the Center for Creative Leadership offers a number of very sophisticated simulations that can test for leadership and managerial skills. For years, AT&T ran a very effective program of management selection and development that used something called an assessment center; over three days, it put managers through a variety of simulated managerial situations.[6]

Training and Development: Acquiring Skills for High Performance

The selection of employees and leaders is crucial to getting the right people in place in an organization. But it is just a first step.

Organizations must also use training and development to create a skill level in their work force that will lead to organizational effectiveness. Training in business strategy and economics is critical to getting employees involved in the organization. Technical training is critical to their developing the skills they need in order to perform their work assignments.

The first task of an organization is to be clear about what skills it needs and how much of each skill it needs. For example, it makes sense to give individuals throughout the organization the opportunity to gain a broad understanding of the business and the organization's purpose, direction, and performance. On the other hand, if an organization needs three experts in statistical process control, there is no reason to offer this learning opportunity to everyone.

I do not think there is any minimum amount of time that should be spent on individual learning and skill development. But it seems to me that allotting at least 5 percent of every employees' time to training may be required to demonstrate an organization-wide commitment to training and development. Unfortunately, many American corporations spend extraordinary amounts of money training and developing their managers but have not done the same for the rest of their employees. An interesting exception is Motorola, which requires that all of its employees receive at least one week of training per year.[7] Another is Saturn, where the contract with the United Auto Workers calls for all union members to receive ninety-two hours of training a year. It also ties a company-wide bonus to meeting this objective.

The most recent data from our continuing study of the Fortune 1000 corporations does show a noticeable increase in the amount of training done.[8] There has been an increase in job skills training as well as in training for problem-solving groups and total quality management programs. But while these increases are encouraging, there are still very few companies that train a majority of their work force in the critical business skills, particularly in the areas of financial analysis and business strategy. As a result, many employees are simply not in a position to participate in business strategy decisions and/or understand information about their organization's financial performance.

To change this, it is not necessary to have a "brick and mortar" training university such as the one that Motorola established at its corporate headquarters (Motorola University). There are other ways to accomplish the same objectives. Organizations can use community colleges, universities, training firms, and other teaching and training organizations to build the skills of their work force. In addition, corporate policies can stipulate that employees be given time off from their jobs with pay to take courses and to learn. Reward systems that increase individuals' pay as they learn new skills are also needed. As will be discussed in the next chapter, rewarding skill growth is not only an important symbolic act but an effective way to motivate employees to learn and further develop their competencies and capabilities.

There are many learning experiences that can be created outside classroom situations. For example, organizations can

- Provide customer service experiences to employees who do not normally interact with customers
- Have an individual do the job of another employee who is away on vacation
- Invite individuals from other parts of the company to come to staff meetings and explain what another department or business unit does
- Have peers train each other in their respective work activities

The challenge is to create multiple learning opportunities for all employees so that they can be continuous learners.

Assessing Skills and Capabilities

A critical component of development is the assessment of skills. Organizations need formal systems to measure the skills of employees. Organizations must also provide ways for employees to assess their own skills. GTE, for example, has developed a test that all employees can take to assess their knowledge of digital communications technology and guide their future training and development activities.

Because knowledge of all kinds is spread broadly throughout new logic organizations, it also makes sense for employees to assess each others' skills and strengths. This is in sharp contrast to the traditional approach where managers evaluate their subordinates from the executive offices on down. Put another way, the new logic assumes that good subordinates know a good manager, or better yet, a good leader because they are the ones being led. The old logic assumes that a high-level manager knows a good manager and that a good manager knows a good worker.

Self-managing teams often take responsibility for determining and assessing the skill profiles of their members. Each individual develops a plan for learning new skills, and each team member acquires his or her portfolio of skills through a combination of classroom and peer training. Teams have skill certification procedures that determine whether their members have mastered particular skills. In essence, skills become an individual's job security in a new logic organization; they determine employability, value to the organization, and pay.

The new logic view of leadership means that when an organization assesses a manager's capabilities and performance, it needs to gather data not just from that individual's boss but also from his or her peers and subordinates, as General Electric does in its 360-degree assessment process. This process provides the variety of perspectives needed to appraise the individual's performance and to guide the future development of his or her skills. Simply asking a manager's manager to assess behavior reinforces the hierarchical process and ignores the reality that some managers manage up much better than they manage down.

Tracking Skills and Capabilities

Because new logic organizations need to give work assignments to individuals on the basis of their skills and capabilities—not just to fill a particular job—they need to maintain a record of their skill levels and capabilities that everyone in the organization can easily access. Increasingly, organizations are developing computerized data bases that provide a skill profile for each individual. With distributed computer technology and personal computers, data bases can be maintained and accessed at the team or work unit level. This allows individuals anywhere in the organization to identify employees with the skills that they need so they can be used as trainers, or brought in to add to the set of skills in a particular work or business unit.

A central skills data base can help senior management keep track of its core competencies and organizational capabilities, identifying where the key resources are within the organization, and what needs to be done to maintain them. This kind of information is central to the challenge of developing organizational capabilities and core competencies. For example, an organization must have data on how many people understand problem solving, statistical process control, and the like to determine how well developed its organizational capability for quality control and continuous improvement is. Similarly, knowing how many individuals understand key business issues, can function in teams, and have worked in multiple functions can be important in deciding whether the organization can use cross-functional work teams to speed new products to market.

In addition to listing skills, the best systems include regularly updated records of everyone's current work assignments, performance goals as well as their performance history. When this information is added, these data bases are extremely valuable tools for managing "jobless" new logic organizations, because they provide widely available information on what everyone is doing and has accomplished. The administrative burden of maintaining these systems can be reduced significantly by making all employees responsible for keeping their records updated. Federal Express and Silicon Graphics are among the companies that have developed state-of-the-art computer-based human resource management systems.

The New Logic of Career Development

In an organization that uses the six principles of the new logic, career development processes must be significantly different. Instead of the organization taking responsibility for the individual's career and managing it, individuals must be in charge of their skill acquisition and career development. Ultimately, individuals must decide for themselves what types of skills they wish to acquire and work to develop them. They may also need to adjust to very different kinds of career moves.

Lateral Moves and Longer Stays

Fast-track or high-potential managers have had careers that consist of a series of upward moves. They were expected to—and they expected to—move up, particularly early in their careers, every two to three years. Moving less frequently was seen as a sign of failing and/or being derailed. If the goal is to get someone to the top of a tall pyramid, it is logical to think of career progress as a series of rapid upward moves. Without them, time runs out for individuals who aspire to a senior management position.

The traditional logic approach to management development was well executed by AT&T. Their management development program during the 1960s and 1970s was clearly world-class.[9] Individuals were hired directly out of college and told that for ten years they could expect a promotion every eighteen months to two years. If they did not get promoted that quickly, they would be retained in the organization, but they understood that it meant they were not heading for a senior management position.

After ten years of rapid moves, the successful managers were put into an advanced program that oversaw their development as a member of senior management. The AT&T program was very attractive to new college graduates and, as a result, enabled it to acquire many talented individuals. In fact, it almost attracted me! I was offered the opportunity to join this ten-year AT&T program when I graduated from college. I would have started as a supervisor of telephone operators in rural New England. AT&T's approach to upward mobility had a lot of appeal for me, but, fortunately for AT&T and for myself, I decided to go to graduate school. In retrospect, I do not think I would have fit well into the management model that AT&T used at the time.

There are some very important limitations to career development systems in which certain individuals are identified as high potential and "crown princes" (or "princesses"). Once identified, they tend to move through positions rapidly, often before anyone can adequately assess their performance in any position. They are simply not in any position long enough for anyone to see the important long-term results of their behavior. They end up being "dipped" in experience and moved on to the next new position. Often they learn how to manage short-term relationships rather than to build long-term organizational capabilities.[10]

In a high-performance organization, since there are few upward career moves and different expectations about learning and leadership, individuals need to stay longer in particular work areas, develop more in-depth skills, and make more horizontal or lateral career moves. Lateral career moves are particularly critical in organizations that emphasize lateral processes. As mentioned earlier, research quite clearly shows that in order for an organization to operate laterally it needs individuals who have worked in different functions and understand multiple specialties.[11] For example, in the discussion of new-product development teams, I noted that it is particularly critical that some members understand both marketing and engineering, while others know both production and design. The only way to develop individuals with this breadth of understanding is to move them horizontally through different functions and to reward them for these moves.

An additional advantage of meaningful lateral career moves and longer stays in particular work areas is that it can help develop strong senior managers and leaders. Managers who have made a series of slow lateral moves know more about the operation of the organization as a business and have the chance to develop better skills in managing long-term relationships with their co-workers. These skills are particularly critical when someone gets to the top of an organization.

All too often, individuals get to senior management positions in large, traditional logic corporations as a result of having gone up a functional silo; that is, they have moved up in finance, production, marketing, or some other function. This usually does a poor job of equipping them to be head of that function because it does not give them the knowledge that is needed to integrate its work with what goes on in other parts of the organization. It is even worse preparation for being a senior executive or CEO. Too often, when individuals with this kind of background become senior executives, they end up focusing on the function that they know best. Thus, instead of the company having a senior executive who integrates the organization and provides overall leadership, it ends up with a CEO who acts as its senior finance officer or its senior marketing manager.

Career Management in the New Logic

Traditionally, organizations have managed the career development of their employees, sometimes without telling them what is planned for them. As was mentioned earlier, in the new logic, individuals are expected to manage their own careers. This fits well with the new logic thinking that individuals should take responsibility for themselves in an environment that is less paternalistic, less entitlement oriented, and more skill and performance oriented. Of course, it is one thing to talk about career self-reliance; it is quite another to establish and manage it in an effective way.

For people who are not used to being in charge of their careers, taking responsibility for career management can be traumatic. Thus, regardless of what methods it uses, it is vital that new logic organizations invest a considerable amount of time and resources to help individuals manage their careers. A computer network of job opportunities and resources, for example, can help, especially if it includes information on the training and learning opportunities that are available throughout the corporation, as well as in the local community.

Some companies—Raychem Corporation, 3COM Corporation, and Sun Microsystems are three good examples—have taken a leading role in developing programs to help their employees become more self-reliant in creating and managing their careers.[12] Raychem has a career center—that includes a library of materials—that is open to all employees. It also has a career counselor who can administer psychological tests and assess skills. Also available is a computerized data base of over 360 people throughout the corporation who are willing to take the time to talk to other employees about the nature of their work and the career opportunities that it provides.

Apple Computer encourages employees to fill in for co-workers who are on sabbaticals or vacations so that they can get a better sense of other career opportunities within the organization. Apple has also created a series of internal programs to make its work force more resilient and self-managing. It provides career information through an "electronic campus" computer network that gives individuals access to lists of books, professional associations, conferences, courses, and articles. Employees can add material that they think will be of interest to their peers.

In order for career self-management to be successful in a corporation, it is important that senior executives both support skill development and serve as role models. A key positive example: in the early days of Raychem's efforts, the company had a senior manager who actively and visibly used the career center. His actions

signaled to the rest of the organization that it was politically acceptable to use the center and not a sign of someone who was failing
or in career trouble.

Finally, organizations can help individuals manage their careers
by giving them the kind of business information that will allow them
to assess where the organization is going and what potential jobs will
exist as a result. Just one example: at 3COM, departments hold
weekly discussion sessions on the status of the business and its implications for the staffing and skills that will be needed. In some cases,
employees are even advised of company plans to exit and enter businesses. Historically, organizations have been very cautious about
revealing such strategic information. However, if an organization
wants its work force to be more resilient and self-managing, individuals need this information to plan their careers. In some cases,
the knowledge may cause them to leave the organization. But in the
long run, it can build trust between employees and the organization.

A case in point: when Procter & Gamble gave employees in the
Los Angeles area a year's notice that their plant would be closed,
it invited them to stay on in order to shut down the plant and to
receive training in new skills that might help them improve their
employability. Most employees stayed until the plant was closed,
and production continued to set records even as the plant was
being closed. Apparently the employees appreciated being treated
as adults who could be trusted and who needed time to develop
new career directions.

Balancing Employment Stability and Strategy

We all remember IBM's famous pledge not to lay off employees.
Digital, Exxon, and AT&T never made such definitive "no layoff"
statements, but they, along with many other corporations, worked
hard to avoid laying anyone off. There is no doubt that employment
security creates a work force loyal to the organization, a perception
of the company as a good employer, and a very long-tenured, stable work force. The deal is clear: in return for their loyalty, employees get job security and employment for life.

The promise of employment security seems like an obvious
good. But the performance problems that forced IBM, Digital,
and AT&T to abandon such policies and lay off hundreds of thousands of employees suggest otherwise. At the very least, a near-

guarantee of employment in combination with fixed base wages and extensive fringe benefit programs tend to insulate employees from the economic realities of the external environment. They also make it difficult for organizations to reduce their labor costs when the business environment requires it. Finally, it puts individuals in a dependent role and contributes to a work climate where employees feel a strong sense of entitlement.

Japanese organizations have often been admired because of their commitment to employment security. It is important to understand, however, that Japanese organizations guarantee employment for all their "regular" employees but not for their large number of temporary employees, and not for many women employees who are expected to have children and leave the work force. They also do not have guaranteed wage levels; their large bonus programs do not pay out if performance is poor. Thus their labor costs can drop significantly without their having to lay off individuals. Incidentally, in their U.S. operations, Japanese companies including Honda, Toyota, and Nissan have tended to practice employment stability without large bonus plans. In business downturns so far, they have used their employees to paint machinery and clean up. They have kept them employed and well paid, much like some American corporations have done in the past.

There is little doubt that employment stability can help some old logic organizations operate more effectively. Nevertheless, it does not even fit all old logic organizations and never existed in most. In cyclical businesses such as autos and appliances, stability was never practiced (except with managers) because it did not fit the companies' rapidly changing production needs. Instead of practicing stability, most organizations followed two simple rules:

- Rule 1: Lay off only in a business crisis or major cyclical downturn.
- Rule 2: Never lay off managers and professionals.

These rules, of course, fit the old logic because they helped assure the loyalty of the high-value-added employees.

But what about employment stability in the new logic? It seems clear that employment security as an absolute right does not fit the new logic. On the other hand, high-performance organizations are not created by mass layoffs or continually churning the work force.

New logic organizations need a work force of people who stay long enough to understand the business, develop appropriate relationships with each other, and acquire the unique skills that will allow them to perform in a way that provides competitive advantage. Effective lateral relationships, minimal hierarchy, and a strong sense of vision and commitment all depend on a relatively stable, highly skilled work force. Stability fosters work relationships among people, relationships that often are the foundations upon which such capabilities as quality and speed to market are built.

Because relatively high levels of employment stability are desirable for most high-performance organizations, they need to take a skills-based approach to employment stability that follows three rules that are consistent with the new logic:

- Rule 1: Reductions are a last option.
- Rule 2: Reductions depend on the skills and performance of individuals.
- Rule 3: Always provide a soft landing for people who lose their jobs.

In order to effectively implement this strategy, an organization must constantly evaluate the skills and performance of its members relative to its need for core competencies and organizational capabilities. This is the only way that an organization can know who is valuable and who is failing to develop and perform appropriately. Those who are failing can be counseled and helped to improve. If they continue to fail, however, they must be let go.

It may make sense for new logic organizations to identify a core group of people who will remain with the organization as long as they continue to meet its performance and skill acquisition requirements.[13] Although this central group should by no means have guaranteed employment, they do need to be protected against economic cycles in the business and kept as part of the organization. This central group should consist of those people who are critical to the maintenance and development of an organization's core competencies and capabilities.

Next to the innermost core group of employees, there may be several rings of employees with different amounts of employment stability. At the outer edges are individuals who are hired for very short periods of time to do a particular task. This group may be hired on a contract basis or obtained through a temporary agency. Companies including AT&T have created their own internal temporary agencies that move a relatively permanent group of flexible employees—including managers—around the organization when and where they are needed.

The nature of the business environment must determine how many rings of employment stability there should be and how many people should be in each one. In a relatively stable business environment, an organization may have a large core with relatively few rings. But if an organization is in a very rapidly changing business, such as the personal computer or fashion business, it may want to have a smaller core and a relatively high percentage of its employees in the rings that surround the core. The challenge is to design an employment stability model that fits the long-term business environment and the demands of a high-performance work setting.

As a totality, human resource practices for new logic organizations must differ significantly from traditional human resource practices. Particularly important are the following:

• *Selection:* Organizations must choose individuals for how they fit the organization, not for jobs. They must offer applicants realistic work previews, obtain input from employees, and create an extensive process that focuses on leadership and management style fit.

• *Training:* There must be a strong organizational commitment to training employees in business skills, leadership skills, and team skills. This involves continued skill assessment for everyone.

• *Careers:* Organizations must provide information and training, but individuals must take responsibility for their own careers in an environment where there will be fewer job changes and more lateral moves.

• *Stability of employment:* There are no employment guarantees, only stability that is based on skills and performance.

How new logic organizations should reward employees is the subject of the next chapter. Later chapters will consider in more detail the new employment contract and consider further the implications of new logic thinking for individuals and their careers.

Chapter Nine

Reward Systems
Paying for Teamwork, Competencies, and Performance

> - Lateral processes are the key to organizational effectiveness.
> - All employees must add significant value.

As a consultant and researcher, I have encountered a great many poorly designed, highly dysfunctional reward systems. I am convinced that this is one of the key areas where organizations are frequently designed in ways that do not contribute to organizational effectiveness.

For example, a major U.S. pharmaceutical company recently introduced a new pay system for its sales force. At the beginning of the year, each salesperson received a sales goal. At year end, supervisors evaluated each person based on how successful he or she was in reaching that goal. Individuals were rated at one of five performance levels based upon how completely they met their goal—which, in theory, determined how much of a pay bonus they got.

If the plan had stopped there, it might have worked. But it did not stop there. After the initial evaluations, the company's head of sales determined how many salespersons should fall into each of the five categories in the rating system and then told the supervisors to re-evaluate their employees. For many, this resulted in a lower rating and a smaller bonus. Not surprisingly, the sales force was in near revolt over this process and was demanding that the system be changed to one that was fairer and more predictable.

Why do organizations continue to introduce ineffective reward systems? I believe there are three primary reasons:

- There is a lack of understanding about how pay systems affect behavior.
- It is difficult and takes a considerable amount of time to design a good reward system.
- A pay system, particularly a good pay-for-performance plan, requires difficult decisions that affect the income levels and the well-being of employees—decisions that managers are often hesitant and poorly trained to make.

Thus, despite the spectacular success of pay-for-performance reward systems at some companies (remember Lincoln Electric), many organizations have not been able to follow suit and as a result do not get a good return on the money they invest in their pay systems. Criticism of traditional pay systems, of course, is not new. Many critics have pointed to their failures. Despite their problems, this chapter will not focus on how to avoid creating dysfunctional reward systems; rather, it will focus on the positive: designing reward systems that effectively support the new logic of organizing.

Why Pay and Reward Systems?

My interest in pay practices goes back to my doctoral dissertation, in which I set out to determine whether managers in large bureaucratic organizations were actually paid for performance and, if so, whether it made a difference in their performance. My research showed a poor relationship between pay and performance. But it did find that when pay is based on performance, it can be a powerful motivator.[1] To wit, managers who were paying for performance clearly got better results from their subordinates than those who were not. This research contradicts the thinking of those motivation theorists who argue that pay systems can only be a source of dissatisfaction and that they cannot motivate employees to perform at a high level.

Indeed, my research over the years has consistently shown that rewards can have a major impact on employee motivation and the skills that individuals develop (or do not). As a result, they can have a critical impact on an organization's effectiveness.

For decades, traditional hierarchical organizations have followed an almost unquestioned set of rules about how to pay individuals. These rules call for pay to be based more on the worth of jobs than on how well they are done. Most studies of the pay rates in major corporations show that getting promoted into a higher-level job is the most highly rewarded behavior.[2] In large U.S. corporations, senior executives make at least 180 times more than the lowest-paid employees. This number has gotten larger virtually every year since 1980 and is the largest for any democratic country.

Length of time in the organization is also an important factor in determining pay, since merit pay increases are annuities that add up over time, and many benefits such as vacation days and retirement pay are tied directly to seniority. While seniority-oriented reward systems promote stability by encouraging individuals to remain with the organization, they often lead to a mentality in which people feel they deserve more rewards simply because they show up and hold a particular job for a period of time. Performing well—particularly, engaging in the kind of performance that contributes to overall organizational effectiveness rather than simply making the individual look good—is often barely rewarded with a small merit pay increase, if it is rewarded at all.

The Old Logic: Individual Jobs and Individual Pay

Traditional job-based reward systems have come under increased criticism now that organizations have begun to incorporate the new logic principles. In several areas, it has served to highlight their failures and limitations. For example, management experts such as the late W. Edwards Deming have been very critical of such traditional reward practices as the management by objective (MBO) performance appraisal systems used by many companies. An especially negative part of the MBO system is the frequent use of forced distribution approaches, like the one employed by the pharmaceutical company that was mentioned at the beginning of this chapter. They cause individuals to compete with each other in order to get pay increases and bonuses and as a result destroy lateral relationships.

In several of my previous books I have been particularly critical of the emphasis by traditional pay systems on paying for the job rather than what the individuals can do and how they perform.[3] I have argued that pay which rewards the size and nature of the job inappropriately rewards people for "growing their job," by increasing their budget and the number of employees reporting to them. Thus individuals with bigger jobs get higher pay, regardless of their skills and their performance. In other words, the pay system ignores person size; it only focuses on job size.

All in all, job-based pay systems fit the traditional logic of organizing. They support designs in which large amounts of power, information, knowledge, and rewards are at the top of an organization. Since the best way to make more money is to get promoted, they tend to motivate individuals to develop skills that help them move up the hierarchy rather than other skills that may be critical to the organization's success because they contribute to key organizational capabilities and core competencies. Of course, this is not all bad, because some individuals clearly do need to develop in this direction. But it is a problem if the pay system does not also reward people for working and managing laterally—behaviors that are central to a high-performance, team-based organization.

Reward system practices in traditional organizations are very hierarchical. At the bottom level of the organization, individuals are paid for the number of hours they work, have time cards, and are rarely paid for their performance. At the top, managers are paid, at least to a certain degree, for the performance of the firm; receive extensive benefits and perks; and are rewarded with compensation that reinforces their hierarchical position.

I could go on endlessly criticizing traditional pay systems. They are too rigid, too seniority driven, too individually oriented, too expensive, and too secret. At this point, however, it is not particularly useful to further criticize the old. It is far more productive to focus on the alternatives that are needed to support the new logic.

Despite the problems with traditional pay systems, organizations have been reluctant to make fundamental changes in them out of fear that the work force might react negatively or that their salary costs might rise. Fortunately, in the last decade, as the failures of the old systems have become apparent, organizations have been much more willing to try different approaches to pay. This has helped my Center for Effective Organizations at USC develop a substantial base of knowledge about alternatives to traditional pay systems. The way to reward individuals in organizations designed around the six principles of the new logic now seems reasonably clear. As will be seen in the remainder of this chapter, it includes placing a strong emphasis on pay for performance and on pay plans that focus on rewarding individuals for increasing their skills and competencies so they can add more value to their organizations.

Creating Reward Systems for the New Logic

It is not enough to simply say, "Well, if the old is bad, let's just pay everyone the same or pay everyone a fair wage," as some have maintained. We know that won't work. What is fair to one person is not fair to another. Thus, rather than being a solution, this approach is likely to create new problems. More importantly, it misses the opportunity to use rewards as an important piece of organization design, a piece that supports the new logic in the context of the Star Model.

In some situations—volunteer work and amateur athletics, for example—people will perform tasks and often perform them well without money or other tangible rewards being a source of motivation. But in the world of both profit-making and public sector organizations, most individuals will not perform at a world-class level for the sheer intrinsic joy of working hard and doing a good job. To perform at their best, most individuals need to have financial or other extrinsic rewards tied to their performance. This is particularly true when sustained high performance is needed and the novelty and the initial excitement of doing something have worn off. Besides, some tasks that need to be done simply cannot be enriched and made intrinsically rewarding or interesting. Most people will not work on a chicken processing line, answer 411 telephone number information requests, and pick cotton because they are intrinsically rewarding. Although people differ, the fact remains that for most people, they are not.

The challenge for high-performance organizations is to design reward systems that both attract and develop the right individuals and motivate the right performance. Reward systems must be able to motivate effective team performance and motivate individuals to develop the kinds of skills that support key organizational capabilities and competencies. As a rule, reward systems can accomplish these objectives if they

- Focus on an individual's skills and competencies (rather than his or her job)
- Are tied to the organization's performance in ways that support its strategy and structure
- Support the organization's architecture

As each of these issues is addressed in this chapter, the major focus will be on pay systems, since they have the greatest potential to drive performance—that is, they offer both purchasing power and recognition. Of course, as was discussed in Chapter Two, pay is just one of the extrinsic rewards that organizations can give. It is quite possible and important to also use other forms of recognition.

Reward Skills and Competencies, Not Job Size

Because pay levels must reflect market realities and because they affect both the cost of doing business and performance, organizations must pay close attention to the amounts as well as how they pay. If organizations pay dramatically more than their competitors, their costs will be out of line, and they will have trouble competing. If they pay less than their competitors, their costs may be lower, but they will have trouble attracting and retaining competent employees.

There is simply no way an organization can ignore the competitive labor costs in its particular industry, whether it is in a local service business, such as gardening, or competing in a global business, such as auto manufacturing. As was discussed earlier, this reality has caused great difficulty for the many companies in the United States, Japan, and Europe that compete with organizations from low-wage countries. It is also why some companies have redesigned their organizations using the principles of the new logic so that individuals can add value that is more in line with their wage rates.

I realize that it is one thing to say that labor costs must be aligned with those of an organization's competitors and quite another to develop systems that set pay levels based on what others are paying. Historically, most major corporations still do this by paying people based on the value of their jobs. They decide what to pay for jobs based on data they get from organizations that have similar types of jobs.

In order to share job and pay data with each other, most organizations use similar job evaluation systems to measure job size and provide salary survey data. A number of consulting firms, such as Hay, collect data from companies and provide them with information about what other organizations pay their employees. At one point, over 90 percent of the largest companies in the United States used the Hay job evaluation system, a clear testimony to the persuasiveness of the old logic of organizing.

The often unchallenged assumption in the job evaluation approach is that an individual's market value can be determined by looking at the value of his or her job. This assumption makes sense in bureaucratic organizations where individuals with job descriptions do prescribed tasks in a standardized way, especially if many of them are doing the same job. It allows an organization a kind of economy of scale in dealing with individuals. They can all be treated the same and compared to the same external standard or benchmark. This is not only logical, efficient, and fair but also supportive of a pay-for-performance system in which individuals are evaluated on how their job performance compares to others doing the same work.

But the very characteristics that make the job evaluation approach appropriate in the old logic—in jobs where people perform prescribed tasks—can create problems in new logic organizations.

First, it rewards job size, rather than rewarding individuals for developing the skills they need to acquire to add value with their performance. As an example, individuals on an assembly line who learn a task further along the line are unlikely to get additional pay. Indeed, if it is a simpler task, they may be paid less while performing it than they would be paid for doing the task they already know. This is in obvious conflict with the new logic approach where workers must know how to perform all the tasks for which their work team is responsible.

Second, job-based pay systems may not accurately reflect the market value of an individual, because that person may have more skills and abilities than are currently being used in the work they are doing. By not paying for the extra skills, the organization runs the risk of losing individuals to an organization that is willing to pay for all of that person's skills.

Third, job-based pay systems create problems where individuals are expected to work in teams, to do what is needed rather than what is prescribed, to manage themselves, and to make horizontal career moves. A pay system based on job descriptions simply is not the best way to reward these behaviors.

Person-Based Pay: The Alternative to Job-Based Pay

The most obvious alternative to job-based pay is to pay employees according to the market value of their skills, knowledge, and competencies—in short, what they can do. Organizations must be careful as they design these skill-based, or as they are also called, competency-based pay systems. They must be designed to encourage people to learn the behaviors that make a high-performance work system operate effectively. But, at the same time, the pay of individuals must be aligned with the external market. The latter point is particularly important in the new logic because jobs do not have a market value—individuals do. They are the ones that add value and change employers, not jobs.

Individuals change jobs, get outside job offers, and test the market to see if they can make more elsewhere. Jobs do not move from one organization to another or test the market to see what they are worth. This point meshes with the frequently made point that it simply does not make a great deal of sense to use the traditional concept of a job. If individuals are to make their maximum contribution to their organization's success, they simply cannot have a static set of duties that can be described and that capture everything that they are expected to do.

When work requires high levels of skill and knowledge, it is particularly important to reward competencies and skills, as individuals often differ dramatically in their abilities. For example, the best software engineers are immeasurably better than the worst software engineers in much the same way that the best second baseman is many times more valuable than an average second baseman. A job description cannot capture this difference in value the way that a "person description" or a skill description can capture it. Thus, if an organization does not reward people for what they can do, it runs the definite risk of losing its best employees to organizations that are able to recognize the value of exceptionally talented and skilled individuals.

How does skill-based pay work? My first experiences with skill-based pay systems occurred when I began working with high-involvement greenfield manufacturing facilities in the late 1960s and early 1970s. These plants typically operated with self-managing work teams and paid individuals according to the number and kinds of skills that the organization needed and that individuals were willing and able to perform. These plants did not develop skill-based pay because of a consulting firm's recommendation or an academic theory. Rather, plant managers saw that traditional job-based pay did not properly reward individuals who could do seven or eight things, each of which used to be a separate job, and that it did not motivate individuals to learn what was needed.

They also saw that traditional pay made it difficult to adjust pay upward as individuals became more competent, capable, and valuable to the organization. So these organizations began to devise pay plans that changed the pay of individuals as they learned, and paid employees for what they could do, not what they were doing at any given moment. They also created systems to measure whether individuals had mastered the skills. Often, engineers, technical experts, or peers did the skill certification assessments.

The pay plans I saw in the Procter & Gamble and General Foods plants where I consulted were often quite simple. They paid individuals an extra twenty-five or fifty cents an hour for learning specific skills. Those skills were carefully identified, and a system was established to measure whether individuals had mastered them. Often, the presence of a skill was measured simply by having an individual do a particular task for a period of time while others who had mastered that skill evaluated the individual's skill mastery. These assessors were engineers, technical experts, or peers, depending upon the skills and who was in the best position to assess mastery.

I still remember my first visit to a Gaines dog food manufacturing plant that had put in a skill-based pay system in the early

1970s. During my first few minutes inside the plant, I was struck by the vitality of the organization and by the overall competence level of the work force. One of the production workers took me on a tour and told me how the whole plant operated. He seemed to know a great deal about the business side of dog food manufacturing (costs, competitors, quality, and productivity). When we began talking about pay systems, he very clearly explained what he had to learn in order to make more money, as well as how his mastery of those skills would be assessed. He also knew how much he could earn if he learned all the skills that his team used to do their work.

When I sat down to talk with the plant manager, Ed Dulworth, I was very curious about the skill-based pay system. He patiently explained to me that it was the only logical pay system, because in the plant's team structure, individuals really did not have jobs, and the key to effectiveness was whether individuals learned more and did more. My initial skepticism gave way to enthusiasm as I realized that I was seeing a whole new logic of how to pay individuals that are part of a lateral, self-managing, team-based organization.

In retrospect, I now realize that organizations have always paid some individuals for their skills or competencies. For example, engineers, lawyers, accountants, and scientists are usually paid based on degree levels, years of experience, and other indicators of their skills and competencies. Universities typically pay professors for their skills and experience rather than for the size of their job. In research and development labs, "technical ladders" reward individuals for greater and greater depth of knowledge in particular technical areas. These deviations from traditional pay practices—necessary because of the unique value these professionals add—were early examples of today's increasingly popular skill- and competency-based pay systems.

Research data suggest that over 50 percent of the Fortune 1000 companies have skill-based pay systems for at least part of their work force, even though only a few companies cover all their employees.[4] Skill-based pay plans have spread far beyond their early application in newly built manufacturing plants. For example, I have helped to install skill-based pay in financial service firms and in a wide range of manufacturing sites that have switched from traditional work designs to ones based on the new logic. In many of these cases, the plans cover managers (where the term *competency-based pay* is more popular) as well as other employees.

Designing Skill-Based Pay Systems

Organizations can use the following approaches to create a pay system that is based on skills, knowledge, and competencies:

- They can tie specific pay raises to learning identified skills. This is the approach that is taken in most of the new high-involvement plants.
- They can create broad pay bands that allow individuals to receive significant pay increases as they learn additional skills. That is, instead of putting people in a pay range in which the top is about 50 percent higher than the bottom, they can use a range in which the top is almost double the bottom. This leaves a great deal of room for pay to rise as employees continue to learn.
- They can give employees one-time lump-sum payments when they develop new skills. This is particularly appropriate where the use of the skills is temporary or short-term, or where pay is already high and it is difficult for the organization to afford an ongoing extra cost.
- They can tie promotions or changes in pay grades to increases in skills. This is the approach that is taken with technical ladders and some competency-based plans for managers.

Some examples: Polaroid has developed a skill-based pay system to cover all of its employees. Frito-Lay has followed Polaroid's lead with a skill-based pay plan for managers. In addition, many organizations are installing broad-banding pay programs for managers. General Electric now has only six management pay grades, as opposed to as many as twelve in the past, and these grades have a range that almost doubles from bottom to top.

Broad-banding by itself does not answer the question of how individuals progress in pay; all it does is make it easier to pay for skills and simplify the problem of putting people and/or jobs into a pay grade. It is easier because there are simply fewer grades in which to put employees or jobs. With forty, fifty, or sixty pay grades, the differences between each grade are small, and thus the decision of where to put an individual or job can be difficult.

In many respects, person-based pay combines nicely with broad-banding if companies use the acquisition of skills or competencies to determine how an individual progresses through a particular pay band. It can encourage individuals to make lateral moves, because the pay system has enough flexibility to reward individuals for this type of career move. As noted earlier, traditional pay systems, in contrast, usually punish someone for making a lateral career move. They get no credit for the skills that they have . learned in their previous job when it is at the same level. They are simply paid based on the size of their new job.

Challenges in Designing Skill-Based Pay

Research over the last twenty years shows that skill- or competency-based pay represents a much better fit with the new logic than does job-based pay.[5] It also shows that competency-based pay works well when organizations:

- Assess skills properly so that individuals are paid only for what they can do
- Identify the skills that individuals need in order to perform effectively (as was discussed in the last chapter, well-developed person descriptions are needed)
- Price both individuals and their skills accurately relative to the external market and avoid the all-too-common practice of using comparisons of one internal job with another to determine pay levels

Admittedly, market pricing can be difficult with skill-based pay, especially since so many organizations still use job-based pay. However, there is always one highly reliable indicator organizations can use: how much successful competitors are actually paying to hire and recruit people like the ones they want to employ.

Individuals in high-performance work systems with skill-based pay are often paid more than their counterparts in traditional organizations. But because of leaner staffing and a flatter hierarchy, the total labor cost for the organization is lower. In short, they are paid more but they add more value. And that is a win-win situation for the organization and for the employees. Both make more money.

Finally, as emphasized so often in earlier chapters, skill-based pay—like the other features of new logic organizational design—should not be adopted without the other features of a high-performance work system. The reason? If skill-based pay is adopted on its own, a bureaucratic organization may prevent people from using their full range of skills to add value to the organization's products. So it may not make good economic sense to pay individuals for most or all of their skills if they cannot use them. In a new logic organization, however, it often does make sense to pay for a wide range of skills, because individuals can use them to add value to their work.

Pay for Performance: Creating a Motivator

Individual pay for performance is as American as apple pie and Thanksgiving turkey. Unfortunately, in many work settings it has become a turkey because it does not motivate employees; in still others, it motivates the wrong behavior.

During the last twenty years, little new or different has been said or written about the problems and potential of pay as a motivator. Still, its usefulness continues to be debated. One of the best books on pay as a motivator, *Money and Motivation*, was written in 1955 by William F. Whyte.[6] It makes all the points about pay as a motivator (how it works, how it misfires, who it motivates, the problems it causes, the way workers defeat the systems that managers develop) that seem to be forgotten and overlooked when organizations design their pay systems. The same problems that Whyte identifies seem to be regularly "discovered" by new critics of pay for performance.

Although Whyte does not say it directly, he shows that one of the greatest problems in creating motivating pay systems is management greed. When systems are successful and employees make more money, management often becomes concerned that employees are making too much money. They then try to see if they can't get the same level of performance for less money by reducing the size of the bonus or by raising the standard an individual must reach in order to earn a particular bonus. He gives example after example of individuals on incentive plans who perform at less than their potential because they fear management will raise the performance standard and thus make it harder for them just to keep their income level where it is.

I am always struck by the contrast between the attitude of managers who are concerned about employees making too much money and the attitudes of managers at Lincoln Electric. Management there is happy when employees make more money, because it means that they are more productive and that the organization, too, will make more money.[7]

Thinkers as diverse as Fred Herzberg, Abraham Maslow, and W. Edwards Deming have argued against pay for performance on the grounds that it usually causes dysfunctional behavior and that people are not motivated by money but by intrinsic rewards. Obviously, both of these arguments cannot be true. If pay motivates dysfunctional behavior, it clearly affects behavior and must be important enough to affect performance. If pay were not a motivator, it would not prompt any kind of behavior, dysfunctional or otherwise.

Even though I argued in Chapter Two that pay can be a positive motivator for most individuals, it is hard to argue with the view that it often motivates dysfunctional behavior. For decades, the literature has been full of cases where pay incentives cause employees to hide work, build the wrong products, optimize short-term profitability, cheat customers, and give poor service. But the dysfunctional behaviors are the fault of poorly designed pay systems, not evidence that pay cannot be an effective motivator. Individuals do these dysfunctional things because, quite simply, their pay plans reward them for it. As was mentioned in Chapter Two, the research literature on motivation shows that organizations get more of the behavior they reward and less of the behavior that they fail to reward.

Two examples: When I studied the sales staff in Sears stores, I discovered that the salespeople had developed a way to allocate customers in order to make sure that everyone had a fair chance to earn the sales commissions that were based on the amount they sold as individuals. To give everyone an equal number of sales opportunities, the employees rotated their contacts with customers who called or walked into the department. When a salesperson "owned" a customer, he or she was responsible for all dealings with that person. This mostly functional practice helped to avoid arguments and disputes among the employees. But it got complicated, as you may well be able to imagine.

Ownership began when customers called on the phone. Since the salesperson who took the call owned the customer, the first question a customer was asked when he or she entered the sales area or called was whether he or she had spoken to any salesperson before. Employees then endeavored to match the customer with the original salesperson—a process that became quite dysfunctional when that salesperson was not available and when the customer simply wanted to be served, often having forgotten whom he or she had dealt with before. The situation was even worse with exchanges. Customers often had to wait until the salesperson who got the commission on the purchase was available to help them. If that salesperson was not in the store, other salespeople would refuse to handle the exchange because they were not rewarded for doing so.

Several years later, I studied an individual pay plan at a ball-bearing plant where incentives kicked in when production exceeded "normal performance." I found that all but four of the 320 individuals in the plant performed at 140 percent of "normal." The others—all union officers—performed at 200 percent of "normal." It seemed obvious to me that pay was motivating behavior, but the question was, why was it producing these particular results?

I found that the employees felt that 140 percent was the amount that one could produce without causing the production standard to be raised. As for the union officials, they felt—and it was apparently true—that because of their status, their standards would not be raised even if they substantially exceeded 140 percent.

As part of an effort to change the pay system in this organization, I held a meeting with the union leadership and management. During that meeting, union officers admitted that the entire performance of the plant could be increased by about 20 to 30 percent if management would agree to freeze the standards so that employees would not be worried about having to work harder in order to make the same amount of money in the future. Management never agreed to this proposition, because they were concerned that employees would "make too much money." Again, the comparison to Lincoln Electric and their attitude about employees making too much is striking.

Motivating with Important Rewards

As discussed in Chapter Two, the research literature on motivation suggests that individuals respond to extrinsic rewards only when those rewards are important to them. That is why money can work well as a reward. It is important to most of us, especially when it involves large amounts, such as a bonus or pay increase of 10 percent or more. The problem with the financial reward programs in most companies is simple: they are underfunded. Most people are simply not motivated by the chance to earn a 5 percent pay increase for exceptional performance when average performers receive a 4 percent increase. Similarly, a five-hundred-dollar year-end bonus is simply not large enough to motivate most people.

The situation is more complex when organizations use non-financial rewards. Many employees do not place a great financial value on the hats, T-shirts, tickets to plays, and trips that companies often give out. Yet these rewards can be of value if they are given out in a way that indicates recognition of a special achievement. But it is important to be cognizant of the culture. For example, in many Western cultures, individuals very much enjoy being singled out for special attention and praise. But in many Eastern and Asian cultures, this is not true. In fact, individual recognition can be painful for people, because it may be seen as showing up other members of the group.

Thus organizations need to be sure that the rewards they use to motivate performance are important to their members. Clearly, as Chapter Two stressed, importance varies from individual to individual and from group to group. For some, a pay increase may be the most meaningful reward, while for others, an all-expenses-paid trip with spouse to a resort may be more valued than its cash equivalent. The challenge, of course, occurs when organizations have diverse work forces: rewards must be customized so that individuals receive the reward they value.

How is it possible to identify the rewards that employees value most? The best way is to let individuals choose their rewards. In some reward-for-performance systems, individuals can choose between stock and cash or between trips and the cash equivalent, or they can choose how they want to invest their profit-sharing funds. With increasingly diverse work forces, choice makes more and more sense, because it is difficult to predict what rewards they will value. Indeed, it may be that only a cash reward will be important enough to motivate all employees.

Another option: create a homogeneous work force and target rewards that appeal to its members. As I mentioned earlier, this can be accomplished with realistic job previews and careful selection. Mary Kay Cosmetics has used this strategy with its "Pink Cadillac" reward for sales excellence. Similarly, Lincoln Electric has developed a work force that values cash compensation.

Connecting Rewards and Desired Behaviors: Line of Sight

No reward—whether it be a pay increase, a promotion, or a desired form of recognition—can be a motivator unless there is a clear line of sight between what the employee is doing and the reward for doing it. Line of sight means that employees believe that there is a direct connection between their performance and the desired reward. As mentioned in Chapter Two, when there is no perceived connection between how individuals perform and how they are rewarded, employees will not be motivated to behave as the organization wants them to, even if they are "lucky" enough to receive the reward.

Ironically, despite their label, traditional merit-pay salary systems are probably the worst offenders with respect to paying for performance and providing motivation. The biggest problem is that even though organizations often say they base merit raises on performance, they administer these programs in a way that creates no clear connection between performance and reward. They suffer from a reliance on subjective performance appraisals and are further damaged by the use of "secret processes" that translate a performance rating into a certain percentage of extra pay. It is not surprising, given the way the systems operate in most companies, that study after study has found that merit pay systems are not motivational.[8] As a result, many organizations end up using an enormous amount of time to allocate small amounts of money to individuals based on an uncertain assessment of performance in the hope that performance will improve. In many ways, it is a kind of corporate fantasy or rain dance that takes time, effort, and resources but has few, if any, positive outcomes.

Paying Teams for Performance

An individual pay-for-performance system does not fit an organization that is designed around processes and teams and that emphasizes the importance of lateral relationships and cooperation. As Deming and many others have pointed out, individuals who need to cooperate and help each other should not be put in a position of competing for the same rewards. Even the common (and ineffective) strategy of adding a performance category on the appraisal form that rates an individual's level of cooperation does not create the desired result. Instead of spending their energy working to reach team performance goals, employees are motivated to compete to see who will be rated the most cooperative.

Individuals on teams need to be rewarded based on the team's performance. This is hard for most American and some European organizations to accept. They immediately become worried about the so-called freeloader who does not perform as well as the rest of the team but gets the same reward and about the individual star who gets the same reward as everyone else. Both of these worries will inevitably arise in a group reward situation, but they are not necessarily dysfunctional.

The "inequity" that results from everyone getting the same reward despite differences in their performance can have a positive impact on the team's behavior. Poor performers can be encouraged by the team either to improve or to leave, and the outstanding performer can be given special social recognition and other rewards by the team.

The design of a group- or team-based pay-for-performance system should follow the groupings in the organization's overall architecture and work design. It is important that pay systems reward individuals who work in a very interdependent manner in the same way. This is critical in order to connect the reward and structure points on the Star Model. There are a variety of approaches that can be used. In highly integrated organizations, employees may well be rewarded primarily for the performance of the entire organization. For organizations with several businesses, pay-for-performance systems should reward business unit performance, team performance, or perhaps both.[9]

In situations where work teams are relatively independent and measurable goals can be set for each team, the simplest way to reward teams is to pay them based on whether they accomplish their team goals. For example, if a team makes an entire product or has sole accountability for serving a particular customer, it makes sense to reward that team for the results that they control (for example, quality, cost, and customer satisfaction).

But in situations where self-managing work teams do not create their own product or do not have complete responsibility for a set of customers, a reward system that focuses on team performance may be counterproductive. Work teams often tend to become very myopic and focus on optimizing their own performance, not their relationships with other teams. Rewarding them for their team's performance can aggravate these tendencies. Often, the best reward system for interdependent teams is one based on the performance of their plant, business unit, or entire organization.

The challenges in rewarding project teams are somewhat different. Members of project teams need to be rewarded for the performance of the team so that they focus their attention and effort on making the project successful.[10] All too often, organizations reward employees for their individual performance during the time that they are on a project team. This can distract them from the team's overall success and motivate them to do the wrong things. For example, if engineers are rewarded as individuals but are assigned to a product development team, they may spend too much of their energy focusing on pleasing their manager in the engineering department rather than focusing on their contributions to the project.

Since project team performance is usually a one-time event, project teams should receive bonuses rather than merit salary increases. Bonuses allow larger rewards because they do not become a permanent cost to the organization. They also ensure that individuals don't get an annuity for what is essentially a one-time contribution (a flaw in all merit pay systems).

Overall, it is probably more important to reward project teams as teams than it is to reward self-managing work teams as teams.

Because self-managing work teams have an ongoing relationship and a sense of permanence about them, they are more likely to be driven by their ongoing interest in the work and by the peer pressures that can develop in a team committed to high performance. But in project teams, because of their temporary nature, there may be a lack of pressure to perform. Regardless of whether there is a team-based pay-for-performance plan, both types of teams can usually be made more effective by a pay system that rewards them for organizational performance.

Rewards for Organizational Performance

Traditional pay systems often create seams in organizations by using different reward systems for different groups. For example, many organizations have special bonus plans for senior managers and different plans for middle managers. The top executives, for example, often receive stock options. Rather than integrating organizations and creating a sense of common direction, purpose, and involvement, these reward programs divide organizations into groups of employees who focus on different objectives and agendas.

The most extreme version of a divisive pay system occurs when only senior management is heavily rewarded for stock performance and short-term profitability. This can mean that senior management earns a large financial reward when it reduces wages and staffing at lower levels, because such short-term moves often improve the organization's cost performance and stock price. But the rest of the individuals in the organization lose in this scenario and quickly realize that what is good for senior management is not necessarily good for them.

I am not saying that individuals at higher organizational levels should not have the highest pay nor that they should not be given stock and stock options. Instead I am arguing that the trajectory of their performance-based rewards (whether it be up or down) should be the same as it is for other members of the organization.

Certain perquisite and benefit programs can also create dysfunctional seams in an organization. Examples include benefit programs that are different for senior managers than for the rest of the organization, tiered plans that give each level in the organization a different set of benefits, and corporate perquisites—

such as parking and country club memberships—that are based on hierarchical levels. Although this kind of stratification may not be as problematic as the stratification produced by different bonus and pay-for-performance systems, it still has no place in a high-performance organization that follows the principles of the new logic, because it works against the key principles of integration, leadership, and involvement. Pay systems should unite an organization, not create unnecessary and dysfunctional divisions.

Making Employees Owners:
Gain Sharing, Profit Sharing, and Stock

One type of collective pay-for-performance system that has proven to be effective is gain sharing.[11] It typically focuses on a business unit, plant, or division of an organization and rewards all individuals for controllable improvements in performance. It works best when it focuses on a relatively small number of people (less than five hundred) and on measures of performance that everyone can influence.[12] For example, in a gold mining organization I studied, individuals were rewarded for increasing their productivity and controlling the cost of mining the gold. It did not reward them based on the sales price of the gold, because that was beyond the control of the work force.

The most positive feature of gain sharing: it includes all employees of the business unit. As a result, it can be a tremendous integrating force for an organization. It does not create the kind of hierarchical stratification that can cause conflict among different levels in the organization. Moreover, since it covers all the individuals who are involved with the product or service, it creates lateral integration.

When gain-sharing plans are in place, I have seen individuals throughout an organization ask other employees about what they are doing and make suggestions about how they can do it better in order to improve the overall performance of the organization. In one organization with which I consulted, production workers talked to the chief financial officer about improving the accounts receivable function, and together they were able to improve the delivery process, which the made accounts receivable more easily collectible.

Motorola, Dana, Monsanto, Herman Miller, and a host of other companies have gain-sharing plans in some or all of their plants. The plants are not in competition with each other, since each plant is measured against its own history, and all plants can be winners. Still, because these plans do not cover an entire organization, they do create seams or divisions among the plants that are on separate plans. The seams, however, are not dysfunctional, when the design of the organization is to have the plants operate independently. If they need to operate in an integrated and cooperative way, the plants should not be on separate plans. They should be on a common plan that encourages them to integrate their efforts.

There are two effective ways to deliver organization-wide pay for performance in a new logic organization: company-wide profit sharing and stock option or stock ownership plans. Such plans integrate the organization vertically and horizontally and help solve the equity issue mentioned earlier, in which only stockholders and senior management who hold options and participate in profit-sharing plans benefit when performance improves.

I am particularly intrigued with the idea of making every employee in high-performance organizations a stockholder. This has been done in some traditional organizations, with mixed results because of the poor fit with the nature of the management systems.[13] It is difficult for individuals in traditional organizations to influence financial performance, so aligning their interests with those of the shareholders has little motivational value. But in high-performance systems, aligning everyone's interests can reduce many of the potential conflicts between what is good for shareholders, what is good for senior management, and what is good for the rest of the work force. It also has the potential to be a more effective motivator.

In high-performance work systems, the extra education, training, information, and power that employees have can dramatically strengthen the line of sight between their behavior and measures of business performance such as profits. With knowledge of the business, individuals can see how their behavior makes a difference in the operating results of their business unit and in many cases of their company. They can also see how they can influence and support others' efforts and how their combined work can result in higher performance and rewards for everyone.

It is critical to emphasize here that there is no reason why an employee cannot be part of more than one pay-for-performance system. It is quite possible to have a nested set of pay-for-performance systems in which an individual may be paid based on two, three, or four levels of organizational performance. They might, for example, be paid based on the performance of their team, their geographical unit, and their business unit. They may also be part of corporate profit-sharing and stock ownership plans.

An important consideration in establishing multiple pay-for-performance plans is the basic architecture of the organization. As noted in Chapters Four and Five, some organizations are designed to operate with multiple independent business units. In these organizations, it makes sense to have separate bonus plans for each of these business units, because they have little need to cooperate with each other. A reward system that creates seams among them may be quite functional because it improves the lines of sight for each of them.

Separate plans also make sense for front-back organizations, where organizational design calls for semi-autonomous units optimizing their performance. In the case of single business organizations that depend on lateral integration across the total organization, the situation is very different. The key issue in these organizations is developing reward systems that cover everyone in the corporation so that they support integration and a common sense of purpose and destiny. A good rule of thumb with respect to reward system design is that the reward system should treat everyone who is highly interdependent in a common manner.

It is important for corporations to develop an organization-wide pay-for-performance system, such as profit sharing, at the beginning of the transition to a high-performance work design. Once this is done, it can prevent situations where senior managers gain tremendously from the conversion to a high-performance work system while the rest of the organization goes through an unrewarded, stressful, and difficult transformation. It can also prevent situations where the reward system slows or blocks the creation of a high-performance organization because this point on the organizational Star Model is not in alignment.

Making Pay for Performance Work

At this point, it may sound as though I am arguing for always having a pay-for-performance system in high-performance work organizations. I am not. I realize that they are not always needed or wanted. In some situations, organizations do not have the ingredients necessary to operate an effective system. Without a good ability to measure performance results, a strong management commitment to pay for performance, and an organizational set of values and philosophies that support it, no pay-for-performance system will work.

I once consulted with a furniture manufacturing plant in which a gain-sharing plan seemed like the obvious addition to its employee involvement efforts. I was never able, however, to convince the plant manager that it was the right thing to do. He consistently said things like, "these guys are already paid well enough," "they should be happy to have a job," "we do not need to bribe them to get them to perform well—they owe it to us." Despite his lack of enthusiasm, I convinced the owner of the plant to go ahead with a gain-sharing plan. Although it was somewhat successful, the plant manager's continuing tendency to call it an "employee bribe program" definitely limited its success.

The most common obstacle to developing a pay-for-performance system is the lack of good performance measures. A notorious instance of improper measurement occurred recently when a number of Sears stores rewarded service order writers in their auto service departments based on the average size of repair bills. This resulted in a dramatic increase in the size of service orders, but it also meant that a lot of unneeded repair work was done. Ultimately, when this "little problem" was discovered by investigators for several states, Sears was fined millions of dollars. The example certainly highlights the point that reward systems can often produce dysfunctional behavior precisely because employees do what they are rewarded for.

There are some advocates of high-performance work systems who strongly oppose the use of all pay-for-performance approaches. They argue that involvement in the business along with challenging work is enough to drive performance, and that pay-for-performance systems will simply cause employees to focus on trying to optimize the payout rather than trying to improve performance and satisfy customers.

None of the very successful Procter & Gamble high-performance manufacturing plants have pay-for-performance plans that cover most of the employees (they do pay their managers on performance-based pay systems, creating a potentially counterproductive seam in the plants). To my way of thinking, this represents a major internal inconsistency in the work design and in the organization's mission. These plants are in business to make money, and I see nothing wrong with the employees sharing in their success.

In fact, I see something quite positive about it. It could cause everyone to focus more on organizational effectiveness and on how useful their behavior is. Senior managers at Procter & Gamble, however, feel that the risks of putting in pay-for-performance plans are great, and they have pointed out to me that the plants are successful, so why risk change? My answer: because success tomorrow depends on getting better and learning to use organizational practices such as pay for performance as a source of competitive advantage.

To summarize this discussion: the challenge for high-performance organizations is to create reward systems that are motivating and at the same time reinforce their structures and design. As has been noted, this can best be done by rewarding teams, business units, and the whole organization. There is little or no room for such traditional pay practices as merit pay. The principles of the new logic instead call for team bonuses, gain-sharing plans, stock option plans, and stock ownership plans.

As with other management systems, pay systems must focus on the skills and competencies of individuals. Why? In order to perform at a high level, an organization needs the right mix of capabilities and competencies to implement its strategy. These will exist only if it attracts, retains, and develops people who have the right skills.

As will be discussed in more detail in the next chapter, critical elements in building effective pay-for-performance systems that mesh with the new logic are the measurement and communication processes of the organization. They must provide information that helps individuals understand the business and that serves as a basis for rewarding people for business performance.

Chapter Ten

Communication and Measurement

Supporting New Logic Management

- Lateral processes are the key to organizational effectiveness.
- Involvement is the most effective source of control.

Measurement and communication processes that fit the new logic are key to the effectiveness of virtually every new logic management practice discussed so far. The new logic makes very different assumptions than the traditional logic does about how this point on the Star Model should be designed. Specifically, it differs with respect to what should be measured and when, how, and to whom performance information should be communicated.

Employees in a business that is structured around the principles of the new logic need to know what goals and targets they should be striving to achieve and also have a good sense of how the organization is performing. The reason? As was highlighted in the Chapter One discussion of the importance of balancing power, information, knowledge, and rewards—unless information about performance moves throughout the organization, widespread employee involvement in the business is impossible.

Measurement and communication are critical, too, in creating a high-performance organization that relies on lateral processes instead of hierarchical ones. Lateral coordination around key processes and customers is possible only if individuals at the same level in the organization can work cooperatively and exchange performance information. In the absence of adequate lateral communication, hierarchy and its vertical communication processes are the only ways to coordinate behavior.

Advocates of profit sharing, employee stock ownership, and gain sharing have long recognized that openly sharing organizational performance information is critical to motivating employees and helping them understand what they are supposed to do. Performance measures indicate what the organization values and what employees should focus on accomplishing. As mentioned in the previous chapter, without widely communicated, well-defined measures of performance, it is impossible to effectively tie rewards such as pay to performance and to the mission of the organization. It is also difficult for employees to contribute to and enjoy the success of the organization.

One organization that has received considerable publicity for its approach to measurement and communication is Springfield Remanufacturing, a small reconditioner of diesel engines. Springfield uses an open-book approach that shares virtually all financial information with the entire work force. Everyone at Springfield knows the return on sales and the costs of doing business. In addition, the company has increased the financial knowledge of its work force. It has developed innovative courses to train employees in how financial data are computed and what they mean to the success of the company.

Springfield certainly deserves credit for its open-book management. But it has not discovered a new breakthrough approach. It is doing exactly what companies that effectively use profit sharing and gain sharing have done—and known about—for decades. When organizations share performance data freely, all employees can understand the payoff from good financial results. Open-book management is fundamental to the whole idea of involving employees in the organization's vision and allowing them to be self-managing. In this chapter, I will expand on this point by first looking at when, how, and to whom performance information should be communicated, and then at what should be measured and how the measures should be used.

The New Logic of Communication

In traditional organizations, information about corporate performance is extremely important to senior management. Measures of organizational performance—such as number of units produced, numbers of defects, return on sales, and performance compared to budget—help senior management direct and control operations. Performance information is carefully guarded, often out of the fear that it may be misused or perhaps even leaked to competitors and the outside world. There is also the belief that with a few exceptions, employees do not need most performance information because the design of the organization is such that most employees are held accountable only for how they handle their particular job responsibilities; communication concerning business performance is put on a "need to know" basis.

Even with more organizations using the principles of the new logic, our ongoing study of the Fortune 1000 indicates that as recently as 1993, only 46 percent of them shared basic profit-and-loss information with all or most of their employees.[1] This lack of information sharing is particularly striking because all these companies are publicly traded, and as a result, these data are hardly proprietary.

To share profit information, organizations would only need to provide annual reports to all of their employees. But they do not. Why? When I ask senior management in most organizations, they are usually surprised by the question and then respond in a way consistent with the old logic. For example: "Employees don't need to know that type of information. (pause) Do you think they would be interested?"

Our study also found that organizations are even more secretive about their business plans, the financial performance of their business units, and comparisons of their performance with the performance of their major competitors. Fewer than 20 percent of the Fortune 1000 companies gave a majority of their employees this type of financial information. Secrecy about performance—especially the failure to talk about the performance of competitors—is particularly damaging. My research indicates that a sense of competitive necessity is a key to overcoming resistance to change. Without this information, it is hard for employees to understand the seriousness of the competition they face. Given that the survival of most organizations depends upon winning in a competitive marketplace, why don't organizations share such information? Again, the old logic suggests employees do not need such information—they simply need to do their jobs well.

Clearly, some organizations do a good job of communicating their plans and business results to their work force. For example, the president of GTE periodically meets with all of his employees through an internal interactive television network that reaches many of the company's locations around the country (tapes are created for employees who cannot attend the live sessions). At a recent meeting, he outlined how he saw GTE evolving over time in terms of its relationship to customers and technology and discussed recent operating results and some major acquisitions that the organization had made. The session ended with a question-and-answer period in which employees could ask the CEO anything they wanted about the business.

GTE is not alone in holding these kinds of sessions. Herman Miller and Hewlett-Packard also share financial information with employees through frequent meetings and televised events. At other companies—Microsoft and Sun Microsystems are just two examples—employees can ask the CEO questions by E-mail, and the CEO typically promises to get an answer to them within a few days.

These companies take these steps for a simple reason: they believe that in order for employees to care about the financial performance of their organization, they need to know about it and be able to compare it to that of other organizations. Of course, simply providing financial information to employees so that they can see how the business is operating financially is not enough to ensure that employees know what to do and are motivated to do it. Employees also need a sense of the company's goals, its competitive strategy, and the consequences of performance for them.

Playing the Game with the New Logic

There are many parallels between the world of sports and the new logic of high-performance organizations. People around the world invest considerable energy in such competitive sports as soccer, football, tennis, basketball, and golf. Many of us participate either directly or vicariously. The great majority of sports participants do not get paid for their efforts. Yet they are willing to devote untold hours to practice so they can perform at higher and higher levels, and when the sport is played, they put forth tremendous effort. Here is why:

- The results are public. Everyone who follows a sport and participates in one knows how each player or team is doing. How else would there be competition?

- Measures of performance are used so that participants can determine how well they did relative to others. In sports such as golf or track and field, fixed performance standards also exist (par for a hole, time records). Measures and standards have meaning because everyone understands how they are set and generally accepts that they are a reasonable benchmark for measuring performance.

- With few exceptions, there is ongoing feedback. Sports performers do not have to wait until the end of the competition to find out whether they are ahead or behind or how other participants are doing.

- Most sports are based on the performance of individuals (as in golf) or on relatively small teams (with one hundred or fewer members). As a result, individuals have strong lines of sight for their performance or their team's performance.

- Performance can be measured at several levels, from individual to group to the entire organization. American football is a good example. It has measures for individual performance; for groups such as offense, defense, and special teams; and for the entire team.

Golf is a classic example of an individually motivating sport. Golfers go out and practice on their own simply because they find it satisfying. A key reason? When they hit a golf ball, they know instantly how well they have hit it. Imagine practicing golf—or any sport for that matter—where no feedback is available. Shooting a basketball, for example, without seeing whether it goes into the basket is unlikely to produce learning, motivation, or aspirations of higher performance. Of course, some individuals play golf because, in addition to intrinsic satisfaction, they can earn millions of dollars. They are in the very desirable position of doing something that they find intrinsically challenging and interesting and that rewards them handsomely when they do it well. Incidentally, I do not know of any evidence which shows that the opportunity to make money decreases their intrinsic motivation to play golf, as might be suggested by motivation theorists who worry that financial rewards damage intrinsic motivation.

I believe that we can learn some important lessons from the measurement and communication processes in sports. It is interesting to compare them to similar processes in business organizations. In the old logic, measurement and communication processes are closed; in sports they are open. In traditional organizations, only those at the top know the results, whereas in sports everyone knows. Old logic measures are often obscure and difficult to understand, and feedback is intermittent or nonexistent. Sports emphasize clearly understood measures and timely feedback.

In sports, measures provide strong lines of sight, whereas workers in traditional organizations often see no connection between their activities and their company's success. Sports cover relatively small groups of individuals; old logic organizations often produce profit-and-loss statements and financial performance reports only for very large groups of people. Traditional command-and-control organizations have problems motivating performance; the same cannot be said for sports. The challenge for new logic, high-performance organizations is clear: create and implement measurement and communication systems similar in nature to those in competitive sports.

Consistently Communicating Goals, Plans, and Performance Results

In the absence of elaborate control systems, an organization can guide employees' behavior only if it consistently and frequently communicates to them what the plans, goals, and objectives are for each work group and for the total organization. Even though this point may seem obvious and certainly has been stated before both in this book and in others, many organizations do not communicate their goals and plans to most employees. Further, they do not involve them in establishing goals and objectives (which is often the best way to communicate and gain commitment to them).

Equally as troublesome, many organizations still fail to let employees know how well they are performing.[2]

For years I have studied individual performance appraisal and performance management systems and have consistently observed what I call the "vanishing performance appraisal." Despite the existence of formal systems, many supervisors simply do not conduct performance appraisals. Even more disappointing, some supervisors who conduct appraisals do not give any meaningful feedback to their subordinates. One reason for this: they are uncomfortable with giving feedback and, in many cases, their subordinates are fearful of receiving it. In their minds, many managers believe they are doing their subordinates a favor by not doing an appraisal that may embarrass either or both of them.

I first discovered the vanishing performance appraisal phenomenon at a research and development lab that I studied. The lab had a requirement that every employee be appraised annually and be given feedback about his or her performance. But my interviews with employees indicated that most of them felt that they had either never had a performance appraisal or certainly not had one within the last few years. Yet when I interviewed their managers, almost without exception they claimed to have appraised all of their subordinates within the last year, and, indeed, a review of the company records showed that appraisal forms had been filled out.

It was not until my follow-up interviews that I discovered why the records showed that the employees had been appraised but the employees did not know it. When asked how appraisals had been done, managers rarely described dedicated meetings at scheduled times during which they and their subordinates discussed either appraisal forms or specific performance results. Instead, the managers said that during "conversations" they had let their subordinates know how they felt about their performance and encouraged them to do well in the future. Not surprisingly, when I talked again to employees they were quite surprised that anyone would have thought of the conversations in question as formal appraisals. They had viewed them simply as casual interactions with their bosses.

The communication problems in most organizations are not confined to the failure to give individuals feedback about their performance and the failure to give them information about corporate performance. The data from our study of the Fortune 1000, which show that employees are much less likely to get information about the operating results of their business units than they are information about corporate results, suggest it is a more general problem. The reason: the traditional logic still dominates in most corporations, leading to the false belief that business unit operating results are so sensitive that only senior management can be trusted with them. But in reality, there may be a greater risk in not communicating them. Failing to share this information creates a seam in an organization between those who know and those who do not and, perhaps more importantly, makes it difficult for employees to measure how they are doing.

The principles of the new logic call for an entirely different approach. As noted in Chapter Seven, performance measurement is a key factor in team effectiveness. It's no surprise then that some of the most successful team-based plants that I have studied post performance results publicly so that everyone on the team and on all other teams can see them. That way the team gets feedback and the organization can recognize and reward good performance.

When I recently visited an auto parts plant that follows the new logic, I saw performance scoreboards throughout the plant that included the pictures of all the employees who worked in each production area or cell. Performance objectives were posted for the day, the week, and the year. Graphs everywhere showed quality, production, and cost numbers for the year. Comparative data was available on how other manufacturers were doing, which included data from J.D. Power, the quality measurement firm, on how the plant's car compared to other cars.

All this is in marked contrast to the old logic information and measurement systems that U.S. organizations used in the 1970s and 1980s. They focused on production numbers and performance against budget with respect to the costs of labor, materials, and supplies. Most employees had no information about these budgets and, in many cases, did not even know the budgets for their own departments or work areas. In addition, production schedules were kept secret for fear that somehow employees would misuse the information and reduce their work pace.

There was no information available on how well competing plants—either foreign or domestic—were doing. Quality data focused on rejects at the end of the production line—not on how customers viewed the quality of the products or services. With this tremendous information vacuum, is it any wonder that many employees in American companies were surprised to find that their plants were not world class when compared to the U.S. plants of Japanese companies or to plants in Japan, Singapore, Germany, and other leading manufacturing countries?

Using Communication to Improve Motivation

The discussion of motivation in Chapter Two stressed that for employees to be intrinsically motivated, they must know how well they and their business are performing. The more immediate the feedback, the more motivating the work.

When individuals can see the results of their efforts, feedback can be direct and immediate; no measurement system is needed. In golf, for example, individuals watch the flight of the ball they have hit and receive direct feedback; other measures such as strokes used and final score also tell golfers how they are doing. In business, there are also examples of direct feedback. Customers make buying decisions after salespeople explain a product to them. Computer programs operate once data have been entered.

But feedback from the work itself is rarely enough. It is also important for organizations to make available other forms of performance feedback—measures of profit, customer satisfaction, and return on investment. These measures are particularly meaningful and powerful when put within the context of an overall strategic plan for the organization.

Pay and recognition systems rely heavily on measurements and communication to establish a motivating line of sight between behavior and rewards. The most common failing of reward systems is that employees are not told how their performance will be measured and are rarely given any detailed information on the connection between the measures of their performance and the amount of financial reward they receive.[3] They are simply told that they earned an X percent merit increase or bonus and that they should accept the fact that pay is based on performance.

With this kind of sketchy information, pay does not motivate performance because people cannot see a relationship between their behavior and the specific amount of their reward. The fact that the relative size of individual pay rewards is seldom communicated further compounds the situation. Individuals must trust that they are being paid in a fair and reasonable manner. When pay rates and performance results are public, individuals know if they are being paid fairly for their performance.

Publicizing pay rates is unacceptable in traditional organizations because it puts too much power into the hands of people who are being appraised and given raises. They are in a position where they can challenge and question the decisions of supervisors on a much more informed basis. Keeping pay information secret concentrates information and knowledge and therefore power at higher levels in the organization. Secrecy has been and continues to be the operating model in Shell, Kellogg, Mobil, IBM, and virtually every major American and European company. At IBM, for example, individuals have been fired for talking about their pay rates because they are considered "company sensitive data" and not for others to know.

Pay secrecy in a traditional logic organization is not always a bad thing. In the traditional logic organizations where I have seen public pay, it typically causes more problems than positives. Making pay public often shows that it is not well administered and diverts a tremendous amount of the organization's time and effort toward explaining how existing pay rates came about. The final result is often a situation in which all employees doing the same job are simply paid the same, with perhaps some allowance for seniority—the same system that is used throughout national, state, and local governments. This occurs because it is difficult to administer performance-based pay in a top-down way and, at the same time, have it in the public domain. When pay becomes public, employees want input and understanding, which is fundamentally inconsistent with the traditional approach to managing.

The new logic starts from an entirely different premise. It argues that for individuals to be full participants in the organization and to add significant value, they need to understand all its operations, including the financial ones. As a result, the organization needs to place a strong emphasis on communicating operating results and reward system data, and tailoring performance measures to provide individuals and teams with feedback. Employees can then develop an understanding of the rationale for doing certain tasks and feel that they are rewarded for performing in ways that contribute to organizational effectiveness.

In the new logic it makes sense for individuals to know measurement and reward information. It allows them to manage their own behavior and can increase their motivation. It is worth repeating: tasks that are measured and rewarded tend to get done. The new logic can only operate if individuals have a clear sense of how their behaviors relate to the effectiveness of the organization and their rewards; public measurement systems help build this connection.

Knowing the Score All the Time

Individuals, groups, and organizations are guided most effectively when they get immediate and continuous feedback on what they are doing. As was mentioned earlier, this is an obvious feature of many competitive sports. In the business world, however, it is often been impossible for teams and business units to get timely and continuous feedback, because the cost is simply too great. So individuals often only know the "score" weeks and even months after the "game" is over. It takes that long to add up the results and give them to people throughout an organization.

But the situation in business is changing, thanks to information technology. With company networks and personal computers, it is possible for individuals throughout an organization to obtain ongoing data about how they and their work teams are performing and, indeed, about how other parts of the organization are performing as well.[4]

For example, the sales representatives who call on stores for Frito-Lay can get almost instant data on how various products are selling through a hand-held computer tied into a network that continuously measures the organization's sales performance. Similarly, Federal Express knows where all of its packages are at any given time. It can continually update its data base and let employees know whether they and the organization are meeting delivery standards. Pier 1 Imports, the retail chain, has developed a continuous feedback system for its stores. At any time, employees can get computer data on daily, weekly, monthly, and annual sales totals for their store. They also get comparisons of their store's sales to daily goals and to last year's performance. As with a sport, they know what a winning score is, and they get continuous feedback about how they are doing.

The growing use and capability of information technology and computers may be the most important development in enabling corporations to become high-performance organizations.[5] When combined with the right measures, the right organization design, and the right types of managerial behavior, information technology can provide support for previously unachievable levels of self-direction and motivation in the following ways:

- Making levels of management unnecessary by creating laterally integrated organizations that operate more rapidly and responsively
- Enabling employees to make operating decisions about such things as pricing, inventory management, and production quickly, without having to check with supervisors or staff support people for information and expertise
- Guiding employees through complex customer service operations such as order administration, insurance claim processing, and bank loan approvals (a computerized data base can put the information and expertise needed to satisfy a customer's request at an employee's fingertips)
- Enabling individuals, via networks, to coordinate their behavior with others in the same work process or business unit without having to go through the hierarchical chain of command

Sometimes a simple but powerful information system can be almost as useful as one based on complex technology. For example, Honda believes it is important that employees understand daily performance goals and are aware of the amount of progress they are making toward reaching them. So when it decided to open its first U.S. automobile assembly plant, Honda placed a scoreboard in plain view that showed the production goal for the day as well as the number of cars already made. Interestingly enough, it looks very much like a basketball or football scoreboard and constantly provides updated information against the performance standard.

It is important to emphasize, however, that having or using information technology does not necessarily create high-performance organizations. An organization must combine information technology with the other features of the new logic if information technology is to be something more than just an expensive addition or a better way to practice the traditional approach to management.

Some traditional organizations have tried to use computers as a way to exercise more effective top-down control. They have created sharply hierarchical, control-oriented information systems rather than systems that allow or encourage lateral communication and self-control. They use computers to record the amount of time salespeople are on the phone and how many calls they take, to automatically allocate calls so there is no downtime for any of them, and to continuously update management on the performance of every individual so they can do a better job of supervising them.

In theory, information technology should help make top-down control more effective; in reality, it usually does not work out that way. A number of studies have found that modern technology can be a fatal disease for traditional, hierarchical approaches to management.[6] Human beings have an impressive ability to defeat the information access controls that are put into information systems. In case after case that I have encountered, individuals seem to be able to get broader and more comprehensive information out of a computer system than its designers intended them to have.

In addition, just like the assembly line workers of past decades, they figure out ways to provide the system with false data about their own performance and to effectively defeat its performance controls. Direct-sales telephone operators, for instance, find ways to go off-line, to fake calls, and to provide inaccurate data in a number of areas when they feel that they are being overly controlled and directed by a hierarchically managed, computerized information system.

Measuring What Counts for Organizational Effectiveness

The emphasis that the new logic places on sharing performance information throughout an organization has implications for what should be measured. Without the right measures, information sharing is at best a waste of time; at worst it may be highly dysfunctional because it will cause the organization to do the wrong things. Remember: organizations get the kinds of behaviors they measure and reward. Thus whatever an organization measures must be consistent with what it wants to accomplish and how it wants to manage its performance. There are two particularly important considerations in developing the right measures: involve what types of performance to measure and whether to measure the performance of individuals, groups, teams, or business units.

Traditional organizations usually measure how well individuals, departments, and groups perform in relation to cost or budget parameters. Large bureaucracies also often devise operational measures of performance for such things as how long it takes an insurance claims representative to answer a customer call or how many claims are processed. They then turn these measures into indexes of performance. These measures are all useful in a top-down management approach, because they give the top the kind of information it needs to direct the bottom.

The "best measured" traditional organization I ever studied was AT&T. Managers at AT&T during the 1970s carefully measured how operators utilized their time (how long they were on a single call, how long it took them to answer a call), and they collected other indicators of operator behavior (tone of voice, words used). The same was true for phone installers. They had targets for the amount of time it should take to do a particular installation, and management collected information about whether they made those targets.

It was time-consuming to keep such records, but AT&T managers had no idea how they would run the organization without them. At the same time, most of the employees I interviewed had little knowledge of the organization's financial budgets and only passing knowledge of many of the performance indicators. One exception was the installers who had figured out how to beat the system by inflating their time budgets and misleading supervisors who came to check on their performance.

The measurement system at AT&T underscores the problems of the old logic approach. It focuses too much on individual behavior. It all too often ignores financial performance and customer satisfaction. Managers focus solely on meeting their operating budgets, ignoring the impact on customers and the costs that are unmeasured. Employees put their efforts into figuring out how to beat the system. Neither the workers nor the managers have good information on either the profitability of the businesses they are in or on how other parts of the company are performing. In short, they have no sense of whether they are winning or losing in the larger sense—only a vague sense of how they are doing against what they often see as arbitrarily established budgets and standards. In order to alter this situation and to develop a measurement system that fits the new logic, different measures must be developed.

Measuring Customer Satisfaction

There is a good reason the old logic approach frequently neglects to measure one very important outcome: customer satisfaction. The assumption is that if operating measures such as the length of time to answer a call are at an acceptable level of performance, customers will be satisfied. This approach is clearly dangerous, since what is measured may not correspond to what the customer wants. For example, it may be more important to a customer to have one person to deal with than to have the phone answered quickly.

Another example: when the Seven-Eleven convenience store chain encouraged employees to be more friendly and talkative, they found it had a surprising negative impact. By measuring customer satisfaction, they discovered that it irritated customers, particularly those who were waiting in line to check out. Most customers preferred a quick and speedy transaction to a conversation with the person behind the cash register. Apparently, people do not go to Seven-Elevens to make a friend; they go to get quick service.

Fortunately, as companies have installed total quality management programs that focus on satisfying and delighting their customer, they have increasingly developed measures of how well they are doing at satisfying customers.[7] They have found that it is important to measure satisfaction with specific services and with identifiable teams and individuals, not simply gauge overall satisfaction with a company and its products and services. The reason for this is that it helps them provide feedback and develop a line of sight for individuals and teams.

For example, when I consulted at Taco Bell on a reorganization that was targeted at reducing the number of levels of management and giving their stores more autonomy, we found they had to change their information system. They started collecting customer satisfaction data for individual stores, they created an 800 number for service problems, and they put in place an on-line financial reporting system. Customer satisfaction data on a store-by-store basis gave employees feedback and also let senior management stay in touch with an important element of the operation and with the performance of all of their stores.

Before introducing the new measurement systems, Taco Bell simply measured overall customer reaction to their products and image. They had data on sales per store, and each store had a budget, but stores did not operate as small businesses with their own profit-and-loss statements and customer satisfaction measures. The introduction of these new measures created much more of a small-business atmosphere in the stores. It helped to get employees more involved and allowed for more local decision making. Finally, it gave management the information it needed to judge how each of its stores (small businesses) was doing.

Measuring Profit

An obvious performance measure that many traditional organizations neglect is that of profit. Of course, they compute profit but all too often only at an aggregate level that is far removed from what employees can control and understand. For example, until recently, Digital Equipment and IBM only computed profit for their total organizations. When profits are measured only at the corporate level, the rest of the organization is judged on its ability to meet budgets, sales objectives, and revenue and cost projections. This produces a focus on internal results and internal customers rather than on external customers and overall results.

When IBM finally began to shift its approach in the 1990s so that particular pieces of the corporation, such as the personal computer business, were measured in terms of their profitability, it was a major change. It meant that the management of the personal computer business had to serve customers successfully—not just negotiate effectively with upper management for budget goals.

Of course, even reporting profits at the level of IBM's personal computer business falls far short of giving employees goals and results that are meaningful for them. As mentioned earlier, ABB, the global firm that manufactures a wide variety of products including railroad cars and electric generators, is a classic example of an organization that has taken the idea of measuring profitability to an extreme. Its six thousand business units all have their own profit-and-loss statements, which, in essence, has created an organization based on mini-enterprise units.

ABB's hope is that this architecture will allow the company to have the enthusiasm and self-control of a small company as well as the multinational global status and power that come from being large. My experiences with them indicate that the approach does go a long way toward accomplishing this goal. It certainly has produced a strong commitment among employees to the success of their business unit. Employees know their unit's profitability and are concerned about its performance.

If anything of value is lost in this approach, it is a focus on the overall success of ABB. In the eyes of most employees, ABB success seems to come second to making their business unit successful. The ABB approach certainly does not fit every organization, but it does provide a good example of how—with the right measures and organizational design—a small business environment can be created within a large multinational corporation.

Measuring the Cost of Doing Business

I am certainly not the first to advocate better measures of organizational performance. Accounting and finance experts, as well as total quality advocates, have also recognized the need for better measures. One of the more interesting new accounting approaches is activity-based costing (ABC), championed by Robert Kaplan, an accountant and professor.[8] Kaplan argues that traditional accounting focuses too much on the costs of departments such as human resources, sales, engineering, and marketing, which in turn leads to the allocation of overhead costs in a way that distorts the real cost of producing a particular product or delivering a service. As a result, organizations do not know how much it costs to make a product or deliver a service; they lack the information they need to decide whether they should make certain products and what they should charge for them. They are also in a poor position to give feedback to individuals and teams about the profit-and-loss performance of their work areas.

Activity-based cost accounting organizes costs around processes, an interesting convergence with the thinking in reengineering and socio-tech work design. The challenge in applying activity-based costing is deciding which processes to focus on. Kaplan suggests that calculating the marketing, sales, and design costs for particular products and services should, in most cases, take precedence over the reengineering approach of focusing on the overall cost of order administration or product development. Placing the focus on the cost of products and services has important advantages. It not only gives individuals feedback but also provides an organization with the information it needs to price its products, evaluate its performance against competitors, and understand the financial performance of its businesses.

Activity-based cost accounting is not widely used, but it is gaining popularity. It fits nicely with the practice of shifting many staff support services to outside vendors. With the right accounting numbers, it is possible to determine the relative internal costs of payroll management, information systems, and other staff activities and to compare them to the costs of purchasing these services from outside vendors.

Beyond the monetary and structural advantages, measuring an organization based on processes and controllable costs can provide a tremendous motivational benefit. An organization can use these measures to offer financial incentives based on a unit's improvements in operating results. Indeed, they can be the foundation of a reward system that relates pay to financial performance.

Measuring Return on Capital

Because corporate finance experts have argued that companies place too little emphasis on the cost of capital in evaluating performance, they have recently come up with a number of new measures that account for cost of capital. One of them, economic value added (EVA), has received a great deal of attention. But it is difficult to understand and even harder to influence. Individuals are not motivated and guided by measures they do not understand and influence. Thus, successfully using an economic return-on-investment measure as the basis for an incentive plan requires extensive communication and education. Even with understanding, measures of financial return often prove to be poor incentives since they are not easily influenced by most employees.

Financial-return measures such as EVA are increasingly being used as a basis for executive compensation plans. There is a defensible logic here, because senior executives can have some influence on them. There can be problems with this use, however, if the same measures are not used to drive the compensation of everyone in the organization. Like some of the executive compensation plans mentioned in the previous chapter, it creates a separation between those who are on the plan and those who are not that can work against integrating everyone's behavior and actions. Simply stated, what is good for individuals who are on the plan may not be good for those who are not on it, and vice versa.

The problems with investment-return measures were driven home for me when I consulted for a large paper company a few years ago. The company had installed a complex return-on-investment incentive plan for the managers in each of its thirty business units. The company's finance department decided that since the company's cost of capital was around 10 percent, any business that performed over 10 percent warranted a substantial bonus, while those that were below that level did not warrant any bonus at all. In theory this sounded good, but it turned out that new business units always had high capital costs (their equipment was being depreciated) and typically generated a negative return, while older operations tended to generate very positive returns because of their low cost of capital.

At the end of the first year of its operation, the plan paid out large amounts of money to many older units that were already performing effectively—even though they did not improve their return. In other cases, it paid nothing at all to new business units that improved their performance dramatically. Ultimately, the organization decided to abandon this cost-of-capital approach, because it could not figure out how to make it "fair" in the eyes of the employees or how to communicate the approach effectively.

Measuring the Human Side of the Organization

Chapter Eight discussed the importance of developing and collecting measures of the organization's competencies and capabilities as part of its human resource management approach. Organizations also need to know the status of its culture and climate as well as the commitment of employees to the company's goals and mission. These can be measured in a number of ways, including attitude surveys and indicators of employee well-being such as absenteeism, turnover, and accident rates.

Motorola has recently introduced an innovative program to measure the condition of its human resources. Every quarter, employees are asked to respond, via an 800 number, to the same six questions concerning how they feel about their work and the management at Motorola. Motorola's plan is to do this for ten years in order to track the company's success in moving forward key strategic initiatives, such as promoting diversity. Motorola also intends to use the data to measure how its work force is responding to the organizational changes the company will make in the next decade. Motorola shares the results of this survey on a regular basis with all the members of the organization, just as it shares quarterly financial information.

Although more organizations are collecting measures of capabilities, culture, and employee well-being, they almost never report the data to investors and the outside world. Despite this, I believe a strong argument can be made that these results should be made known. I once participated in an experiment that was intended to test the validity of this argument. Graphic Controls, a technical printing and manufacturing company, agreed to develop an annual report to its shareholders that included data on employee satisfaction and turnover as well as financial results. My study of shareholders and financial analysts who got the data indicated they thought the information was important and that they wished to keep getting it.[9] Graphic Controls intended to report these data annually, but soon after they published the first year's results, they were acquired by the Times Mirror Company, and the practice ended. Recently, Ben and Jerry's Homemade began issuing their version of a human resources report.

The idea of companies reporting on their human and organizational resources has surfaced in the writings and speeches of

Robert Reich, secretary of labor in the Clinton administration. He has tried to persuade large investors, such as the California Public Employees Retirement fund, to ask companies for data on their management practices and on how their employees react to these practices. Some investment firms have followed his suggestion and are circulating questionnaires that ask companies to report on their management approaches. In addition, they are asking companies how their boards of directors operate and what major organizational effectiveness initiatives they have under way.

Overall, the idea of developing a more balanced scorecard for company performance seems to hold a tremendous amount of promise. The challenge is to develop the right mix of measures so that employees and investors can get an accurate idea of how an organization is performing and what its future prospects are. All too often, the only information available reflects short-term financial performance as measured by traditional accounting methods. These measures are too narrow and only reflect the old logic. Because the organization and its competencies and capabilities are an important source of competitive advantage, measures are needed that provide a broad and balanced overview of its condition to everyone who has a stake in it.

Measuring Performance Against a Standard

Measures of performance can be meaningfully interpreted only when they can be calibrated against some standard. In the old logic of measurement, most standards are negotiated hierarchically within the organization. The budget process is a perfect example. Individuals throughout the organization spend weeks, sometimes months preparing a budget that will survive an extensive set of budget reviews. Performance in this system often depends on how well managers negotiate their budgets. No doubt, it takes considerable skill and knowledge to build a budget and to tell a credible story up the hierarchy for why it should be accepted.

The new logic emphasizes the importance of standards that come from outside the organization, often from comparisons with competitors' performance. Whether the measure is customer satisfaction or defects per car, the same logic applies. Comparisons with competitors' performance provide the most important basis for judging what is adequate and what is not. They also help to focus employee attention on what needs to be done in order to win in the marketplace.

Even though focusing on competitor performance seems highly desirable, data from our research on the Fortune 1000 indicate that most of them do not communicate this kind of information to employees. Less than a quarter of them give the majority of their employees information about how their performance rates in comparison to their competitors.

In situations where it is not easy to get competitor data, an organization may have to focus on improving its performance in comparison with its history. Total quality management programs emphasize continuous improvement over last year's, last month's, and last week's performance. In gain-sharing pay plans, employees are rewarded when they exceed historical performance standards. A major problem with focusing on performance improvements against a historical standard is that they may not be big enough, particularly if performance has been low compared to an external competitive standard. For example, in the 1980s, the American automobile industry needed to do more than just continuously improve. To compete with Toyota, Honda, and Nissan, it had to increase quality by 50 percent or more.

One way to set a standard that is not based on historical measures or on competitors' performance is to create a transformative goal that asks the organization to dramatically change its levels of performance. This is difficult to do, but when done well it can be very powerful. Motorola's 6-Sigma goal is an example of a transformative quality standard (6-Sigma is the statistical probability that there will be a certain number of defects per part or per operation; Motorola's goal is less than one defect per million parts). This standard was not based on continuous improvement or on what competitors were doing. As was mentioned earlier, it was simply a part of the vision that Bob Galvin, the CEO of Motorola at that time, had for the level of quality that his corporation could achieve. He set it as a corporate goal and through his leadership was able to get most members of the corporation to buy into it and work toward achieving it.

The major risk in setting a goal like 6-Sigma is that employees will see it as unreachable and thus not worth their time and effort. The challenge for senior managers in creating and implementing a transformational goal, therefore, is threefold: set a goal that requires substantial reach, persuade the members of the organization that it can be reached, and communicate why achieving the goal should be an important business objective.

Measuring Performance at the Right Organization Levels

On every level of an organization, from the individual to the team to the business unit, performance can be measured and the results communicated, depending, of course, on the fit between the organization's architecture and the measurement system. The key: measurements must be appropriate for the architecture of the organization. The measures need to focus on the key units or groupings in the organization, whether it is a front-back organization, a network organization, or a heavily matrixed organization, to mention three examples.

If the organization is broken into a number of small business units like the example of ABB, it is vital to measure the performance of each one. As already discussed, if the organization uses teams for new product development or running production facilities such as oil refineries and chemical plants, research on teams suggests that it is critical to measure team performance.[10]

Recently, I spent several days consulting with a large organization that had moved to a front-back structure a year earlier. They felt it was not working well. The reason for this soon became obvious: the performance measurement process had not been changed so that the success of each of the parts in the front and back of the organization could be determined. Since performance was still measured on the basis of the old functional-organization approach, most employees still behaved as if the front-back organization did not exist.

One of the trickiest measurement issues concerns staff groups such as those working on legal matters, human resources, or information systems. Historically, the performance of these groups has rarely been measured separately except in terms of whether they have met their budgets. This is changing because of the pressure on them to add value and the growing trend to focus more on service processes. Once the key staff service processes are identified and individuals are made responsible for them, they can be measured and, as was mentioned in Chapter Eight, rewarded as performing units. They can also be compared to external competitors on cost and service quality. Some organizations—Xerox and Enron are examples—have decided to use outside vendors and to cut back their information and computer systems corporate staff after comparing the cost and quality of services that can be obtained internally and externally.

Comparison with outside suppliers is a logical step toward measuring, and establishing accountability for, all of an organization's activities. It applies well to some of the activities that are done by staff groups (such as payroll processing, information system maintenance, legal service). A word of caution is in order, however. It does not fit staff activities that need to be done in a business partner approach, such as planning for the marketing of new products and developing business strategy. Separately measuring and rewarding staff groups that help the organization do these may be dysfunctional because it fails to integrate them and their work with the rest of the organization.

Tying Performance Measures to Rewards

As previously discussed, when financial rewards—such as pay and stock—are tied to performance measures, those rewards can become motivators and can drive behavior. The challenge is to pick measures that lend themselves to being tied to a financial reward. I believe it makes sense to have some portion of every individual's financial rewards tied to profit in high-performance organizations. This linkage makes sure that everyone in the organization has a common goal, and it creates a performance-based culture. It also provides yet another reason for all employees to be aware of and understand the organization's profitability.

It is important to note here that for reward purposes, an organization may decide to use a different profit measure from the one reported to the external world. Publically reported accounting profits often reflect write-offs for bad businesses, capital gains from the sale of divisions or businesses, and a host of other things which weaken the line of sight for most employees. So it may make sense to focus measurement and reward systems on operating results rather than on publically reported profits.

It is worth once again mentioning the importance of getting stock into the hands of all employees. It directly aligns employees' self-interest with the interests of the other important stakeholders in the organization: the shareholders and investors. Fortunately, more and more corporations are realizing the importance of making their employees stock owners. Merck, PepsiCo, Intel, Monsanto, and United Airlines are among the many corporations in which most employees either own stock or have stock options.

In a large organization, extrinsic rewards can be and often need to be tied to performance at several levels. Profit sharing and stock ownership take care of the total corporation, but they do not deal with team, plant, office, or business unit performance. In a new logic organization, individuals need rewards that are tied to measures that they can influence and that reflect "their" businesses. Thus, as was stressed in the discussion of rewards, it is important to measure and, in most cases, to reward teams, plants, offices, and business units.

Measures at different levels serve different but complementary purposes. For example, measuring and rewarding the performance of the entire organization through profit sharing creates an overall sense of direction and commitment. Measuring and rewarding performance at the team or profit center level is better for motivating and guiding individuals and teams, because they have a stronger line of sight to this performance.

Fit Is the Key

In many respects, the information and performance measurement systems in an organization are like the cables that connect servers, workstations, and personal computers in a network. They determine what kinds of information individuals will receive about the organization and what kinds of information can be sent. The traditional logic emphasizes secrecy and hierarchy. Thus information systems are designed to measure and communicate upward what top-level managers need to know so they can add value by controlling the organization.

The new logic emphasizes open communication and the measurement of performance in a number of new and different ways. Keep in mind that the effectiveness of these new approaches depends on how they fit with other elements of the Star Model. No performance measurement makes sense unless it supports the business strategy and reinforces the organization's basic architecture. Since the principles of the new logic emphasize that employees throughout the organization must add value, it follows that employees need much more information—information that allows them to manage themselves and that gives them a line of sight to controllable business performance.

This completes the discussion of the five points of the Star Model. In the next chapter, the focus shifts to the complex and critical task of managing organizational change. Because an existing organization typically must alter all points on the star in order to adopt the new logic and become a high-performance organization, the change process can be difficult to manage. But when completed, it can give an organization capabilities and competencies that are difficult to copy and that provide a powerful source of competitive advantage.

Part Four

Managing Change
The New Logic Corporation and Beyond

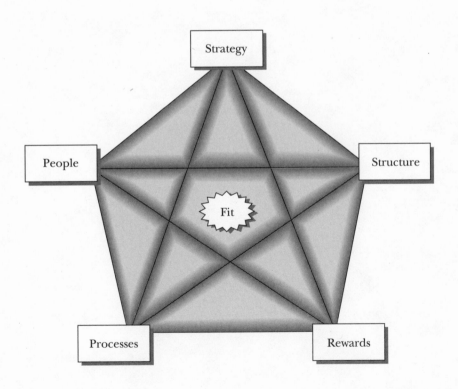

Chapter Eleven

Making It Happen
Creating the New Logic Corporation

- Organization can be the ultimate competitive advantage.
- Effective leadership is the key to organizational effectiveness.

Organizational change has become a big business, with major corporations spending billions of dollars a year on change management consulting services. Firms such as Gemini, Index, and Andersen Consulting employ thousands of consultants and have a worldwide reach. This represents a dramatic change from just a decade or two ago, when most firms in this field were small (two- or three-person) "virtual" firms that billed corporations between $100,000 and $200,000 for a change management project. It was a craft industry with little size and few established programs and products.

But with the advent of total quality management and then reengineering, the corporate change management consulting scene changed dramatically. There is one experience that stands out in my mind as illustrating the dramatic increase in the size of change management projects. In 1991, a strategy consulting firm called MAC—with projects largely under a couple of hundred thousand dollars (and where I was a faculty associate)—was acquired by the French firm CAP-Gemini Sogeti. CAP-Gemini also acquired a rapidly growing change management consulting firm,

United Research. They quickly recognized that there was a potential synergy between the strategy work of MAC and the change consulting work of United Research—perhaps they had seen the Star
Model!—and set out to integrate the two firms.

I attended an early meeting between the two organizations in
which two United Research consultants talked about several projects that they had done that billed out at several million dollars a
year. The MAC consultants were amazed at these numbers and
continually asked the United Research consultants what they did
to produce billings of this amount. The United Research consultants responded that they facilitated change. The more they gave
this and similar answers, the more frustrated the MAC people got.

After the United Research consultants left, the MAC consultants spent a great deal of time talking about what United Research
actually did to warrant such large billings. They tended to dismiss
change management as some kind of black magic that organizations were being sold. It is easy to see why they reacted this way,
since their experience was with an entirely different kind of consulting, but they were very definitely wrong. Admittedly, change
management at times involves some mystery and luck, but there is
no doubt in my mind that there exists considerable knowledge
about how to do it. Incidentally, MAC and United Research ultimately merged to form Gemini Consulting, which now has a number of strategic change management consulting projects that bill
over a million dollars a year.

There is a good reason why there is a booming consulting business in change management: it is difficult to design a change
process that creates major management and organizational
changes in large corporations. Stating the principles of the new
logic is one thing; putting them in place is another matter. But it
can be done, and in some cases, consultants can help. As mentioned in the Introduction, there are many examples of organizations that have successfully transformed themselves—from giants
such as Xerox, Motorola, Honeywell, Hewlett-Packard, Corning,
and TRW to smaller firms such as Harley-Davidson, Springfield
Remanufacturing, and Progressive Insurance, and IDS.

In this chapter, the focus is on how organizations can use the
principles of the new logic to transform the way they operate.
There is no magical formula for changing traditional organizations

to high-performance ones. The change process is difficult to manage, but it is manageable. Based on a number of studies of organizational transformations, there appear to be some general guidelines that, when followed, can increase the chances for a successful transformation to a high-performance organization.[1] It is perhaps a bit too bold to call these principles, but they are at least good predictors of successful change.

1. Establish Compelling Business Reasons for Change

The organizational change literature is full of suggestions about how to motivate change.[2] Most focus on the importance of making people feel that there is a need for change and the importance of providing a vision of a new more attractive world toward which the organization should be heading. There is no question that these points apply to adoption of the new logic. Organizations are most likely to change when there is a commonly accepted view that the current ways of operating are not likely to lead to success—but that a new, better way will lead to success.

Organizations that decide to change to the new logic do so for a number of reasons. Some find it more aesthetically pleasing. Others agree with its underlying values. Still more believe that it provides the kind of culture that they prefer. All of these reasons are valid and can lead to change. But in my experience the most effective way to motivate change is to establish a compelling business reason. Survival, competition, and winning in the marketplace are the kinds of compelling reasons that consistently generate energy around change and also provide a sense of direction. In the absence of these, change becomes a luxury or a hobby rather than a business necessity. This is particularly true in large, complex organizations that have a strong vested interest in maintaining the status quo. In these organizations, change needs to have compelling reasons behind it, not just a vague sense that it is something "nice to do."

Often the best way to establish a business justification for change is to analyze the competitive environment. A careful benchmarking of how an organization compares to its competition can often provide good evidence of the shortfalls of an organization's performance and highlight the kinds of improvements that need to be made. It is important in this exercise to look not just at direct business competitors but at anyone who is using similar business processes and activities. This is the only way to accurately assess an organization's long-term competitiveness. Once this activity has been completed, the organization should be in a position to identify its weak points and the threats to its continuing success and survival.

New technology such as computers or automation in the workplace, the start-up of operations, new business ventures, and new territories or locations also can provide a felt need for change. All of these sources of instability in the organization can actually create the energy and provide an opportunity for an organizational transformation. A "start-up" mentality can take hold, making it easier to create new designs and systems for an organization. When I consult with organizations, I strongly recommend that they look upon every major change in technology and/or physical location as a prime opportunity to redesign themselves and move toward a high-performance approach to organizing.

Any effort to justify change for business reasons must consider all four points of the Diamond Model presented in Chapter Three. That is, it must analyze the business environment and determine how the organization must behave in order to perform successfully in it. Further, it must identify the kinds of organizational capabilities and core competencies needed to reach a winning performance level.

One of the most important things that an effective manager or leader can do is to help generate the feeling within an organization that there is a need for change. Jack Welch did it at General Electric, Larry Bossidy did it at AlliedSignal, and David Kearns did it at Xerox. For many years before significant change began in these organizations, some people within them were dissatisfied with the existing state of affairs. But it took an effective CEO to crystallize the discontent into a strongly felt need for change and ultimately to provide a vision of how the change process should play out.

The example of Jack Welch and General Electric is particularly impressive in terms of making the business case for change.[3] When he took over as CEO of General Electric in the early 1980s, it was a successful firm and viewed as world-class in terms of its management practices. But Welch believed that in order for GE to continue to be successful, he had to lead a major transformation process. His first challenge: draw attention to the need for change and define the kinds of changes that were needed. Welch believed that unless GE's businesses were first or second in their competitive markets, they were unlikely to produce high levels of financial return. He therefore made a bold statement: "Only those parts of General Electric that are number one or two in their business will be retained; others will be sold or shut down." This rather dramatic statement mobilized energy for change within GE and shows how leadership can create successful change.

2. Leaders Must Guide the Change

Hierarchical, autocratic institutions and organizations can change through only two fundamentally different processes: top management–driven initiatives and revolution. Top management–driven change has a number of advantages over revolution when it comes to transforming corporations. The major one is that managers at the top have the power to make it happen in a programmatic, focused way.[4] Unless senior management strongly supports and guides change, it is likely to be fragmented, not driven by a vision, and ultimately threatening to them.

All too often when I have been involved with change efforts where a middle-level manager decides to change to the new logic without senior management support, the outcome has been far from satisfactory. Remember the plant manager mentioned earlier who created a new plant based on teams and new logic principles? He was the "rebel leader" who successfully started his new high-performance plant. Unfortunately, support for his "guerrilla action" was limited to the individuals at his location. He was eventually ousted from the organization. Indeed, this is the fate of most rebel leaders.

Senior managers are uniquely positioned to supply the kind of strategic leadership that is critical to a successful transformation to the new logic. They are in a position to help define the mission of the organization and to establish a link between that mission and the type of management and organization principles that are used. In this situation, leadership—not managership—is needed. Indeed, sometimes a larger-than-life transformational leader— a "magic" leader—can be a significant help.

The best transformational leaders have the ability to clearly articulate a new mission for the organization, the ability to provide a sense of how to achieve results, and the ability to use their own behavior to provide examples of the new behavior. They also know how to carefully articulate their expectations for others, and they consistently follow up with appropriate rewards for those who adopt the new behaviors.

A good example of this kind of leadership is the way David Kearns led the change process at Xerox. He made a clear business case for the change and then spent a considerable amount of time working with his own senior management team to be sure that they understood the new behaviors that would be needed in order for the organization to be successful. He next persuaded his senior management team to train their subordinates in the right behaviors and to spread the principles and leadership behaviors of the new logic throughout the total corporation by having managers at all levels train their subordinates.

3.   Take a Long-Term View of the Change Process

Because changes in an organization's management approach happen slowly and take time to pay dividends, it is important to take a long-term view. How long? Depending upon the size of the organization and the urgency for change, the amount of time required can vary from a few years to more than a decade.

Xerox, which is often cited as having undertaken one of the most successful corporate change efforts, has been working on its transformation for well over a decade, and it is far from finished. Significant, positive results began to show after a few years, so it is not now a question of whether change will pay off for Xerox. They long ago regained some market share from the Japanese copier makers. The question now is what additional changes they need to make in order to achieve further gains.

Results from AlliedSignal, General Electric, Corning, Rockwell, and Harley-Davidson are encouraging. For these companies, it did not take five years for positive results to appear. Some positive results appeared in less than a year in areas such as product quality. Indeed, their experience suggests that investments in new work and organization structures, training, and the development of new information technology and management systems can produce new organizational capabilities and better financial performance within two years. As noted in Chapter One, a growing body of academic literature shows a direct relationship between the adoption of the new principles for organizing and the overall financial performance of the organizations. It does not tell us how quickly organizational change impacts on performance, but it does suggest that introducing changes takes time and that performance will continue to improve as new behaviors and systems take hold. Thus it is critical that organizations make a long-term commitment to adopting the new logic—a commitment that involves continuous change.

4.   Create a Climate of Continuous Change

The most popular models of change management involve three phases:[5]

- Create dissatisfaction with the existing state of affairs.
- Make needed changes.
- Return stability by "refreezing" so that the organization operates with its newly created organizational practices and structure.

It is hard to argue with the first two. I have already pointed out that organizations need to "unfreeze" or develop the need for change and, of course, adopt new practices. However, in this era of rapid environmental change, I question whether refreezing is the best third step. I think it is better to think of the final phase as continuous change and organizational learning.[6]

Change is not a process that an organization should undergo in order to freeze new practices and then settle back into a new way of doing business as usual. Change is an opportunity for an organization to learn and to develop its capabilities and competencies through trying new approaches and assessing how well they work. An organization needs to continue the change process, constantly making changes, experimenting, and assessing the results of change with a continuous improvement mindset.

We are in a very fertile period of new ideas and new technologies concerned with organizational design and management. An organization that freezes or locks in its management practices and policies at this point in time is in very great danger of being unable to take advantage of what are likely to be significant developments in the future.

It is important to keep in mind that there is a significant distinction between locking in the new logic approach to building organizational capabilities and locking in particular management practices. The former is usually positive, the latter is often not. Most organizations can continue to improve their organizational capabilities only by introducing new management practices that support or create them. For example, in creating a quality capability, the challenge is to find the best combination of practices to support it. Motorola and other organizations that have been pursuing a quality capability for over a decade are still making new discoveries and learning new ways to improve their capability. Their ongoing pursuit of improvement demonstrates a focus on developing the capabilities of the organization and a healthy willingness to search for the right mix of practices. They are open to learning about the positive and negative effects of particular practices and are not wed to a "we have to do it this way" mentality. They are wed, however, to having a world-class capability in quality and to creating a high-performance organization.

Given the current levels of organizational experimentation and the evolution of information and computer technology, there is no doubt in my mind that many valuable ideas are going to emerge in the next decade about how to manage new logic organizations. Organizations need to be aware of these new developments and, where appropriate, put them into practice. The challenge will be to utilize them as a way to enhance organizational capabilities and to integrate them into the organization.

On the down side, a real danger is that organizations will automatically adopt technologies and new approaches to management without determining how well they fit their business strategy and their need for certain organizational capabilities. This can clearly lead to an instability that is more dysfunctional than functional and can ultimately lead to the reduction of an organization's capabilities. Effective continuous change requires that an organization strike a careful balance between being open to learning new practices and maintaining constancy in its key capabilities and its sense of mission and strategy. Indeed, this may turn out to be the ultimate organizational capability in an era of rapid technological and political change.

5. Avoid Fads

In many respects, management practices have become a consumer product. Individuals, companies, and publications vigorously market new ideas about how to manage. Books on management can sell a million copies or more, and magazines such as *Fortune, Business Week, The Economist,* and *Industry Week* regularly report on new management practices. There are also hundreds of thousands of workshops on management practices as well as a multitude of consulting firms that claim to offer the management equivalents of better mousetraps. The market for management innovation is large and seemingly insatiable, particularly if the innovation can be summarized in a very short form and taught in a one- or two-day training course.

But this is very much a buyer-beware market. All too often, organizations adopt such ideas as speed to market, total quality management, reengineering, organizational learning, and many others on a short-term basis. After a while, all of their new programs seem like the flavor of the month (or perhaps year).[7] The net result is that each time the emphasis shifts to the next new program, with its "silver bullet" solutions, much of what was learned in the old program is discarded and forgotten. Individuals who did not commit to the previous program feel reinforced for not accepting it and not participating in it. As they so often say to me when I interview them, "I knew it was a passing fad, so why invest my time and energy in it?"

It is impossible to predict what the next fad will be. The only safe prediction is that fads will come and go just as management by objectives, zero-based budgeting, and a host of other management innovations disappeared because they did not focus on the kinds of fundamental changes that organizations require in order to become high-performance organizations.

Can organizations inoculate themselves against the fad- or flavor-of-the-month syndrome? I believe they can. For organizations, the challenge is to identify the useful new practices and reject the large number of new practices, recycled old practices, and current fads that dominate the management field but are not a good fit for them or are simply not very useful. The place to start: determine whether the practices lead to the development of organizational capabilities that are key to business success.

Hewlett-Packard provides a good example. Its careful analysis of its markets and products found that speed to market is critical to the profitability of its products. In many of its businesses, the greatest profits (by a wide margin) are made by organizations that get products to market just a few months ahead of the competition. This led Hewlett-Packard to identify speed to market as critical and to work hard to develop its capability in this area. They test new management practices to see if they will improve speed and adopt only those that do.

A second step in guarding against being a victim of faddism: test all new management practice against the new logic. The best way to do this is by asking the following set of questions which follow directly from the principles of the new logic:

- Does the change increase the degree to which employees throughout the organization are involved in the business? To be more specific, does it lead to a broader sharing of information, knowledge, power, and rewards with respect to key business decisions and processes?
- Does it improve the degree to which employees throughout the organization can add value through their work? For example, does it allow employees to work with less supervision, to coordinate key lateral processes, or to make decisions and use knowledge that previously would have been reserved for managers at a higher level in the organization?
- Does it improve the lateral communication and coordination processes among interdependent employees in customer service, product development, or the production of a particular product?
- Does it move the organization toward a greater focus on products and customers so the employees will increasingly feel associated with a piece of the business rather than with a specialized function?
- Does it improve the leadership capability in the organization either because it helps improve the capability of leaders or because it provides them with an opportunity to model effec-

tive behavior and communicate with the organization about its mission and its strategy?

- Does it help leaders focus on organizational effectiveness and how they can add to the organization's core competencies and capabilities?

Literally any management practice can be tested by asking these questions. If the practice does not pass this test, it should not be adopted.

Finally, senior management must play a critical role in preventing fad-embracing behavior. It needs to have a constancy of purpose and focus on developing multiple capabilities that position new practices and policies as a part of the organization's long-term business strategy. If senior management has a short attention span and does not behave strategically, it is almost inevitable that the rest of the organization will also be easily entrapped by the latest fads.

Designing an effective organization is a journey without end. Yesterday's performance is unlikely to be good enough tomorrow, so organizations must continuously think of ways to improve their performance. This means change, experimentation, strategic alignment, and a willingness to adopt a learning stance toward the development of organizational capabilities. It does not mean a faddish, ever-changing, flavor-of-the-month approach to organizational effectiveness.

6. Focus on Where Change Goes and What Points It Covers

One of the clear implications of the Star Model is that change to the new logic usually requires changing all the important systems and practices of an organization.[8] At the start-up of a new organization or business unit, it is relatively easy to create a new logic organization. All the major systems can be designed according to the new logic, and thus there is no sequencing issue with respect to which point to change first, second, and so on. Just the opposite is true when a traditional organization is being changed. A critical question concerns where to start the change process. The answer to this question is both simple and perhaps not very satisfying to someone undertaking the change process.

There is no one right way or place to start the change process. It is not always right to start with changing the reward system, the structure, or any other feature of the organization. Typically, the best place to start the change process is where the organization is open to change. If there are complaints and pains with respect to the pay system, this most likely is the right place to start change. If there is a major technological change occurring, the design of work and the organization's structures may be the right place to start the change. The critical issue in changing to the new logic is that change does not end with just one point on the Star Model. It needs to continue until all points on the Star Model have been changed and aligned with the principles of the new logic.

7. Don't Wait for Heroes

An all-too-common belief is that change can happen only if a single hero emerges to lead the process. This so-called magic leader phenomenon is dominant in American mythology. John Wayne and other great heroes in American popular culture were sole operators. So we expect the same to be true in the business world, and we see the image of the magic leader reinforced by the mythology surrounding the impact that Lee Iaccoca had on Chrysler, Michael Eisner on Disney, and Jack Welch on General Electric. Stories about the success of these companies often picture these individuals as almost single-handedly turning them around. There is no question that each of these individuals played a critical role in improving their corporations. But they also had a talented group of people surrounding them to provide the overall sense of senior leadership and direction that was critical to a successful change effort.

Not every senior manager can lead a complex change process, but I believe that many can and that in the case of organizational change there is considerable strength in numbers. Highly successful organizations such as 3M and Hewlett-Packard have had strong leaders, but more than anything, they have had strong groups of individuals at the top who provide an ongoing sense of leadership. Texas Instruments and Rockwell are other examples of large organizations that have moved toward the new logic without having highly visible "magic" leaders. Waiting for a great leader to produce change is not only foolhardy but potentially fatal in an era in which rapid change is badly needed.

8. Avoid Corporate Anorexia from Excessive Downsizing

In the 1960s and 1970s, many large, successful organizations began to suffer from a corporate disease that has been called the dinosaur syndrome, a set of practices and beliefs that made them unwilling and unable to adapt to a rapidly changing business environment.[9] The disease most commonly affected large and very successful corporations that were praised for and extremely comfortable with their ways of doing business and their results. They were dinosaurs because their self-satisfaction prevented them from changing in response to environmental change and created the opportunity for new and old competitors to take business away from them.

The dinosaur syndrome seems to be on the decline. The fate of dinosaurs like Pan Am, RCA, Westinghouse, and Kmart has graphically shown to all that today's successful organization can be tomorrow's disaster if it fails to change. Unfortunately, the very focus on change, which has helped eliminate the dinosaur syndrome, has produced a new disease that threatens to be equally debilitating for many large corporations: corporate anorexia.

Corporate downsizing and reengineering became popular in the 1980s for a very good reason: many organizations simply had too many managers, too many employees, and staff support groups that were too large. Their high-cost organization structures kept them from competing with leaner, more efficient, and lower-cost competitors. In response, many corporations downsized, which did indeed reduce their costs and produce short-term increases in their profitability. This in turn produced a positive reaction from the investment community and greatly rewarded managers who ordered the downsizing by increasing the value of their stock, stock options, profit-sharing plans, and compensation packages.

Some companies have followed their initial reductions with more and still more downsizings. A kind of corporate anorexia seems to have developed in some of these companies that I believe will lead to their destruction if it does not stop. The pattern resembles the human disease of anorexia in which individuals continue to lose weight even though they have gone far beyond the weight loss that is healthy for them. In the corporate world, the initial downsizing often makes the organization leaner and meaner, but continued downsizings, as with human beings, make them weak and emaciated, which leads to decreased performance and then to further downsizing as business losses mount. If an organization is not careful, it can enter a death spiral in which it continues to downsize as it continues to lose revenues because its earlier downsizings have caused it to lose customers.

In my experience, a death spiral is particularly likely to happen when downsizing improves only the cost structure of an organization. Downsizing that is driven strictly by cost reductions is unlikely to add key organizational capabilities and, as a result, will fail to improve long-term performance. It can help an organization become a lower-cost competitor, but usually this is not enough to win in the marketplace. It often sets off demands for lower and lower costs in order to remain competitive. These demands, in turn, can lead to a spiral of cost reductions that cause the organization to lose its performance capabilities and ultimately to lose business.

A recent interview I had with the CEO of a major corporation underscores how powerful the culture of downsizing has become. He had just returned from a retreat where many Fortune 500 CEOs were present and said that the major topic of conversation was how much more downsizing was possible. CEO after CEO told him they felt they could eliminate another 20 percent or more of their employees and still perform at their present level. His concern, and mine as well, is that these CEOs may be sacrificing the long-term performance capabilities of their corporations in order to gain a short-term cost-reduction advantage.

You cannot shrink to greatness. At some point in a transformation process, an organization needs to begin to gain a competitive advantage because of the improvements it has made in speed, quality, and innovation. At that point, it should be able to grow and capture market share, and the critical issue becomes not continued downsizing but structuring the organization to grow and develop additional capabilities. If downsizing remains the major theme, it can be dumbsizing, and the organization risks losing the initial advantages it gained from its downsizing.

9.   Replace Downsizing with a Growth Strategy

The challenge for an organization is to understand when it has downsized to the point that it is well positioned in terms of its cost structure and its ability to perform. It must then not go beyond this point or it will begin to cut into muscle and, ultimately, bone.

Corporations often have a hard time recognizing this stopping point, particularly when the stock market seems to immediately reward every corporate downsizing announcement. But there are some clear signs that indicate when an organization is beginning to become anorexic. A first warning sign: an automatic tendency to downsize regardless of business conditions and the cost structure of the organization. For example, one organization I studied automatically downsized by 10 percent each year. In this particular organization the business continued to grow, but the work force began to question the necessity for these repeated downsizings and indeed the integrity of the senior management team. Finally, it stopped growing and entered what looks like a death spiral.

A second warning sign: a loss of employee commitment. If valued employees are regularly looking for jobs elsewhere or opting for voluntary retirement, there is a good chance that they have lost faith in the organization's ability to manage downsizing appropriately.

A third warning sign: an organization has no time or money to invest in the future. When an organization cannot commit resources to work restructuring, process improvement, training, and other aspects of its infrastructure, it has gone too far. Likewise, if an organization cannot find time to invest in creating new products or improving its products and services, it is suffering from too much downsizing. It will soon find that it cannot introduce new products, a decreasing percentage of its revenue comes from new products and services, and levels of customer dissatisfaction are increasing.

A fourth warning sign: loss of business (particularly new business) from the downsizing of the sales force. It makes sense to carefully examine the staffing of the sales force as well as how they carry out their work. In my experience, they often spend too much time preparing sales reports, doing bureaucratic work, and entertaining customers in ways that do not lead to new business. As a result, sales forces often incur high expenses and are prime candidates for cost reduction efforts. However, cutting the sales force is potentially very dangerous. The loss of a close relationship between a salesperson and a customer may not show up in the immediate loss of business, because an order taker can, for a while, substitute for the relationship that a salesperson had. But this lost relationship can eventually mean that new business opportunities—as well as information about what the customer wants—is lost to the organization.

A fifth warning sign: an organization needs to rehire fired workers. All too often companies cut too far and too precipitously until they have no choice but to rehire people who know how to do the work and who are readily available. These so-called ghost workers are often hired as consultants at a higher pay than they earned before they were laid off or encouraged to take early retirement. Sometimes these rehired workers really are only temporary. But all too often the need for them is a clear symptom that the organization has simply cut too far and that it is at the beginning of a downward spiral. This is particularly likely to be true when innovation has disappeared from the organization and it is relying more and more on its already established products and customers for its continuing existence.

10. Do Not Downsize Repeatedly

My research indicates that downsizing is most effective (less damaging to employee commitment and organizational capabilities) when it is not repeated regularly. An initial downsizing can even be positive, especially when individuals feel that only excess and poorly performing employees are removed. I recently interviewed a number of employees in an organization that had gone through a 20 percent staff reduction. Virtually every employee reported positive results from the reduction. They argued that the organization had improved from a cost point of view and from a speed and quality perspective. There were now, they said, fewer checks and balances in the system and less bureaucracy to fight. By and large, they felt that they had more freedom and autonomy—to do their work as it needed to be done—as well as better career opportunities.

On the other hand, repeated downsizings can be devastating. They cause a number of problems that lead to lower capabilities and competencies. They can, for example, be terribly destructive of employee commitment. In organizations where I have interviewed employees who have survived multiple downsizings, they don't talk about the guilt of being a survivor, as some have suggested. Rather they talk about the fear of being the next victim. In some cases, this fear can motivate good performance. But it is more likely to motivate wrong behaviors. The employees that I have interviewed report that they spend time looking for an escape route from the organization, that they take few risks, and that they look for ways to defend any decision or action they take.

11. De-Layer, Don't Just Downsize

An organization's short-term financial performance will almost always improve after a downsizing because its costs are reduced. Removing individuals based on voluntary retirement and the targeted outplacement of less competent performers and layoffs does reduce costs.[10] But the reduction of costs is just a one-time gain. A successful downsizing puts the emphasis on preparing the organization to move toward becoming a high-performance organization. Taking out levels of management is a key to accomplishing this. It not only lowers costs but lets people act more quickly, with greater agility. As was discussed in Chapter Four, with fewer levels, power can be moved downward and employees can add greater value at the lower levels of the organization. Taking out levels of management also creates the need to change and improve work processes.

The change process at General Electric in the early 1980s is a classic example of a multi-phase effort that moved from downsizing to changing work processes. Jack Welch first eliminated staff and layers of management. At that point he had the rather unflattering name of Neutron Jack. The standard joke at General Electric was that after Jack Welch visited your GE business, the people were gone but the buildings and the work remained.

The reality, of course, was that some people still remained, and they were struggling to do work in the old way, with the old systems. This did not go on for very long, however, since they were literally overworked and unable to cope with the remaining volume of work. Realizing this, Welch launched the "workout program"—which I mentioned earlier—it was specifically targeted at eliminating unnecessary work and, therefore, making the organization capable of operating with fewer people and fewer levels of management. By doing away with the requirement of extra signatures on travel requests, unnecessary reports, and other meaningless controls, it has ultimately helped General Electric adopt most or all of the principles of the new logic.

One of the things I like about the GE workout process is the three questions it suggests managers ask about approvals they give:

- How many signatures are already on documents when I receive them? Suggestion: if there are already two, then in the future, get out of the approval loop.
- How many times have you failed to approve a request like this one? Suggestion: if the answer is never or almost never, get out of the approval loop.
- Can this decision be made by someone lower in the organization? Suggestion: if it can, have them make it; they are paid less and it is a cheaper way to get it made.

Many organizations that have followed the General Electric example have simply done the downsizing part of the GE approach. They realize that they are overstaffed with managers and with corporate staff personnel and begin the change process by getting rid of them. They often fail, however, to significantly change the organization's processes, communication infrastructure, and other systems that must change in order for the organization to operate effectively in a different, downsized, and less layered way. As a result, they run the risk of developing corporate anorexia and downsizing themselves out of existence.

We are just at the beginning of rethinking how corporations can operate outside the constraints created by the bureaucratic approach to organizing. The new logic is not a passing fad; it represents a fundamental rethinking of the way complex organizations need to be designed and managed. It is replacing a logic of organizing that has been dominant for almost a century with a new logic that will be in place for decades. Like the old principles of bureaucratic management, the principles of the new logic need to be supported by a variety of sometimes changing practices, organization structures, and management behaviors. It is important not to confuse these, however, with the key principles that lead to high-performance organizations. They are right—and essential—for these turbulent times. I believe as we become more and more a society of knowledge work and information technology, the correctness of the new logic principles will be even more apparent and will, as discussed in the next chapter, require fundamental changes in how societies and governments interface with corporations.

Chapter Twelve

Beyond the Corporation
The Impact of the New Logic on Society

> - Organization can be the ultimate competitive advantage.
> - All employees must add significant value.

I am still a bit surprised and very concerned when I get a phone call from an executive who has been laid off as a result of yet another corporate downsizing. Most of the people who call me are competent, effective managers with twenty years or more of service in major corporations. Even though most of these individuals end up with a good job, some don't.

Managers who lose their jobs as part of an organizational change represent just one very visible and disturbing sign of the impact that the new global business environment has had on society. To be sure, there have been layoffs as long as there has been capitalism, but they have usually involved production workers, not managers and executives. What's more, most previous layoffs were not the result of changes that made highly paid work and managerial skills obsolete: the changes that are taking place today do just this.

For a variety of other reasons, the changes occurring in organizations today are more profound and fundamental than any I have experienced. In order for them to eventually have a positive impact on society and most individuals, there need to be major changes in the way people think about their careers and work as well as changes in the way governments relate to people and organizations.

The subject of this final chapter is the impact of the growth of new logic organizations on careers and career management, pay systems, legislation and public policy, education, the types of skills and training that are needed, and unions. The impact of the new logic is neither all good nor all bad. It is, however, significant and needs to be understood, discussed, and shaped if corporations and societies are to operate in ways that create both effective organizations and a high quality of life.

The New Logic of Careers: Skills, Job Markets, and Management

Fundamental to the new logic is a change in the relationship between individuals and their work organizations. In traditionally managed organizations, the longtime employer-employee covenant was that the organization would provide stable (if not lifetime) employment and would manage individuals' careers if they were loyal.

With corporate downsizing and restructuring, however, this traditional covenant has given way to a world in which large corporations lay off tens of thousands of employees at a time and temporary employment agencies are growing more rapidly than any other business. Indeed, one of the largest employers in the United States is now Manpower, a temporary-employment agency. Just a decade ago, Manpower employed only a small fraction of the numbers that AT&T employed, but now it employs more than either AT&T or IBM.

In many organizations, although it is clear that the "old deal" is gone, it is not clear that it has been replaced by a new deal that fits the new logic. The current "deal" in many companies goes something like this:

IF YOU:
  Stay
  Do your job plus someone else's
  "Volunteer" for task forces

We'll Provide:
   A job if we can
   Gestures that we care
   The same pay

And You'll Be Part of:
   A business trying to survive a crisis

The unsatisfactory nature of this "deal" brings up the very important question of whether a better mutual relationship is possible in new logic organizations. I am optimistic enough to believe that it is.

Many employment situations in new logic organizations can resemble the stable, traditional employee-employer relationship. New logic organizations need long-term employees, particularly those with skills that are critical to their core competencies and organizational capabilities. To keep and develop employees with the right skills and competencies, organizations need to make the requisite commitments and provide the right incentives.

High-performance organizations need clear, mutually beneficial relationships with most of their employees that look something like this:

If You:
   Develop the skills we need
   Apply them in ways that help the company succeed
   Behave consistently with our values

We'll Provide:
   A challenging work environment
   Support for your development
   Rewards for your contribution

And You'll Be Part of:
   A high-performance organization

I prefer to call this a "skill-based employment relationship," because skills are the foundation of it. As was discussed in Chapter Eight, people are asked to join a new logic organization because their skills match what is needed—or asked to leave because that match is no longer there. Organizations whose skill needs are relatively stable can make relatively long-term commitments to many employees. Indeed, they may have to make those commitments to assure that they have the competencies they need to be successful. In other organizations, however, where rapid changes in the market, technology, or business strategy make it difficult to predict the needs for particular skills, it may not be possible or desirable to make long-term commitments to more than a small number of employees.[1]

When I think of what it is like—and will be like—to work in a high-performance work organization, these adjectives come to mind: challenging, exciting, demanding, stressful, uncertain, and even bewildering. People are bound to feel more stress in a high-performance work environment simply because there are so few givens and there is so much more at risk in this world of much greater ambiguity and uncertainty. After all, workers are now responsible for how their organization is performing as well as for their lives at work and their careers.

Downsizing in the Future

Downsizing will continue. It may not be as dramatic or as frequent as it was during the 1980s and 1990s at Sears, GM, IBM, Digital, AT&T, Mobil, British Petroleum, Phillips, and a host of other large corporations. That downsizing was a consequence of corporations reducing the costs of the bureaucratic model of operating, as well as the result of companies losing market share in the new global economy. Layers of management and excess staff had to be removed in order for corporations to be cost-competitive.

In many cases, downsizing has not moved organizations to a high-performance management model. It has only stopped the fiscal bleeding that was due to too much managerial and administrative overhead. Thus many organizations may have to downsize further as they lose market share because they have not solved their performance problems. Other corporations who have still not addressed their competitiveness issues will have to downsize as well just to get their costs in line with the realities of their markets. They need to eliminate the massive control systems and bureaucracies they built while following the principles of the old logic.

As market changes create the need for different organizational capabilities and core competencies, it is inevitable that some new logic organizations will have to change the skill mix of their work force. Thus some employment instability will exist even in high-performance organizations. Overall, the form and nature of terminations and layoffs will likely change as organizations enter new businesses, exit old ones, or simply become more competitive in existing ones. They are less likely to be driven by a simple desire to reduce costs and more likely to be driven by a desire to get the organization's skill mix correct. The implication of continuing job insecurity for individuals is clear: career self-management must be a priority.

Career Self-Management

More and more individuals are, for all practical purposes, going to be self-employed. They may, at any point in time, be working for a large corporation or doing a piece of contract labor on a temporary basis—it does not matter. In both cases, they are in temporary, skill-based employment situations. In the short and long term, the market value of their skills is what really matters. As a result, individuals must be able to

- Develop marketable skills
- Assess and compare their skill levels to those of others
- Manage their own careers

In this new logic world, career management means knowing both your own skills—and those of others—and how much the employment market values and needs them. In addition, individuals must recognize that they can no longer reasonably expect most organizations to guide them through the white water of updating skills and/or converting from one skill set to another. Individuals will have to manage these tasks themselves.

As discussed in Chapter Eight, some organizations—Motorola, Raychem, and Texas Instruments—are committed to helping employees navigate the treacherous waters of the new workplace, but relatively few others have taken this stance. It is not realistic to expect most companies to absorb this cost in the foreseeable future—even though I believe that organizations should and that it can help contribute to a positive work culture. The reason for this organizational reluctance is simple: helping individuals develop the right skills is expensive. And although it will produce long-term payoffs for organizations, it may not produce short-term performance improvements. It is often much cheaper to hire someone who already has the new skills.

Those who do a good job of managing their careers stand to prosper in this new world. In fact, they should be able to have more control over their work lives and take advantage of the wide variety of work options available to individuals with marketable skills. Such options include working part-time, working through a temporary agency, developing an individual-contractor relationship with an organization, creating a virtual organization, joining an organization as a regular employee—in short, doing whatever meets an individual's needs. In the future, there are likely to be even more options available to people as corporations develop new ways to both meet their needs and attract the right talent.

Of course, access to all these options depends on whether individuals have marketable skills and can manage themselves and their development. Those who do not adapt to this new skill-based employment relationship are likely to pay a heavy price.

The income levels of employees who perform low-skill work are already falling further and further behind those of more highly skilled workers.[2] They are also losing purchasing power. This is essentially a problem of supply and demand. People who do not have skills that are in demand have minimal bargaining power in the labor market. In many cases they are also competing for work with billions of relatively unskilled employees all over the world. Their wages are being forced down to the global standard for people who are eager and willing to work but who lack technical skills and competencies.

Keys to Managing a Skill-Based Career

What can individuals do to manage their own skill-based careers? One obvious answer is to take the continuing-education courses offered by professional associations, universities, or other groups. In the United States, for example, the American Compensation Association has grown dramatically in the last decade by offering certification programs in pay administration. As the education market responds to the societal need for more work-related education, educational opportunities are increasing. The number of MBA programs, for example, has increased dramatically worldwide as more attention is paid to the need for a business education. Indeed, there are so many educational opportunities that it is difficult to be a wise consumer of them.

Individuals must learn to evaluate the market value of the educational opportunities that are available. Often, this depends on the credibility of an educational institution, because employers rely on certifications, degrees, and program reputations in order to determine how skilled an individual is. In essence, an individual who learns a great deal but does not do it in a way a company can easily see may have difficulty converting those skills into a good job opportunity or a higher pay rate.

It is critical that individuals regularly assess their skills to be sure that they are still at a world-class level. How? Skill-based pay systems can give individuals good feedback about their current competency levels. Individuals working full-time for an organization should be particularly active in gathering feedback about performance (ask for it!) and in attending relevant company training courses. Managers can attend skill assessment programs or participate in simulations of managerial situations that provide intensive feedback on how effectively participants handle a wide variety of situations.

In order to manage their own careers, individuals need to know about the job market—how to test it, how to identify changes in it, how to stay in touch with it, and how to build a network of individuals who can help them develop the skills and contacts needed to thrive in it. A variety of resources are available for individuals who want to maintain their skills and understand the job market. There are unions, as well as professional associations and clubs, that bring individuals together who have common interests in finance, human resources, and other specialty areas. In addition, considerable information about skills, work opportunities, and organizations is available in both the electronic media and the business press. Anyone who is not regularly reading the business press and finding out what is going on in the hiring world is at great risk of being unable to manage his or her career successfully.

Individuals can also help themselves by applying for new positions in their present organization and in others. In many respects, this is the best way for individuals to gain data about their market value and to learn what they need to do to manage their careers.

Commitment and Loyalty in New Logic Organizations

A good piece of advice for most people is to be happy and enthusiastic about your current job and employer but be prepared to leave. In other words, see your current job as an opportunity to show what you can do and as an opportunity to increase what you can do, not as a comfortable long-term niche.

A number of articles have suggested that because individuals cannot count on an organization for permanent employment, they should be, and inevitably will be, somewhat less committed and loyal. This may be inevitable, but it is also potentially counterproductive for all concerned. If an employee fails to fully commit to doing a good job, he or she may be more likely to be let go and may find it more difficult to get a new job. Failing to perform may also prevent individuals from developing the kinds of skills and competencies that will position them to get jobs elsewhere. Besides, a commitment to high performance is different from loyalty to an organization.

If loyalty means staying with an organization regardless of how you are treated or the prospects it offers, then it is clearly inappropriate to be "loyal," if an organization is not "loyal" to you. Loyalty and commitment is a two-way street and can only be reasonably expected of individuals when organizations commit to offering stable employment and developing the skills of their employees.

One thing individuals can and should do is clearly establish the nature of the employment relationship with their employer. In some cases the relationship is obvious because they are working through a temporary agency. But the relationship may not be so obvious when they have a "regular job" in a large organization. It can be especially confusing if the organization has a "rings strategy" of employment security, which identifies some employees as permanent and others as subject to layoffs and staff reductions. Knowing your position in the organization is critical to developing a sense of what kind of skills to develop and how to orient yourself toward the external labor market. A good rule of thumb: unless the organization says that you are a long-term employee and have a job for life, it is wise to assume that you are self-employed and to behave accordingly.

Management Careers in the New Logic

The new logic has already had a major effect on managerial career opportunities, and there is every reason to believe that it will have a greater impact in the future. Bluntly stated, there are going to be fewer and fewer managerial job opportunities. But let me qualify this a bit. When I say fewer managerial job opportunities, I mean fewer traditional career opportunities that involve upward movement from one management level to another. In particular, the classic linear career that emphasizes upward mobility within a single function (accounting, manufacturing, or marketing and sales) is simply not going to be as available. There will, however, be more work assignments in which individuals have the opportunity to use management skills as they lead work teams, project teams, and problem-solving activities.

Historically, the most popular and highly compensated career tracks for college graduates have included the management development programs of large companies. In high-performance work organizations, this type of career track is virtually nonexistent. Some individuals still need to be prepared for high-level management jobs, but their career moves are likely to be lateral and less frequent than in the traditional hierarchical model.

Although this change in available career tracks has negative implications for people who want a linear, ascending career, it can be positive for many others. Fewer and fewer individuals are going to be supervised by fast-track managers who emphasize short-term performance results. With fewer managers, there is also more of an opportunity for everyone to take on managerial responsibilities and to add value that will justify higher compensation levels and provide broader development opportunities.

In addition, there will be more opportunities for individuals to be part-time or quasi-managers as they lead work teams that do technical, production, and customer service work. On some teams, individuals may be team leaders and take on many management responsibilities, while on others they will be individual contributors because of their subject matter expertise.

The Impact of New Logic Pay Systems

The pay systems used in many high-performance work organizations give employees more control over the growth of their pay, but they also introduce more risk to the pay equation.[3] Skill-based pay fits well with the emphasis of the new logic upon individual skill development and career management. Moreover, new skill-based pay systems tend to result in somewhat higher pay rates, because they raise the market value of workers who acquire additional skills.

Variable pay can offer people the opportunity to make much more money than is possible under a traditional merit salary system (remember the Lincoln Electric example). Through profit sharing and stock ownership, individuals have the potential to reach much higher total compensation levels than if they are paid a salary only.

On the less positive side, the pay-for-performance approaches that are part of the new logic can potentially create much more risk (swings in pay are inevitable in profit-sharing plans and stock ownership plans) for individuals than is present with traditional merit pay systems. For those who like secure, predictable growth in their pay, such a system is a negative.

Variability in pay can also pose significant challenges for people in managing their personal finances. It can—and probably should—mean that individuals will be more conservative in taking on substantial debt that can only be covered if variable compensation plans pay off. Financial self-management—just like the self-management of work and career—is a skill that individuals will need to develop to a much higher level.

Perhaps the most serious compensation issue that is raised by the new logic concerns benefits. It is a relevant issue for all individuals who do not work full-time for a corporation that offers a long-term employment commitment. The benefit programs in most U.S. corporations and the government regulations that cover them are very much targeted toward protecting and supporting full-time, long-term employees. Many part-time and temporary employees are not eligible for retirement plans, disability insurance, health care benefits, and so on.

Today, people who change jobs frequently often find that they lose their retirement plan benefits every time they change employers. Typically, these plans require five or more years of employment with the same firm before benefits are actually earned. Unfortunately, there is little that individuals can do to protect themselves against the possibility of not having retirement and medical benefits. As will be discussed later, solutions to this problem depend largely on changes in company policy and on new legislation.

Educating the New Logic Work Force

Much has been written in the last decade about the importance of education in providing individuals with the kinds of technical skills that are needed in a high-tech workplace.[4] In high-performance organizations, workers need more than technical skills; they need skills that support important organizational capabilities. They must have skills that allow them to add value by managing themselves. The ability to work with others, to set goals, to get feedback about performance, to solve problems, and to understand group processes are all important self-management skills. Most of these skills are best developed early in an individual's education, not encountered first at the university level or after joining the work force.

A number of studies have pointed out that the U.S. educational system needs to be improved in order to support high-performance work organizations.[5] There is little question of the overall validity of this conclusion, particularly for kindergarten through high school, where the quality of education is often embarrassingly poor. However, I would argue that the situation with respect to university education is different. The United States has world-class universities. The problem is that they do not always prepare students to work in high-performance organizations.

Improving the educational system in the United States does not necessarily mean that most students will need to spend more years in school. Already, over 40 percent of the population attends school beyond high school, and more people receive college degrees than can be employed in jobs that require a college education. However, the high dropout rates in many big cities must be reduced. In a world dominated by high-performance companies, there will be little work for individuals who fail to complete high school and who have not developed work-relevant skills.

One thing that needs to change in most schools is the way students learn. Too many schools in the United States still emphasize rote learning, individual study, and disciplined, controlled environments. The classrooms in many respects look like the workplaces of the 1940s. To prepare students for high-performance work organizations, schools must create learning environments that include training in group problem-solving, peer training and coaching, and self-management. Teaching students to use information technology is also critical, because work will be increasingly done by individuals using networks and operating in virtual-reality work groups.

Schools also need to encourage students to adopt an attitude of openness to lifelong learning. There is no question that in order to have marketable skills, individuals must pursue ongoing educational experiences—whether inside the classroom, via computerized training systems, or through co-workers. The educational arena has to turn out adults who, for their lifetimes, are receptive to learning, want to learn, and can learn.

Business Education in the Future

In order to be effective managers and leaders in new logic organizations, individuals will need a much different kind of preparation than is provided by traditional master's degree programs in business administration. They do a good job of preparing students for linear careers in such functions as finance and marketing. But future managers will need to learn how to deal with groups, how to work on issues of strategy, how to articulate a business vision, how to build consensus, and how to work with peers in a mutually supportive manner. They need to learn not only to be good managers but also to be good team members and individual contributors.

Given the increasing importance of lateral processes in organizations, it is also very important that managers make cross-functional career moves. In the future, a good manager (or a good employee, for that matter) is unlikely to be someone who has spent his or her entire career in finance, human resource management, or marketing. Instead, a good manager will be someone who will have spent four or five years in each of several functions and who is capable of performing an important integrative role as a member of a product development team or a task force. That manager's expertise may look like a T—that is, deep in one area such as finance or human resource management, but broad in knowledge of a number of functions. With this type of background, an individual should be well prepared to move back and forth between the roles of individual contributor and manager.

Business schools can play an important part in providing individuals with a broad understanding of how business operates, a good grasp of the different functions, and in-depth knowledge of at least one functional area. But perhaps the most important thing a business school education can give a student is an idea of how complex organizations work and the necessary skills to get things done in a new logic organization. In essence, it can help students become leaders, doers, and creators of key value-added processes in complex organizations.

The Job of Senior Management

The new logic suggests that senior managers will need a different type of background than they historically have had. This is particularly true for the president and chief executive officer. In essence, the senior executive or executive team needs to be the chief organizational effectiveness officer (COEO). This requires a very different preparation than is needed to be a chief technologist, finance officer, or CEO of an old logic firm. COEOs need to develop in-depth skills in dealing with people, organizational architecture (and its interfaces with information systems and measurement processes), business strategy, and the many other organizational effectiveness issues that have been discussed. Instead of a single-function career, the COEO needs to have a career that provides him or her with a broad understanding of how organizations work and how they can be designed and led.

After all, providing the right core competencies, organizational capabilities, strategy, design, and leadership is the critical value-added process that must come from the top. It simply cannot be done elsewhere in the organization. If senior management does not add value in this way—or if those at the top do it poorly because they are not well prepared for the responsibility—the organization's performance is inevitably going to suffer.

I recently consulted with a technology organization whose CEO had worked in sales before becoming CEO. He had little interest in and tolerance for organizational issues. He wanted a simple organizational design that was easy to operate. In many cases, of course, this is desirable, but in the case of his firm it simply was not possible. The firm was trying to do complex systems integration work in the field of computers, and a simple organization's structure could not accomplish what they wanted to do. Indeed, if it was simple to organize and manage, many of the firm's customers would do it themselves. Because the customers could not, his firm had the chance to earn a nice profit margin on its business. Unfortunately, in this case, the CEO's interests and skills simply did not match the demands his organization faced, and, as a result, his firm was struggling to develop the organizational capabilities it needed.

There are some outstanding CEOs who have played the role of COEO for their corporations. Indeed, many of them have become so well known that they have taken on an almost superhuman quality. Earlier, I mentioned such examples as Larry Bossidy of AlliedSignal, the now retired Max De Pree of Herman Miller, Rich Teerlink of Harley-Davidson, and Bob Galvin of Motorola. There are many more who are not as well known but are equally impressive.

The Changing Role of Unions in the New Logic

Unions around the world developed during the era of bureaucratic and scientific management. Once they understood how traditional logic organizations operated, they found a very effective role for themselves. They adopted an adversarial stance with management and positioned themselves as the advocates for employees, arguing—correctly—that employees who have little power need to be protected against management's substantial and, at times, arbitrary use of power. There is little doubt that, as a result of unions, employees today are better paid, are safer, and, overall, enjoy a better quality of life.[6]

By countering the bureaucratic management step-by-step in its assumptions and processes, unions carved a very effective role for themselves. When management wanted to use job descriptions, unions proceeded to negotiate more and more carefully defined job descriptions that became descriptions both of what someone is responsible for and what they are not responsible for. As workers became more specialized and less flexible over time, the high levels of specialization led to the need for more employees, who, of course, joined unions and made the existing work force even more inflexible. Job descriptions also allowed unions to expand their role by filing grievances concerning individuals working outside of their job descriptions or about the design and assignment of new work.

Given the apparent success of unions, why has union membership declined in the United States in the last three decades? Why have workers at the new greenfield plants of Procter & Gamble and a host of other organizations, and workers at new, high-performance organizations such as Nucor, Chapparal Steel, Compaq, Dell, Wal-Mart, W.L. Gore, and Home Depot not joined the union movement? When I ask them, they say something like this: "I have a better deal here. Why should I pay union dues and be restricted by union rules and regulations? Here I am in control."

The decline of the union movement and the inability of unions to organize high-performance work organizations has led some to conclude that unions are obsolete and no longer have a meaningful role to play in the United States (fewer than 15 percent of employees are members). I only partially agree. In traditionally managed organizations in the United States and elsewhere in the developed world, unions are critically important because they still contribute to the quality of work life and help protect employees' rights. Without the presence of unions, rogue managers in these organizations would undoubtedly be more likely to mistreat employees and be unwilling to offer them fair wages and reasonable working conditions.

But are traditional unions needed in high-performance work organizations? I believe the answer to this question is clear: no. I say this because they are unlikely to make the organization more effective or improve the work life of employees. In the absence of unions, these employees already have more information, knowledge, and power than unionized employees typically have. In effect, they already "run the organization," so there is nothing left for a traditional union to do except get in the way.

One might argue that because high-performance work organizations do not and will not always treat people fairly, unions are needed. But the body of laws in the United States and other developed countries provides the protection employees need in most situations. Laws protect employees from wrongful discharge, age and racial discrimination, and the unfair administration of pay and benefits.

What employees do need in new logic organizations is the institutionalization of the employee involvement and participative practices that are often "discretionary"—and thus subject to cancellation. They also need help in dealing with the complexities of health care and retirement programs, and with career planning and skill development. Although unions could provide help in all of these areas, most traditional unions do not, which is why I conclude that they are not needed in high-performance organizations. However, a new kind of union might play a quite positive role.[7]

With respect to career development and training, as well as the certification of skills, unions are already active in some industries. For example, in the motion picture industry and in the construction trades, unions train employees, certify their competency, and virtually act as employment agencies to help firms meet their needs for temporary labor as projects form and advance through different stages. Unions in these industries also have a history of helping temporary employees obtain retirement and health care benefits and of creating their own benefit plans to make up for the unwillingness of companies to offer such plans. Unions could potentially expand their reach beyond the industries where they are now active in these areas by offering skill development and certification to businesses that use skilled temporary employees to do such jobs as write software and handle customer service calls.

Unions can also remain viable by working with businesses to create high-performance organizations. The United Auto Workers, for example, joined with General Motors to launch the new Saturn car company. In this effort to create a new logic organization, the union took on the role of ensuring that the employee involvement systems and practices would operate effectively and help contribute to organizational performance. In addition, it played an important part in communicating and developing the mission and vision of the organization. The UAW also played a key role in helping its members develop the skills necessary to do the work at Saturn.

Despite examples such as Saturn, the American labor movement has been slow to recognize the importance of high-performance organizations and has had considerable difficulty figuring out what its role should be in them. Most unions do not see the Saturn example as something to be emulated; it is, in fact, still a subject of some controversy within the UAW and, I should add, within the rest of General Motors as well.

I am convinced that part of the union resistance to high-performance organizations stems from the fundamental change that union leaders have to make in order to play a meaningful role in them. The senior leadership in the union movement, in many respects, has the same problem as senior management in corporations when it comes to accepting the change to the new logic. In both cases, many of the primary skills they have relied on become obsolete.

Instead of being adversarial, union leaders need to be cooperative. Instead of filing grievances, they need to make suggestions on how to improve organizational effectiveness. Instead of focusing on how to get employees a greater percentage of the profits and gains, they need to figure out how to help the organization make gains. In short, they need to become partners in the business and, at the same time, represent an important group of stakeholders, the employees.

To make sure that employees share fairly in the organization's success and play an important role in achieving that success, union leaders need to understand the business. They need to learn how to communicate business results and information to the work force. Union leaders need to provide direction as to how the organization can become more effective and how the skills and capabilities of their members can be developed and utilized. Finally, union leaders need to transform their organizations, because as employees learn about the new logic, they will not accept unions that operate in a traditional, autocratic way.

Changing Unions

When I first began working with union leaders, I was part of a group at the University of Michigan that started eight labor-management cooperation programs across the United States in the 1970s.[8] Several of these programs were quite successful and helped convince

Irving Bluestone and Doug Fraser of the United Auto Workers, as well as other union leaders, that it was vital that they move in this direction. Unfortunately, these pioneering union leaders were never able to convince a majority of union leaders in the United States to change. Apparently the thought of adopting a whole new role was simply too frightening. Indeed, some unions such as the International Association of Machinists even adopted policies that condemned the idea of high-performance work organizations as a management trick to exploit the work force.

An encouraging event did occur in 1994. The AFL-CIO, which represents most unions in the United States, finally adopted a policy statement that acknowledged the growing prevalence of high-performance work organizations and described the role that the union movement can and should play in them.[9] This statement may be an important first step in the union movement recognizing that it must change in order to survive.

The opportunity now exists for unions to play a key role in creating high-performance management practices. I believe that if unions take on this challenge they can help create new logic organizations. After all, studies have shown for decades that most employees want more participation and a greater voice in their organizations.[10] So employees are ready for their unions to change.

Given the long-standing failure of unions to respond positively to the issues raised by the new logic, it is hardly surprising that unions are declining in the United States and that most employees today do not see unions as helpful to them. Thus, if unions fail to change, I believe they will continue to decline and ultimately cease to be a significant factor in most organizations in the United States. One exception: the public sector, which is likely to continue to be managed in a predominantly traditional way and, therefore, is a fertile ground for an adversarial union-management relationship. A second possible exception is that part of the service sector that pays low wages, provides poor or no benefits, and is traditionally managed. Here also there is a need for traditional unions.

High-Performance Organizations and Public Policy

In the United States and in many other developed countries, laws and government regulations have played a major role in institutionalizing traditional management practices. Legislators may not have set out with this goal in mind, but that has been their impact. Frequently the legislative solution to problems in the workplace has been to specify that organizations use fair, reasonable, and well-administered traditional practices.

There has been relatively little appetite to try to change the fundamental way that organizations operate by passing laws that encourage them to adopt the new logic. The situation is somewhat different outside the United States—western Europe in particular. There, legislation has been passed that encourages and, in some cases, mandates profit sharing and participative management practices that are supportive of the new logic.

The U.S. laws concerning the creation and operation of trade unions are classic examples of government support for the traditional logic. These laws are effective in telling employers and employees how to deal with each other in an adversarial manner. They detail, for example, how both sides must act when employees set out to organize themselves into a union. They regulate a union's dealings with management and provide courts and hearings to resolve disputes. Labor law legislation in the United States is almost entirely lacking in provisions that try to create a climate of cooperation. In important ways, some laws and regulations actually make it difficult for an organization to operate in a high-performance manner. This needs to change. Let me give you three examples of laws put in place in the 1930s to make the point that in order for a society to have high-performance work organizations, laws and regulations need to support them.

U.S. law requires that so-called non-exempt employees receive overtime pay. This law was designed to protect non-management employees from being asked to work excessive, uncompensated overtime hours. It clearly made sense when it was written into law because in every organization at that time, there was a clear line of distinction between managers who perhaps did not need this protection and employees who did. In high-performance work organizations, the distinction between managers and employees is intentionally blurred and, for all practical purposes, is often nonexistent. In fact, central to the very design of new logic organizations is the idea of creating a single, seamless "all-managerial" work force. But current law does not recognize this work design.

Some workers must be classified as non-exempt employees and be paid accordingly.

Another example is a provision in the National Labor Relations Act that limits the degree to which employees who are not organized into unions can participate in decision making concerning such conditions of employment as hours of work and wages. This law was originally designed to protect employees from companies creating company-dominated or sham unions in order to make it more difficult for legitimate unions to organize the work force. It has the effect now of limiting the degree to which companies can engage employees in participative decision making—which is in direct conflict with the spirit and intent of the new logic. Thus, companies are faced with violating either the law or the new logic of high-performance organizations. The law clearly must be changed in order to support and encourage all employees to participate in decision making about their conditions of employment.

A third example is the lack of retirement benefits for part-time, temporary, and short-term employees. As previously noted, they are a rapidly growing group, as fewer employees have long-term, stable relationships with a single organization. The situation with retirement benefits will undoubtedly become a greater concern as more and more individuals who have changed organizations frequently or have not had coverage begin to retire without retirement benefits. To a degree, individuals can manage these problems themselves if they are good savers and responsible in preparing for their retirement. It is unrealistic, however, to expect all employees to do this.

The solution seems obvious. Change the law to make retirement benefits portable. This solution is already in place for university faculty and many others who work for nonprofit organizations. It could work for all individuals, whether they work for large organizations and change jobs or work on a part-time or temporary basis. Some employees might have to pay more of their own money into a retirement plan, but the employer could still be required to make a contribution.

Supportive retirement plans are critical to any society that wishes to have a flexible, high-performance work force. The government must develop and put into place mechanisms that protect the economic welfare of employees, whether these individuals are literally working on their own or working for an organization. If this is not done, society will end up with far too many people who continue to work for the same organization just to protect their benefits. There will also be far too many individuals who do not have the income that they need for a decent retirement. It simply is not right to ask employees to sacrifice their retirement years in order to build high-performance organizations and a flexible work force.

Winners and Losers in the New Logic

In the traditional logic, the clear winners have been senior management, mid-level managers, and relatively low-skilled manufacturing employees. Senior management, for example, has been extremely well paid, particularly so in the United States, and given enormous amounts of power and prestige. Although their job security has lessened in the last decade, senior management has still gained in pay overall and, in most cases, been handsomely compensated through "golden parachutes" when they have been let go.

Managers at most levels below the senior management level have also been well compensated, although in the United States they have not necessarily been paid better than their peers in other developed countries. They have also received numerous perks and privileges and, until recently, enjoyed high levels of job security with growing reward levels and well-funded retirements. Despite their extensive compensation packages, they have had relatively little accountability for profitability and business success. They have only had to manage the behavior of those who report to them or worry about how the managers they supervise are supervising those below them.

Relatively low-skilled manufacturing employees in the United States and other developed countries, including Germany and France, have also been winners under the traditional management approach. Because of the effectiveness of their unions and the dominance of their manufacturing firms, these workers have enjoyed a very high standard of living compared to workers in most of the rest of the world. In some cases, given the world market value of their skills, they have actually been dramatically overpaid. Employee wages in the service sector have not been as high. Nevertheless, even in the service sector, many employees in Europe and the United States are highly paid given the world market value of their skills.

What about the future? First, I believe that senior managers are likely to continue to be winners in high-performance organizations. But the skills required by the new logic may mean that different individuals will end up in executive positions. Given the strong egalitarian emphasis in the new logic, senior managers may not be as highly paid as they have been in the past (or at least not see the increases in their pay that they have seen in the last decade). This should be particularly true in the United States, where executives are the most highly compensated in the world. Already, for example, there is a clear trend toward fewer perquisites and special benefits for managers in the United States.

Second, I expect to see a radical change in the world of middle- and lower-level managers. There are already fewer of them because of downsizing. As the new logic spreads, self-managing teams and information technology will do much of the work of these managers. What's more, the command-and-control behaviors as well as the reports and the information these managers have created will no longer be needed or valued. The result: in many cases, these jobs will simply be eliminated because they are unnecessary and do not add value.

The most important change for the middle- and lower-level managers who remain will be in the kinds of skills they need in order to be successful. In the new logic, it is much more important for them to be able to lead groups and teams and to develop advanced technical skills and competencies. This means that many of the individuals who succeeded in old logic management jobs are unlikely to match that success in the new logic.

I am already seeing many situations where individuals who have worked for years to obtain very desirable lower and middle management positions now find that the management jobs which remain require skills that they have not acquired because they were not important in the past. Thus some people have spent fifteen or twenty years of their careers getting ready for a position only to find that it is suddenly beyond their reach or nonexistent. Given this situation, it is not surprising that many middle- and lower-level managers feel insecure and disenfranchised and, in fact, end up as significant opponents of change because they are the ones who will end up losing out.

Third, there is growing evidence that many relatively unskilled production and service employees in developed countries will not be winners. Their wages are increasingly moving toward world standards, which are substantially lower than those in the United States, Japan, and much of Europe.

We have already seen decreases in the wages of many low-skilled workers in steel, aluminum, auto assembly, and other industries that were slow to move to high-performance work organizations. In some cases, entire industries have disappeared from developed countries because the work could not be done at the existing wage rates and could not be changed to fit the high-performance model. Therefore, it could only be done in low-wage countries. For example, much simple assembly work—such as the assembly of televisions and the manufacture of athletic shoes—has essentially disappeared from the United States as a consequence of global competition.

As discussed in earlier chapters, some work does not allow employees to add enough value for it to be done in a high-wage country. However, work can be done in high-wage countries if the work is designed so that people at all levels in the organization can add significant value. It also can be done if the value of labor is a small fraction of the total cost of doing business, as with paper manufacturing and gasoline refining. Companies in high-wage countries must develop the right management approach and focus on the right industries, and individuals must have the right skills and competencies. When this happens, individuals throughout an organization can enjoy a high standard of living and profit from the new logic of organizing.

Workers who can learn different skills and adapt to the new organizational forms should do well. But the future is not bright for those who cannot adapt to situations that require them to deal with ambiguity, to manage themselves and others, to handle change, to add to their skills, and to develop significant technical and organizational expertise. For some relatively low-skilled workers, the new skills they need to learn may be beyond their learning capabilities, or they may simply be too invested in the status quo to give it up. For those who are unwilling or unable to change, I do not believe anything can be done to assure that they will continue to enjoy the same standard of living.

I agree with those who argue that the "gold collar" knowledge worker is going to be one of the winners in the future.[11] There is little doubt in my mind that individuals who have high levels of technical knowledge in the right core competency areas, such as health care, computer programming, consulting, entertainment, and design, will be winners in the future. Particularly in developed countries, knowledge work that requires individuals to have extensive training and specific expertise will become more and more common. Those who have the right skills gain considerable bargaining power in knowledge work situations because they are not easily replaced and their performance can have a big impact on an organization's performance. Just the opposite is true when work and skills are easy to learn and many have them.

But focusing only on the increased power of highly skilled gold-collar workers misses an important implication of the new logic. The new logic creates the potential for more and more individuals—from production workers in auto plants to customer service representatives in financial service businesses—to add significant value and thus become silver-collar, if not gold-collar, workers. In this respect, adoption of the new logic can be quite positive for those people who can accept change, who can work to achieve continuous improvement, and who can focus on improving and upgrading their skills and competencies.

High-Performance Work Organizations: Changing Our Society

This last chapter has focused on the changes that the creation of high-performance work organizations will bring about for individuals, unions, education, and public policy. Added together, the changes will produce a significantly different society from the one that has existed since the advent of traditional bureaucratic organizations. In a number of respects, this society is likely to be a better one as more individuals play meaningful roles and have a chance to grow, to develop, and to use their skills and abilities. But it will not be positive for everyone, and the change is likely to be difficult for many of us.

People without the fundamental skills and aptitudes to work in a high-performance organization are likely to experience the most obvious negative consequences. For them, the stress and insecurity will be great and the learning difficult—particularly if their attachment to the status quo is too strong to give up. As I have already said, I do not believe that anything can be done to ensure that individuals who do not adapt can maintain the same standard of living.

The new economic reality of global competition and the new logic of organizing represent major societal disruptions. They are bound to make life much more difficult for the middle managers, semiskilled production operators, and first-level supervisors who prospered in traditional work organizations. These individuals make up a large portion of what is considered the stable middle class in the United States and other industrialized nations. The social fallout that will occur as these groups face a much different environment than the one under which they prospered is likely to be substantial and long-lasting. They are already feeling anxious about the changes they face. They both need and deserve help in adjusting to the realities of a new economy and a new way of working. Among other things, they need a safety net that provides medical coverage, retirement income, and opportunities to learn needed skills.

Given the potential negative impact of organizations moving toward high-performance structures based on the new logic, it is reasonable to ask whether this transformation is worth it. I would suggest that it is not only advisable but necessary for developed countries that wish to maintain and/or increase their standard of living. Developed countries that fail to adopt the new logic will lose out to developing countries that have competitive advantages such as low wages or abundant natural resources. Even more significantly, not adopting the new logic will ultimately mean losing not only routine jobs but other jobs that can be done by well-educated work forces in lower-wage countries.

In competing to retain work, countries and companies need a competitive advantage. One distinct and not altogether widespread advantage is the ability to organize and manage people to do complex work. Those who have this ability need to capitalize on it and structure their organizations and societies accordingly. Economic competitiveness will increasingly rest on organizational meritocracy. Those businesses and societies that are best at creating effective organizations will also be best at ensuring a high standard of living and quality of life. The key question, then, is not whether high-performance, new logic organizations should be created, but how fast they can be created.

Notes

Introduction

1. Kuhn, T. S. *The Structure of Scientific Revolutions.* Chicago: University of Chicago Press, 1970.
2. Lawler, E. E., Mohrman, S. A., and Ledford, G. E. *Creating High Performance Organizations: Practices and Results of Employee Involvement and Total Quality Management in Fortune 1000 Companies.* San Francisco: Jossey-Bass, 1995.
3. Taylor, F. W. *The Principles of Scientific Management.* New York: Norton, 1911.
4. Ulrich, D., and Lake, D. *Organizational Capability.* New York: Wiley, 1990.
5. Prahalad, C. K., and Hamel, G. "The Core Competence of the Corporation." *Harvard Business Review,* 1990, *68*(3), 79–91.

Chapter One

1. McGregor, D. *The Human Side of Enterprise.* New York: McGraw-Hill, 1960.
2. Argyris, C. *Personality and Organization.* New York: HarperCollins, 1957.
   Likert, R. *New Patterns of Management.* New York: McGraw-Hill, 1961.
3. Pfeffer, J. *Competitive Advantage Through People.* Boston: Harvard Business School Press, 1994.
   Huselid, M. A. "The Impact of Human Resource Management Practices on Turnover, Productivity, and Corporate Financial Performance." *Academy of Management Journal,* 1995, *38*(3), 635–672.
4. Lawler, E. E., Mohrman, S. A., and Ledford, G. E. *Creating High Performance Organizations: Practices and Results of Employee Involvement and Total Quality Management in Fortune 1000 Companies.* San Francisco: Jossey-Bass, 1995.
5. Womack, J. P., Jones, D. T., and Roos, D. *The Machine That Changed the World.* New York: Macmillan, 1990.
6. Lawler, E. E. *The Ultimate Advantage: Creating the High-Involvement Organization.* San Francisco: Jossey-Bass, 1992.

291

7. Reich, R. B. *The Work of Nations.* New York: Knopf, 1991.

8. Schneider, B., and Bowen, D. E. *Winning the Service Game.* Boston: Harvard Business School Press, 1995.

9. Conger, J. A. *The Charismatic Leader: Behind the Mystique of Exceptional Leadership.* San Francisco: Jossey-Bass, 1989.
   Bennis, W. G., and Nanus, B. *Leaders: The Strategies for Taking Charge.* New York: HarperCollins, 1985.

10. Collins, J. C., and Porras, J. I. *Built to Last.* New York: HarperCollins, 1994.

11. McCall, M. W., Jr., Lombardo, M. M., and Morrison, A. M. *The Lessons of Experience: How Successful Executives Develop on the Job.* San Francisco: New Lexington Press, 1988.

Chapter Two

1. Galbraith, J. R. *Designing Organizations: An Executive Briefing on Strategy, Structure, and Process.* San Francisco: Jossey-Bass, 1995.

2. Schein, E. H. *Organizational Culture and Leadership.* San Francisco: Jossey-Bass, 1985.

3. Lawler, E. E., Mohrman, S. A., and Ledford, G. E. *Creating High Performance Organizations: Practices and Results of Employee Involvement and Total Quality Management in Fortune 1000 Companies.* San Francisco: Jossey-Bass, 1995.

4. Dunnette, M. D., Campbell, J. P., Lawler, E. E., and Weick, K. E. *Managerial Behavior, Performance and Effectiveness.* New York: McGraw-Hill, 1970.

5. Lawler, E. E. *Motivation in Work Organizations.* San Francisco: Jossey-Bass, 1994.

6. Vroom, V. H. *Work and Motivation.* New York: Wiley, 1964.

7. Herzberg, F. *Work and the Nature of Man.* Cleveland, Ohio: World, 1966.

8. Lincoln, J. F. *Incentive Management.* Cleveland, Ohio: Lincoln Electric Company, 1951.

9. Maslow, A. H. "A Theory of Human Motivation." *Psychological Review,* 1943, *50,* 370–396.
   Maslow, A. H. *Motivation and Personality.* New York: HarperCollins, 1954.

10. Lawler, E. E. S*trategic Pay: Aligning Organizational Strategies and Pay Systems.* San Francisco: Jossey-Bass, 1990.

Chapter Three

1. Mintzberg, H. *The Rise and Fall of Strategic Planning.* New York: Free Press, 1994.

2. Collins, J. C., and Porras, J. I. *Built to Last.* New York: HarperCollins, 1994.
3. Hamel, G., and Prahalad, C. K. "Strategic Intent." *Harvard Business Review,* 1989, *67*(3), 63–76.
4. Locke, E., and Latham, G. *A Theory of Goal Setting and Task Performance.* Englewood Cliffs, N.J.: Prentice-Hall, 1990.
5. Hamel, G., and Prahalad, C. K. *Competing for the Future.* Boston: Harvard Business School Press, 1994.
6. Lawler, E. E., and Galbraith, J. R. "Avoiding the Corporate Dinosaur Syndrome." *Organizational Dynamics,* 1994, *23*(2), 5–17.
7. O'Toole, J. *The Executive's Compass.* New York: Oxford University Press, 1993.
8. Selznick, P. *Leadership in Administration.* New York: HarperCollins, 1957.
9. Weisbord, M. *Discovering Common Ground.* San Francisco: Berrett-Koehler, 1992.
10. Ledford, G. E., Wendenhof, J., and Strahley, J. "Realizing a Corporate Philosophy." *Organizational Dynamics,* 1995, *23*(3), 5–19.
11. Prahalad, C. K., and Hamel, G. "The Core Competence of the Corporation." *Harvard Business Review,* 1990, *68*(3), 79–91.

Chapter Four

1. Nadler, D. A., Gerstein, M. C., Shaw, R. B., and Associates. *Organizational Architecture: Designs for Changing Organizations.* San Francisco: Jossey-Bass, 1992.
2. Ashkenas, R., Ulrich, D., Jick, T., and Kerr, S. *The Boundaryless Organization: Crossing the Barrier to Outstanding Performance.* San Francisco: Jossey-Bass, 1995.
3. Deming, W. E. *Out of the Crisis.* Cambridge, Mass.: MIT Press, 1986.
4. Adams, W., and Brock, J. W. *The Bigness Complex.* New York: Pantheon, 1986.
5. Galbraith, J. R., Lawler, E. E., and Associates. *Organizing for the Future: The New Logic for Managing Complex Organizations.* San Francisco: Jossey-Bass, 1993.
6. Mohrman, S. A., Cohen, S. G., and Mohrman, A. M. *Designing Team-Based Organizations: New Forms for Knowledge Work.* San Francisco: Jossey-Bass, 1995.

Chapter Five

1. Galbraith, J. R. *Organization Design.* Reading, Mass.: Addison-Wesley, 1977.
2. Galbraith, J. R. *Competing with Flexible Lateral Organizations.* (2nd ed.) Reading, Mass.: Addison-Wesley, 1994.

3. Galbraith, J. R., Lawler, E. E., and Associates. *Organizing for the Future: The New Logic for Managing Complex Organizations.* San Francisco: Jossey-Bass, 1993.
4. Hammer, M., and Champy, J. *Reengineering the Corporation: A Manifesto for Business Revolution.* New York: Harper Business, 1993.
5. Miles, R. E., and Snow, C. "Organizations: New Concepts for New Forms." *California Management Review,* 1986, *28,* 62–73.
6. Davidow, W. H., and Malone, M. S. *The Virtual Corporation.* New York: HarperCollins, 1992.
7. Davis, S. M., and Lawrence, P. R. *Matrix.* Reading, Mass.: Addison-Wesley, 1977.

Chapter Six

1. Hackman, J. R., and Oldham, G. R. *Work Redesign.* Reading, Mass.: Addison-Wesley, 1980.
2. Mowday, R. T., Porter, L. W., and Steers, R. M. *Employee-Organization Linkages.* San Diego, Calif.: Academic Press, 1982.
3. Herzberg, F. *Work and the Nature of Man.* Cleveland, Ohio: World, 1966.
4. Hackman, J. R., and Lawler, E. E. "Employee Reactions to Job Characteristics." *Journal of Applied Psychology,* 1971, *55,* 259–286.
5. Lawler, E. E., Mohrman, S. A., and Ledford, G. E. *Creating High Performance Organizations: Practices and Results of Employee Involvement and Total Quality Management in Fortune 1000 Companies.* San Francisco: Jossey-Bass, 1995.
6. Lawler, E. E. *High-Involvement Management: Participative Strategies for Improving Organizational Performance.* San Francisco: Jossey-Bass, 1986.
7. Hackman, J. R., and Oldham, G. R. *Work Redesign.* Reading, Mass.: Addison-Wesley, 1980.
8. Lawler, E. E., Mohrman, S. A., and Ledford, G. E. *Creating High Performance Organizations.* San Francisco: Jossey-Bass, 1995.
9. Lawler, E. E. *The Ultimate Advantage: Creating the High-Involvement Organization.* San Francisco: Jossey-Bass, 1992.
10. Lawler, E. E., Mohrman, S. A., and Ledford, G. E. *Creating High Performance Organizations.* San Francisco: Jossey-Bass, 1995.
11. Lawler, E. E., and Mohrman, S. A. "Quality Circles After the Fad." *Harvard Business Review,* 1985, *85*(1), 64–71.
12. Lawler, E. E. "The New Plant Revolution." *Organizational Dynamics,* 1978, *6*(3), 2–12.
13. Seashore, S. *Group Cohesiveness in the Industrial Work Group.* Ann Arbor: Survey Research Center, Institute for Social Research, University of Michigan, 1954.

14. Mohrman, S. A., Cohen, S. G., and Mohrman, A. M. *Designing Team-Based Organizations: New Forms for Knowledge Work.* San Francisco: Jossey-Bass, 1995.

Chapter Seven

1. Seashore, S. *Group Cohesiveness in the Industrial Work Group.* Ann Arbor: Survey Research Center, Institute for Social Research, University of Michigan, 1954.
2. Mohrman, S. A., Cohen, S. G., and Mohrman, A. M. *Designing Team-Based Organizations: New Forms for Knowledge Work.* San Francisco: Jossey-Bass, 1995.
3. Pasmore, W. A. *Designing Effective Organizations.* New York: Wiley, 1988.
4. Hammer, M., and Champy, J. *Reengineering the Corporation.* New York: Harper Business, 1993.
5. Mankin, D., Cohen, S. G., and Bikson, T. K. *Teams and Technology: Fulfilling the Promise of the New Organization.* Boston: Harvard Business School Press, 1996.
   Walton, R. E. *Up and Running: Integrating Information Technology and the Organization.* Cambridge, Mass.: Harvard Business School Press, 1989.
   Zuboff, S. *In the Age of the Smart Machine: The Future of Work and Power.* New York: Basic Books, 1988.
6. Adler, P. S., and Cole, R. E. "Designed for Learning: A Tale of Two Auto Plants." *Sloan Management Review,* 1993, *34*(3), 85–94.
   Berggren, C. "NUMMI vs. Uddevalla." *Sloan Management Review,* 1994, *35*(2), 37–49.
7. Womack, J. P., Jones, D. T., and Roos, D. *The Machine That Changed the World.* New York: Macmillan, 1990.
8. Ashkenas, R., Ulrich, D., Jick, T., and Kerr, S. *The Boundaryless Organization: Crossing the Barrier to Outstanding Performance.* San Francisco: Jossey-Bass, 1995.
9. Mohrman, S. A., Cohen, S. G., and Mohrman, A. M. *Designing Team-Based Organizations.* San Francisco: Jossey-Bass, 1995.
10. Mohrman, S. A., Cohen, S. G., and Mohrman, A. M. *Designing Team-Based Organizations.* San Francisco: Jossey-Bass, 1995.
11. Bowen, D. E., and Lawler, E. E. "The Empowerment of Service Workers: What, Why, How, and When." *Sloan Management Review,* 1992, *33*(3), 31–39.
12. Becker, F., and Steele, F. *Workplace by Design: Mapping the High-Performance Workscape.* San Francisco: Jossey-Bass, 1995.
13. Mankin, D., Cohen, S. G., and Bikson, T. K. *Teams and Technology.* Boston: Harvard Business School Press, 1996.

14. Pelz, D. C., and Andrews, F. M. *Scientists in Organizations.* New York: Wiley, 1966.

Chapter Eight

1. Lawler, E. E. "From Job-Based to Competency-Based Organizations." *Journal of Organizational Behavior,* 1994, *15,* 3–15.
2. Lawler, E. E., Mohrman, S. A., and Ledford, G. E. *Creating High Performance Organizations: Practices and Results of Employee Involvement and Total Quality Management in Fortune 1000 Companies.* San Francisco: Jossey-Bass, 1995.
3. Bowen, D. E., Ledford, G. E., Jr., and Nathan, B. R. "Hiring for the Organization, Not the Job." *Academy of Management Executive,* 1991, *5*(4), 35–51.
4. Wanous, J. P. *Organizational Entry.* Reading, Mass.: Addison-Wesley, 1980.
5. Schneider, B., and Schmitt, N. *Staffing Organizations.* (2nd ed.) Prospect Heights, Ill.: Waveland Press, 1992.
   Heneman, H. H., and Heneman, R. L. *Staffing Organizations.* Middleton, Wis.: Mendoti House, 1994.
6. Bray, D. W., Campbell, R. J., and Grant, D. L. *Formative Years in Business: A Long Term Study of Managerial Lives.* New York: Wiley-Interscience, 1974.
7. Wiggenhorn, W. "Motorola U.: When Training Becomes an Education." *Harvard Business Review, 68*(4), 71–83.
8. Lawler, E. E., Mohrman, S. A., and Ledford, G. E. *Creating High Performance Organizations.* San Francisco: Jossey-Bass, 1995.
9. Dunnette, M. D., Campbell, J. P., Lawler, E. E., and Weick, K. E. *Managerial Behavior, Performance and Effectiveness.* New York: McGraw-Hill, 1970.
10. McCall, M. W., Jr., Lombardo, M. M., and Morrison, A. M. *The Lessons of Experience: How Successful Executives Develop on the Job.* San Francisco: New Lexington Press, 1988.
11. Galbraith, J. R. *Competing with Flexible Lateral Organizations.* (2nd ed.) Reading, Mass.: Addison-Wesley, 1994.
12. Waterman, R. H., Jr., Waterman, J. A., and Collard, B. A. "Toward a Career-Resilient Workforce." *Harvard Business Review,* 1994, *72*(4), 87–95.
13. Handy, C. *The Age of Unreason.* Boston: Harvard Business School Press, 1990.
   Handy, C. *The Age of Paradox.* Boston: Harvard Business School Press, 1994.

Chapter Nine

1. Porter, L. W., and Lawler, E. E. *Managerial Attitudes and Performance.* Homewood, Ill.: Irwin-Dorsey Press, 1968.
2. Lawler, E. E. *Strategic Pay: Aligning Organizational Strategies and Pay Systems.* San Francisco: Jossey-Bass, 1990.
3. Lawler, E. E. *Strategic Pay.* San Francisco: Jossey-Bass, 1990. Lawler, E. E. *Pay and Organizational Development.* Reading, Mass.: Addison Wesley, 1980.
4. Lawler, E. E., Mohrman, S. A., and Ledford, G. E. *Creating High Performance Organizations: Practices and Results of Employee Involvement and Quality Management in Fortune 1000 Companies.* San Francisco: Jossey-Bass, 1995.
5. Gupta, N., Ledford, G. E., Jenkins, G. D., Jr., and Doty, D. H. "Survey-Based Prescriptions for Skill-Based Pay." *ACA Journal,* 1992, *1*(1), 50–61.
6. Whyte, W. F. (ed.). *Money and Motivation: An Analysis of Incentives in Industry.* New York: HarperCollins, 1955.
7. Lincoln, J. F. *Incentive Management.* Cleveland, Ohio: Lincoln Electric Company, 1951.
8. Heneman, R. L. *Merit Pay.* Reading, Mass.: Addison-Wesley, 1992.
9. Lawler, E. E. *Strategic Pay.* San Francisco: Jossey-Bass, 1990.
10. Mohrman, S. A., Cohen, S. G., and Mohrman, A. M. *Designing Team-Based Organizations: New Forms for Knowledge Work.* San Francisco: Jossey-Bass, 1995.
11. Lawler, E. E. *Strategic Pay.* San Francisco: Jossey-Bass, 1990.
12. Schuster, J. R., and Zingheim, P. K. *The New Pay.* San Francisco: New Lexington Press, 1992.
13. Blinder, A. S. (ed.). *Paying for Productivity: A Look at the Evidence.* Washington, D.C.: Brookings Institution, 1990.

Chapter Ten

1. Lawler, E. E., Mohrman, S. A., and Ledford, G. E. *Creating High Performance Organizations: Practices and Results of Employee Involvement and Total Quality Management in Fortune 1000 Companies.* San Francisco: Jossey-Bass, 1995.
2. Mohrman, A. M., Resnick-West, S. M., and Lawler, E. E. *Designing Performance Appraisal Systems: Aligning Appraisals and Organizational Realities.* San Francisco: Jossey-Bass, 1989.
3. Lawler, E. E. *Strategic Pay: Aligning Organizational Strategies and Pay Systems.* San Francisco: Jossey-Bass, 1990.
4. Mankin, D., Cohen, S. G., and Bikson, T. K. *Teams and Technology:*

Fulfilling the Promise of the New Organization. Boston: Harvard Business School Press, 1996.

5. Zuboff, S. *In the Age of the Smart Machine: The Future of Work and Power.* New York: Basic Books, 1988.

6. Mankin, D., Cohen, S. G., and Bikson, T. K. *Teams and Technology.* Boston: Harvard Business School Press, 1996.

7. Deming, W. E. *Out of the Crisis.* Cambridge, Mass.: MIT Press, 1986.

8. Cooper, R., and Kaplan, R. S. "Profit Priorities from Activity-Based Costing." *Harvard Business Review,* 1991, *69*(3), 130–135.

9. Lawler, E. E., and Mirvis, P. H. "How Graphic Controls Assesses the Human Side of the Corporation." *Management Review,* 1981, *70*(10), 540–563.

10. Mohrman, S. A., Cohen, S. G., and Mohrman, A. M. *Designing Team-Based Organizations: New Forms for Knowledge Work.* San Francisco: Jossey-Bass, 1995.

Chapter Eleven

1. Lawler, E. E., Mohrman, S. A., and Ledford, G. E. *Creating High Performance Organizations: Practices and Results of Employee Involvement and Total Quality Management in Fortune 1000 Companies.* San Francisco: Jossey-Bass, 1995.

2. Mohrman, S. A., and Cummings, T. G. *Self-Designing Organizations: Learning How to Create High Performance Organizations.* Reading, Mass.: Addison-Wesley, 1989.

3. Tichy, N. M., and Sherman, S. *Control Your Destiny or Someone Else Will.* New York: Currency Doubleday, 1993.

4. Tichy, N. M., and Devanna, M. A. *The Transformational Leader.* New York: Wiley, 1986.

   O'Toole, J. *Leading Change.* San Francisco: Jossey-Bass, 1995.

5. Beckhard, R., and Harris, R. T. *Organization Transitions: Managing Complex Change.* (2nd ed.) Reading, Mass.: Addison-Wesley, 1987.

6. Mohrman, S. A., and Cummings, T. G. *Self-Designing Organizations.* Reading, Mass.: Addison-Wesley, 1989.

7. Kotter, J. P. "Leading Change: Why Transformation Efforts Fail." *Harvard Business Review,* 1995, *73*(2), 59–67.

   Shapiro, E. C. *Fad Surfing in the Boardroom.* Reading, Mass.: Addison-Wesley, 1995.

8. Nadler, D. A., Shaw, R. B., Walton, A. E., and Associates. *Discontinuous Change: Leading Organizational Transformation.* San Francisco: Jossey-Bass, 1995.

9. Lawler, E. E., and Galbraith, J. R. "Avoiding the Corporate Dinosaur Syndrome." *Organizational Dynamics,* 1994, *23*(2), 5–17.

10. Lawler, E. E., Mohrman, S. A., and Ledford, G. E. *Creating High Performance Organizations.* San Francisco: Jossey-Bass, 1995.

Chapter Twelve
 1. Handy, C. *The Age of Unreason.* Boston: Harvard Business School Press, 1990.
 2. Thurow, L. C. *The Future of Capitalism: How Today's Economic Forces Shape Tomorrow's World.* New York: Morrow, 1996.
    Karoly, L. A. "Anatomy of the U.S. Income Distribution: Two Decades of Change." *Oxford Review of Economic Policy,* 1996, *12*(1), 77–96.
 3. Jenkins, G. D., Jr., Ledford, G. E., Jr., Gupta, N., and Doty, D. H. *Skill-Based Pay: Practices, Payoffs, Pitfalls, and Prospects.* Scottsdale, Ariz.: American Compensation Association, 1992.
    Lawler, E. E. *Strategic Pay: Aligning Organizational Strategies and Pay Systems.* San Francisco: Jossey-Bass, 1990.
 4. Reich, R. B. *The Work of Nations.* New York: Knopf, 1991.
    Pfeffer, J. *Competitive Advantage Through People.* Boston: Harvard Business School Press, 1994.
 5. Commission on the Skills of the American Workforce. *America's Choice: High Skills or Low Wages.* Rochester, N.Y.: National Center on Education and the Economy, 1990.
    Secretary's Commission on Achieving Necessary Skills. *What Work Requires of Schools.* Washington, D.C.: U.S. Dept. of Labor, 1991.
 6. Bluestone, B., and Bluestone, I. *Negotiating the Future.* New York: Basic Books, 1992.
 7. Kochan, T. A., and Osterman, P. *The Mutual Gains Enterprise.* Boston: Harvard Business School Press, 1995.
    Levine, D. I. *Reinventing the Workplace: How Business and Employees Can Both Win.* Washington, D.C.: Brookings Institution, 1995.
 8. Lawler, E. E. *High-Involvement Management: Participative Strategies for Improving Organizational Performance.* San Francisco: Jossey-Bass, 1986.
 9. AFL-CIO. *The New American Workplace: A Labor Perspective.* Washington, D.C.: AFL-CIO, 1994.
10. Freeman, R. B., and Rogers, J. *Worker Representation and Participation Survey: Report on the Findings.* Princeton, N.J.: Princeton Survey Research Associates, 1994.
11. Doyle, F. P. "People-Power: The Global Human Resource Challenge for the 90s." *Columbia World Business,* 1990, *25*, 36–45.
    Marshall, R., and Tucker, M. *Thinking for a Living.* New York: Basic Books, 1992.
    Quinn, J. B. *Intelligent Enterprise.* New York: Free Press, 1992.

Index

Skills: assessment of, 184–185, 272; central data base of, 185–186; cross-training in, 159–161; and employment stability, 192; focus on, in human resource management, 172–174; needed by managers of teams, 162; needed by new logic work force, 276–277; needed in teams, 158–159; tracking of, 185–186. *See also* Expertise; Training

Small-business approaches, in large organizations: in business unit model, 103–111; in front-back model, 111–115; in network model, 115–117. *See also* Business units; Front-back organization

Small organizations: advantages and disadvantages of, 91–93; networking approaches of, 94, 115–117

Social responsibility, 69–70

Society: and changing role of unions, 279–283, 285; and education, 276–278; impact of new logic on, 266–267, 289–290; impact of new logic careers on, 267–274, 278–279; impact of new logic pay systems on, 275–276; and public policy, 283–286

Socio-tech approach, 145–146

Solectron, 86, 116–117

Sony, 14, 75

Southwest Airlines, 2, 71, 161

Spaghetti Model, 118

Specialties. *See* Expertise

Sports, 222–224

Springfield Remanufacturing, 220, 248

Staff support and service groups. *See* Support and service staff

Standard, measurement against, 239–241

Standardization, of jobs, 123–125

Star Model, 45–50, 100; and organizational change, 257–258. *See also* Communication; Human resource management; Measure-

ment; Reward systems; Strategy; Structure

Status, 87

Stock ownership, 213, 214–216, 243, 275

Strategic planning: employee involvement in, 72–75; formal, 62–65, 67

Strategy, 61–81; alignment of, with capabilities and competencies, 61–62, 75–78; alignment of, with employee commitment, 71–75; communication of, 78–79; versus downsizing, 261–262; and employment stability guarantees, 190–193; for growth, 261–262; keys to developing, 80–81; leadership role in, 78–80; mission statement and, 65–67, 70–75; in organizational design, 46–48; and organizational structure, 85, 102–103; versus planning, 63, 67; relationship of, to environment, 62; and shared understanding of the future, 66–67; value statement and, 67–75. *See also* Organizational design

Structure. *See* Organizational structure

Sun Microsystems, 25, 112, 176, 189, 222

Supervisors, 129

Support and service staff, 94–97; as business spin-offs, 97; outsourcing of, 96–97, 242; performance measurement of, 241–242

T

Taco Bell, 233–234

Tandem Computers, 86

Tasks: appropriateness of, to teams, 150–151; versus jobs, 99–100, 123; setting of, for teams, 144–149

Taylor, F. W., 172

TBWA Chiat/Day, 86

Team-based organization, 99–100, 141–142; keys to success of, 143–167; problems of, within tra-

Other Titles by Edward E. Lawler III

Rewarding Excellence: Pay Strategies for the New Economy
Edward E. Lawler III
Hardcover ISBN 0-7879-5074-2

High-Involvement Management: Participative Strategies for Improving Organizational Performance
Edward E. Lawler III
Hardcover ISBN 0-87589-686-3
Paperback ISBN 1-55542-330-2

Designing Performance Appraisal Systems: Aligning Appraisals and Organizational Realities
Allan M. Mohrman Jr., Susan Resnick-West, Edward E. Lawler III
Hardcover ISBN 1-55542-149-0

Large-Scale Organizational Change
Allan M. Mohrman Jr., Susan Albers Mohrman, Gerald E. Ledford Jr., Thomas G. Cummings, Edward E. Lawler III, and Associates
Hardcover ISBN 1-55542-164-4

Strategic Pay: Aligning Organizational Strategies and Pay Systems
Edward E. Lawler III
Hardcover ISBN 1-55542-262-4

The Ultimate Advantage: Creating the High-Involvement Organization
Edward E. Lawler III
Hardcover ISBN 1-55542-414-7

Organizing for the Future: The New Logic for Managing Complex Organizations
Jay R. Galbraith, Edward E. Lawler III, and Associates
Hardcover ISBN 1-55542-528-3

Motivation in Work Organizations
Edward E. Lawler III
Paperback ISBN 1-55542-661-1

Tomorrow's Organization: Crafting Winning Capabilities in a Dynamic World
Susan Albers Mohrman, Jay R. Galbraith, Edward E. Lawler III, and Associates
Hardcover ISBN 0-7879-4004-6

The Leader's Change Handbook: An Essential Guide to Setting Direction and Taking Action
Jay A. Conger, Gretchen M. Spreitzer, Edward E. Lawler III, Editors
Hardcover ISBN 0-7879-4351-7

Strategies for High Performance Organizations—The CEO Report: Employee Involvement, TQM, and Reengineering Programs in Fortune 1000 Corporations
Edward E. Lawler III, Susan Albers Mohrman, Gerald E. Ledford Jr.
Paperback ISBN 0-7879-4397-5

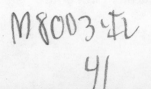